The
Reference Shelf®

The Arab Spring

Edited by
Paul McCaffrey

The Reference Shelf
Volume 84 • Number 2
H. W. Wilson
A Division of EBSCO Publishing, Inc.
Ipswich, Massachusetts
2012

The Reference Shelf

The books in this series contain reprints of articles, excerpts from books, addresses on current issues, and studies of social trends in the United States and other countries. There are six separately bound numbers in each volume, all of which are usually published in the same calendar year. Numbers one through five are each devoted to a single subject, providing background information and discussion from various points of view and concluding with an index and comprehensive bibliography that lists books, pamphlets, and articles on the subject. The final number of each volume is a collection of recent speeches, and it contains a cumulative speaker index. Books in the series may be purchased individually or on subscription.

Library of Congress has catalogued this serial title as follows:

The Arab Spring / editor, Paul McCaffrey.
    p. cm. — (The reference shelf ; v. 84, no. 2)
  Includes bibliographical references and index.
  ISBN 978-0-8242-1116-5 — ISBN 978-0-8242-1249-0 (series)
  1. Arab countries—Politics and government—21st century. 2. Democratization—Arab countries—History—21st century. 3. Protest movements—Arab countries—History—21st century. I. McCaffrey, Paul, 1977–
  JQ1850.A91A74 2012
  909'.097492708312--dc23

2012004021

Cover: Egypt protest. © ANDRE PAIN/epa/Corbis

Visit: www.salempress.com/hwwilson

Printed in the United States of America

Contents

3

Egypt: Tahrir Square and After

4

Libya: Qaddafi's Downfall

5

Syria: Twilight of the Assad Regime?

6

Elsewhere on the Arabian Peninsula: Bahrain and Yemen

7

The Poltical Economy of Revolution

Preface: The Arab Revolution

Why Men and Women Rebel

The so-called Arab Spring began in Tunisia on December 17, 2010, when a young vegetable vendor, Muhammad Bouazizi, lit himself on fire in one of the least turbulent states in the Arab world. This act of protest resulted from being repeatedly denied a license to ply his modest trade at the impoverished interior town of Sidi Bouzid. The twenty-six-year-old harbored the frustrations of an unemployed university graduate denied a license for the second time by a female government employee. This tragic encounter unleashed an uprising of the common people against Tunisia's economic, political, and social elites, triggering a wider seismic shift in the internal and external political alignments of this troubled part of the world. In the final analysis, the young vegetable vendor may have been the match that lit a revolution long in the making, seeking political reforms in a part of the world where the deficit of human rights and democracy outweighed the area's rich cultural heritage.

Conceptualizing the Uprising

Although some journals, such as the *Nation* and the British *Financial Times*, opted for such terms as "Arab Awakening" and the "Great Arab Revolt" to describe the events of early 2011 in the greater Middle East, US Secretary of State Hillary Clinton and others repeatedly referred to these events as the "Arab Spring." The Western media added such terms as "social networks" and "Facebook revolution," as well as "youth rebellion." "Arab Spring" was soon surpassed by more authentic frames of reference, particularly in Egypt.

In Egypt, both the occasion that triggered the uprising and the terms used to describe it proved to be as true to the country's history as Giza's pyramids. The avalanche of popular protest in Egypt materialized as a result of the observance on January 25, 2011, of Police Day, which commemorates an incident during the Revolt of 1952 in which occupying British troops fired on a contingent of Egyptian police at Ismailia. The Egyptian media, therefore, named the uprising the "Revolution of January 25." Events in Egypt quickly eclipsed the earlier uprising in Tunisia, a country that was not involved in the Arab-Israeli conflict and thus offered little magnetism for Western journalists and commentators. Although Tunisia supplied the model of how to engineer the toppling of a corrupt family regime, the subsequent forced removal of the Mubarak dynasty in Egypt was fraught with potential dangers for the Western architects of the tentative Arab-Israeli peace.

In Tunisia, Egypt, and other locations, the disempowered elements of society rushed to tear down the symbols of their oppressive regimes, repeatedly dubbed "securitocracies" by observers of the human rights deficit. Outside commentators explained that this was civil society at work, finally mimicking examples of Western democracies where ordinary people constantly took their own governments to task. However, local commentators refuted this line of analysis. To begin with, even though many of the young revolutionaries had recently studied the works of American political theorist Gene Sharp, particularly *From Dictatorship to Democracy* (1993), they were also taking their cue from examples closer to home, namely, the Palestinian intifadas of 1987 and 2000. That young Palestinians were able to confront the mightiest military machine in the region, namely, the Israeli Defense Forces, was an important lesson in how to translate weakness into strength. Revolutionaries called it "breaking the fear barrier." The civil society paradigm stuck as women, both veiled and modern, took up their positions on the front lines of revolutions from Cairo to Sana'a to Manama. Arab youth were not only in evidence but were in the leadership position of these popular tremors, along with the unrepresented religious minorities of Egypt, the Shiite majorities of Bahrain, and the Sunni majority of Syria.

But once Islamic movements with dubious democratic credentials began to throw their numbers and their funds into these uprisings, emerging on top in the democratic elections of Tunisia and Egypt, the "civil society" paradigm began to fade away. In reality, this term was extremely suspect to people of this region since it conjured up images of foreign political actors set on exporting American-style democracy to other parts of the world. There is extensive literature about native versus foreign civil society which appeared in the wake of President George W. Bush's doctrine of exporting American democracy abroad. As attractive as democracy was to the area's oppressed masses, the Arab people in general were not in a receptive mood when democracy was proposed within the context of the US invasion of Iraq.

Arab historians have always argued that the "civil society" concept did not begin with Hegel and de Tocqueville but went back to the glory days of the Abbasid Empire, which, until its destruction in 945, experienced the highest stages of urbanization and commercialization. The Abbasid state gave rise to a thriving bourgeoisie that prospered due to long-distance trade outside the reach of governments. These were also joined by trade guilds, Sufi orders, and an independent clerical class to counterbalance the power of the state. Indeed, the great Tunisian sociologist and historian Ibn Khaldoun (1332–1406) wrote that "the state was the greatest commercial market," in reference to the highest stage of Arab and Islamic development. But, alas, Western political sociologists like Max Weber (1864–1920) chose to focus on Arab states in the worst stages of decline, such as the Mamluk period in seventeenth-century Egypt, as the prototype of what he termed "patrimonialism." This was an early version of royal autocracy where the center of political life was the palace and not parliament. Had Weber focused on the great periods of Arab history, we may not have been addicted to the practice of ascribing every modernizing tendency to Western influence.

Why Men and Women Rebel

One of the most frequently heard explanations for the Arab uprisings is the need to restore people's dignity. The early waves of protesters who demolished the fear barrier were not the starving masses but children of the semi-affluent classes who were generally well-educated and technologically sophisticated. Their main complaint was loss of personal dignity at the hands of the enforcers of decrepit and corrupt regimes. Experts in the psychological aspects of rebellions, like American political sociologist Ted Gurr, have explained the psychological underpinnings of uprisings in rapidly modernizing societies of the developing world in terms of a phenomenon called "relative deprivation." This refers to a people's awareness of the lack of political freedoms enjoyed by people in other countries and witnessed on a daily basis through mass media. Thus, the uprisings were not the result of attraction to the American model of democracy as such, but a general feeling of deprivation resulting from living in harsh authoritarian states while witnessing how other people lived in more open and free societies through available means of technological communications.

Variations on a Common Theme

Is it possible to claim a similar background to these various uprisings just because they shared the same time period and the same general characteristics? Or is this a case of deceptive homogeneity overlaying a complex set of differences? A third possibility would be a copycat effect producing a checkered map of winners and losers.

Tunisia

The uprising began here in protest over the self-immolation of a victim of bureaucratic corruption, but as the revolt widened, all sectors of the Tunisian political community participated in a show of national unity that was sustained through the procrastinations of at least two transitional cabinets. Women, unionists, and members of suppressed Islamic parties like the Ennahda Movement came out in full force. Women who played a leading role in this revolution included Amal Qarami, Aalifeh Yousef, and Rajaa bin Salamah. Yet Tunisia is not typical of its Arab neighbors due to its unusually homogeneous population, powerful trade union movement, and a weak military with no history of political involvement. The fact that the revolution midwifed an Islamically dominated constituent assembly is currently explained as a phenomenon similar to Egypt's case, where the social-welfare program of these parties built grassroots support among the destitute masses.

Currently, Ennahda leads a coalition of three parties headed by President Muncef Marzouki, a moderate ex-physician and human rights activist. Marzouki appears to be a conciliatory figure heading this temporary government pending the writing of a new constitution. For now, the head of Ennahda, Rashid Ghannushi, seems to be content to play the role of éminence grise, directing his party without the benefit of an official title. The chances of such an arrangement succeeding in the long-run are minimal, given the example of similar power partnerships as between Omar al-Bashir of Sudan and his spiritual guide, Hassan al-Turabi, who has since been stripped of all power. Tunisia is also blessed by an absence of an Arab-Israeli factor due to its distance from the so-called confrontation states, which bodes well for not antagonizing Western powers. But women, youth, and the press seem to be intent on staying vigilant over political developments, ready to start another uprising if the Islamic government endangers their hard-won liberties.

Egypt

The revolution of January 25, 2011, began as a civil society uprising and ended as a successful Islamic climb to the pinnacle of political power. One could argue that the early leaders of the uprising, acting mostly on behalf of oppressed and under-represented labor groups—as in the case of the April 6 Movement, which represented the strikers of the textile industries at al-Mahilla al-Kubra—were woefully unprepared to exercise power. Egypt's labor movement had a history of fragmentation and leftist leadership, suffering the wrath of several Egyptian regimes, including that of Gamal Abdel Nasser. In addition, it always lacked the same level of funding that Islamic groups seemed to enjoy. The early leadership of the uprising, being mostly made up of women like Asma Mahfouz and Amal Sharaf, as well as young Coptic activists and youthful members of the Muslim Brotherhood, fought largely in order to force a redefinition of citizenship. They fought in order to bring about a change from the corrupt politics of the regime of Hosni Mubarak.

The second phase of the uprising saw the Muslim Brotherhood and the Salafi extremist groups enter the political stage from its widest door, by winning general elections overseen by the caretaker military council. This leaves many questions unanswered, the main ones being: Will these traditional and conservative groups adhere to their declared social agenda, which threatens the civil rights of women and minorities? Or will the liberal wing of the Muslim Brotherhood prevail and transform the movement into something resembling Turkey's Justice and Development Party? The bigger question also remains: Will there be a general revamping of Egypt's unpopular foreign policy, especially in light of the Brotherhood's long opposition to the Camp David Agreement with Israel, or will the military council assert its control over this area of Egyptian politics?

Libya

The case of the regime of Muammar Qaddafi in Libya stood out against the rest as an extreme tribal system of autocratic government that eventually turned into the usual Arab-style dynastic republic. The absence of any independent political and social institutions diminished any possibility of a civilian uprising. The revolt that erupted in 2011 played out within the context of the historic regional rivalry between Tripoli in the west and Benghazi in the east, the two centers of, respectively, the historic regions of Tripolitania and Cyrenaica. Each enjoyed its own set of loyalties and attachments, with Benghazi having served as the seat of the previous Sanusi dynasty.

Qaddafi's dismal human rights record did not bode well for a peaceful resolution of the protests that broke out in Benghazi and other cities in January and February 2011. What Qaddafi failed to understand, apparently, was the impact of his violent reaction to the uprising, particularly his violent rhetoric, on international public opinion. This is not to dismiss the lure of Libya's rich oil resources, which had frequently invited outside military intervention in the past. Thus, NATO began its air attacks on his country, assuring the dissident movement of eventual victory. However, the chaotic period that followed, ending with the public lynching of Qaddafi and his son, in contrast to Tunisia's utter lack of reprisals and vengeance killings, detracted from the legitimacy of the new revolutionary government. Inevitably, the revolutionary group's endorsement of NATO's attacks and its inability to fashion some kind of unity out of its various fighting factions eroded its authority and its legitimacy. Qaddafi's regime, in addition, had not been without its virtues, primarily in providing Libya with one of the highest standards of living and wage structures in all of Africa. Libya's was an economy that attracted thousands of foreign workers and earned a high position on the UN Human Development Index.

Syria

If the Tunisian and Egyptian uprisings were able to inspire others, Syria's rebellion may have cooled the ardor of many. There are several issues distinguishing Syria from the matrix of the Arab uprisings, not the least of which is the use of force by both sides, resulting not in a civilian uprising, but in a militant armed conflict. There were some elements here that mimicked earlier uprisings: the use of Facebook by human rights groups; brutal government attacks on the youths of Diraa, a town in southern Syria, which galvanized the nation into action; the rise of Islamic opposition groups in traditionally hostile and antigovernment centers such as Homs and Hama; and the early participation by female human rights activists such as Razan Zeitoun. But the rebels here will find it difficult to wrap themselves in the mantle of civil society, given their militancy and readiness to receive outside support.

Although the Syrian Muslim Brotherhood seems to be driving the resistance, it would be difficult to compare its role to that of the Egyptian Brotherhood since unlike the Egyptian case, the Syrians did participate in parliamentary elections during the 1940s and 1950s. The Brotherhood lost out to competition from other popular ideologies such as the pan-Arabism of the Baath Party and the Greater Syria project of the Syrian Social National Party. The Brotherhood's leaders fled to Germany in the 1980s, settling mostly in the city of Aachen. Throughout their turbulent history in Syria, the Brothers were known to favor a conservative social agenda over support for the popular Palestinian cause. Operating from the outside, they are still finding it difficult to destabilize a regime boasting a pan-Arab foreign policy that continues to attract the support of Arab elites throughout the region. The minority-controlled Baath regime seems to enjoy alliances with some of the most rejectionist, anti-Israel, and anti-American powers, such as Iran and Hizbollah. Added to this are its strong ties to the Russian Federation, which continues to be the government's main source of weapons. Other hidden assets of the regime include its historic and unique ability to integrate its Arab Christian population into the main fabric of politics and society, thereby neutralizing one of the West's frequent arguments against Middle Eastern despotic regimes. Syria's complex foreign policy, which is the outcome of its central geographic position in the region, has given rise to many fears regarding its possible disintegration and fragmentation. The Syrian regime apparently can still mount a powerful argument against any sustained outside intervention—a prospect that has been considered by the League of Arab States, with the Syrian situation approaching a full civil war.

Bahrain

The significance of the situation in Bahrain is that it is emerging as a test case for uprisings in the Persian Gulf region, most of which will inevitably be mounted by Shiite groups. The tendency of Shiite populations to oppose Sunni regimes is too common to ignore, ranging from a Shiite opposition bloc in the Kuwaiti parliament to the sizeable Shiite population in Saudi Arabia's Eastern Province. These Shiite populations may find themselves energized by other Arab uprisings, but they will be facing the military might of Saudi Arabia, as well as that of US troops in the Gulf area. Both of these forces are increasingly fearful of intervention by Iran in these oil-rich and Shiite-populated Gulf countries and will not hesitate to use maximum firepower to quell any challenges. Some of the contentious issues in Bahrain's uprising have a familiar ring. These include attacks on unarmed civilians in Lulu Square, Manama's equivalent of Tahrir Square, and the pivotal role of women such as the human rights activist Ghada Jamsheer. So far, plans by the al-Khalifa ruling family to buy time with a mixture of repression and royal reforms have failed to convince the Shiite majority to abandon their struggle and move on.

The American Factor, the Israeli Echo Chamber

In examining each of these cases of the Arab uprisings, one invariably comes across the American factor, or US options in a rapidly changing landscape. Can the United States gamble on the fate of its erstwhile allies and embrace the new revolutionaries, especially when some of those regard Western democratic ideals with considerable derision? Another imponderable question is whether it would be in the US national interest to intervene militarily in these upheavals in order to restructure its system of alliances in this crucial region. One American academic has suggested adopting a certain criterion to determine, not if an emerging group is committed to the United States, but rather whether or not such regimes are committed to opposing terrorism in their dealings with former enemies and new allies. Amitai Etzioni said as much in a recent article in which he referred to powerful groups such as the Muslim Brotherhood as "illiberal moderates," whose ideology is not totally compatible with the West, but who are moderate on the essential elements such as the use of violence to achieve their foreign policy objectives. Such an argument, nevertheless, raises the issue of prejudging movements prior to their assumption of power and branding them as undemocratic simply on the basis of their religious orientation. Hillary Clinton rejected this approach once, suggesting that it bordered on racism.

The Israeli factor is enormously significant under these conditions, for several reasons, among them Israel's role as the surrogate of the United States and guardian of Western interests in the region. Israel is expected to react harshly to any major change in the area's strategic status quo. Israelis are already displaying considerable anxiety over the uncertainty and unpredictability resulting from the Arab uprisings. The United States would be wise to follow its own hunch and not be moved solely by the ambitions of its non-Arab ally in the Middle East. It should be noted that the relative ease with which Tunisia achieved the goals of its uprising is already a clear demonstration of its irrelevance to Israel's security. The Arab uprisings, as expected, are already forcing a reassessment of who will be US allies in the upcoming half century.

Ghada Hashem Talhami
January 2012

1

Whither the Arab Spring?

On January 25, 2012, tens of thousands Egyptians gather in Tahrir Square to mark the one-year anniversary of the revolution that toppled President Hosni Mubarak.

Government in the Arab World: Monarchy, Pan-Arab Socialism, and Islamism

By Paul McCaffrey

The Arab world is composed of twenty-two nations encompassing all of North Africa and much of the Middle East. The Arab people number over 360 million and while they share a common language, there is a surprising degree of diversity among them, whether in terms of nationality, culture, religion, economics, or politics. The Arab Spring uprisings of the past two years have brought renewed attention to the political landscape of the region, as long-reigning dictators and monarchs have endured vigorous challenges to their rule, with some, in Tunisia, Egypt, and Libya, succumbing to the pressure. Though generalizations about such a broad spectrum of countries can be difficult, the political regimes and movements operating in the Arab world today generally fall into three main categories—monarchy, pan-Arab socialism, and Islamism—with some examples embracing more hybrid approaches incorporating aspects of two subgroups. For the most part, however, these categories exist in opposition to one another, and the Arab Spring uprisings often developed when competing currents swept into one another.

Though these subdivisions seem simple on the surface, their expression is unique from country to country. Islamism in Iraq is different from Islamism in Tunisia; pan-Arab socialism in Syria is distinct from the Egyptian variety; and the Moroccan monarchy is not in all ways analogous to the Saudi form. Furthermore, in their individual application, there is often an underlying complexity. Frequently, the political structure, whatever its professed ideology, serves more sectarian purposes and illustrates the larger religious and cultural rifts within a country.

The lack of a democratic option is noteworthy, too, and may seem to support the cliché that the Arab world is "immune" to democracy. While this cliché holds true in some cases more than others, there are notable exceptions. Syria enjoyed a brief era of democratic governments soon after achieving independence, while Lebanon had a more robust and lengthy experience with a parliamentary system. In each country, however, democracy remained a sectarian affair, with political parties representing religious interests, until the system could no longer keep the peace and was overturned by a series of coups and a civil war, respectively. Sectarianism can also be seen in representative governments more recently established by the Palestinian Authority and Iraq. The major competition in the Palestinian Authority elections is between Hamas, an Islamist party, and Fatah, a secular, pan-Arab, and socialistic organization. Iraqi elections are similarly sectarian in outcome, with various Islamist parties and Kurdish organizations vying for influence. The results of post–Arab Spring elections in Egypt and Tunisia have resulted in victory for Islamist parties.

Democracy in the Arab world tends to reflect the sectarian makeup of the particular country and the struggle between Islamist and pan-Arab socialist approaches to government.

The political dimension is essential to understanding the Arab Spring phenomena, but it is not the only dimension. Demography also had an undeniable influence. One common trait shared by the various nations of the Arab world is a rapidly expanding population, with a demonstrable "youth bulge." In many Arab countries, more than half of the people are under the age of thirty. Such circumstances have historically contributed to social upheaval, both in the Arab world and elsewhere. Compounding the problem is a largely stagnant economic climate. Vast numbers of unemployed young people constitute a destabilizing element in any society.

The monarchical category is especially prominent in the oil-rich states of the Arabian Peninsula, applying to Saudi Arabia, Oman, Qatar, the United Arab Emirates, Kuwait, and Bahrain. In these states, the monarchies are absolute in nature. Whatever legislative structures are in place exercise little real power. Morocco and Jordan also have monarchies, but these are of the constitutional variety, so influential parliaments play prominent roles in affairs of state. In the early years of the post-colonial era, Iraq, Egypt, Yemen, and Libya each had monarchies as well, though pan-Arab socialist movements toppled them.

Of the nations that currently have the monarchical political structure, the only one to experience serious Arab Spring–related unrest is Bahrain, which at first glance, may seem an outlier. With the other Gulf oil monarchies, a small population coupled with vast oil wealth—or just vast oil wealth—was enough to ensure stability during the Arab Spring. Why was Bahrain the exception? As it turns out, a sizeable majority of Bahrain's population subscribes to the Shia branch of the Islamic faith. The ruling Al-Khalifa family, on the other hand, is Sunni and, demonstrators contend, has favored fellow Sunnis at the expense of the Shia in distributing the wealth of the kingdom. Despite their majority status, the largely Shia protestors failed to overthrow the regime or persuade it to reform. Confronted by the demonstrations, the authorities instituted a brutal crackdown, and with Saudi assistance, stamped them out.

The Sunni-Shia divide that emerges in Bahrain is a common theme in the Arab Spring and in the larger context of Arab politics. Along with other religious schisms, it often influences the various Arab political institutions and movements, whether they are outwardly monarchical, pan-Arab, or Islamist. Over a thousand years old, the Sunni-Shia distinction has its origins in a dispute over the successor to the Prophet Muhammad. Sunni believe that Abu Bakr, an advisor to Muhammad and the consensus choice among the Prophet's companions, is the rightful heir. Shia maintain that Ali, the Prophet's cousin and son-in-law, is Muhammad's true successor. In subsequent centuries, the religious and cultural practices of Sunni and Shia have diverged, while the succession debate has evolved into larger disagreements about the nature of religious authority and the relationship between humanity and the divine.

Though an accurate breakdown is hard to come by, the vast majority of the Arab world is Sunni Muslim. Shia Arabs are the largest demographic in Iraq and Bahrain and make up sizeable minorities in Lebanon, Yemen, Saudi Arabia, and, through the Alawite sect, Syria. The Arab world is not uniformly Muslim, however. Though Egypt, the Palestinian Territories, Syria, and Jordan are all predominantly Sunni, they do have notable Christian populations. Lebanon's population is around 40 percent Christian, the largest proportion in the Arab world.

An example of a hybrid regime, Saudi Arabia is ruled by an absolute monarchy, with members of the large royal family monopolizing the levers of wealth and power. It is also, however, a devoutly Muslim nation, one that contains Mecca and Medina, the two holiest sites in all of Islam; consequently, the Saudi monarchy has long embraced political Islamism. The form of Islam practiced in Saudi Arabia and written into its legal code is Wahhabism, an especially austere and strict variety. Thanks to its vast oil wealth, Saudi Arabia has exported this sort of political Islamism to Pakistan, Afghanistan, and elsewhere.

Aside from the protests and repression in Bahrain, the oil-rich Gulf monarchies avoided the worst of the Arab Spring disturbances. This suggests that oil wealth and an absence of major sectarian divisions had a palliative effect on potential resistance to the ruling order in each monarchy and helped preserve the peace. It also indicates that vast oil reserves alone may safeguard a regime, or at least a monarchy, from the threat of revolution.

The Libyan example contradicts these conclusions. In 1968, the Free Officers, led by Colonel Muammar Qaddafi, overthrew King Idris I. There was no sectarian motive to Qaddafi's coup. Then as now, Libya was around 99 percent Sunni Muslim. Forty-odd years later, with Libya's oil wealth and homogenous population still intact, Qaddafi himself was deposed. Facing an Arab Spring–inspired insurrection supported by foreign airpower, he could not maintain his position and was eventually killed by insurgents.

Qaddafi's regime, like the others that fell in the Arab Spring—Hosni Mubarak's Egypt and Zine El Abidine Ben Ali's Tunisia—and one that may yet crumble—Bashar el-Assad's Syria—did not base their rule on heredity or religion but on more secular considerations. Mubarak, Qaddafi, Assad, and, to a lesser extent, Ben Ali, are all heirs of Egyptian president Gamal Abdel Nasser and his ideology. Pan-Arab socialism—Nasserism and its close relative, the Baathism of Syria and Iraq—developed in the 1940s and 1950s as a response to the schisms within the Arab community and to the perceived humiliations of the colonial era.

As an ethos, Nasserism and other forms of Pan-Arab socialism make more sense in the abstract than in the actual, in word more than deed. There was and remains a unifying sense of Arab identity, of Arab nationalism. But as the structures of the colonial era were dismantled, the new institutions that replaced them ignored this impulse. Instead, artificial boundaries were imposed, creating fresh divisions among the Arab people on top of the old sectarian ones. The new governments were corrupt and ineffectual, the full extent of their incompetence illustrated by the 1948 Arab-Israeli War, when the outnumbered Israelis crushed the combined Arab armies. Pan-Arab socialism sought to reverse these outcomes. It brought about Arab unity by removing foreign and imperial influences, constructing socialist economies, and confronting Israel.

Pan-Arab socialism enjoyed some early successes. Upon coming to power in the early 1950s, Nasser eloquently championed the Arab poor, who had been variously ignored or exploited by their leaders for centuries. With his handling of the Suez Crisis in 1956, Nasser became a truly transcendent figure. But his domestic policies came up short. His pan-Arab unity projects failed. His brinkmanship with Israel led to one of the more crushing defeats in military history.

Nasser's successors in Egypt altered his doctrine, excising most of the socialism and much of the pan-Arabism. They retained his repressive security apparatus. As Hosni Mubarak's tenure entered its thirtieth year, Nasserism in Egypt was a spent force. Little remained but the regime's avowed secularism and its police-state cruelty. But as pan-Arab socialism stagnated, Egypt grew increasingly religious. The Muslim Brotherhood and other Islamist groups expanded their influence and presented a challenge to the dictatorship. With major victories in the elections following Mubarak's downfall, the Islamist parties—and political Islam—have for now eclipsed Nasser's pan-Arabism and its offspring and risen to the forefront of Egyptian politics.

A similar dynamic may be at work in Tunisia. Following the demise of the corrupt and repressive but distinctly secular Ben Ali regime, the ensuing elections resulted in strong showings for Islamist parties. If this pattern holds, Islamists will perform well in the upcoming Libyan elections.

Though nominally a pan-Arab socialist state ruled by the Baath Party, Syria is a compelling example of how the pan-Arab designation can be subverted for sectarian ends—and how Arab Spring uprisings may, as in the Bahraini example, reflect underlying religious and ethnic tensions. Syria's population is largely Sunni Arab, but the country's governing elite is composed of Alawites, a historically marginalized community as well as a distinct minority in Syria. Throughout the forty years of the Assad dictatorship, opposition to the regime has developed mostly among Sunni Arabs and manifested itself as Muslim Brotherhood Islamism. The regime has responded with brutal repression, killing tens of thousands. While the Arab Spring demonstrations in Syria are not openly Islamist, they are centered in the predominantly Sunni Arab cities of Damascus and Homs, so it is likely, given democratic alternatives, Sunni Arabs in Syria would vote their faith, as they have in Egypt and Tunisia.

Whether Bashar el-Assad retains his power or falls like Mubarak, Qaddafi, and Ben Ali, the underlying lesson is that the Arab Spring uprisings, whatever their root causes—religious discrimination, economic stagnation, official corruption, repression, a youth bulge—their immediate outcome thus far is the downfall of secular, pan-Arab socialistic regimes and the empowerment of Islamist political parties. Political Islam is still very much a work in progress and its early expressions, in Turkey, for example, leave cause for hope, whereas the history of pan-Arab socialist regimes is largely one of grave excess compounded by failure.

The Long Revolt

By Rami G. Khouri
The Wilson Quarterly, Summer 2011

The Arab world's wave of change was a century in the making. Why expect its effects to become clear in the space of months?

We are witnessing today the culmination of a century of Arab popular struggle for freedom and sovereignty. That struggle was interrupted by many decades of often illusory statehood under the reign of autocrats who were enthusiastically supported by foreign powers. Today's struggle is the single most significant movement of Arab citizens and citizenries since the modern Arab world was created in the early 20th century.

That world was born amid revolts against the region's Ottoman and European overlords. When the European colonial powers finally retreated, the Ottomans having been swept aside by their defeat in World War I, they left behind a collection of Arab countries they essentially had manufactured for their own convenience out of their particular dominions. Twenty-two nominally sovereign Arab states ultimately emerged, and they limped into the 21st century battered and tattered by a combination of forces: their own economic mismanagement and corruption; regional wars and occupations involving Israel, Iran, and recurring invasions by the United States and Britain; severe income disparities resulting from the misuse of oil and gas wealth; and a stunning record of sustained autocracy and authoritarianism unmatched by any other region of the world.

Now Arab countries finally are being born of their own volition rather than through the false-birth handicraft of audacious European officials. The momentous process that is under way today is so complex and was so long in the making that it is not surprising that we have a hard time finding a name for it. "Arab Spring" is the tag used in the West. "Revolution" (thawra) is the preferred name among those protesting and sometimes battling in the streets in Egypt, Tunisia, Libya, Syria, and Yemen. In some countries people speak of their "intifada" (uprising), the name popularized by the two Palestinian intifadas against Israeli occupation. Others speak of a "citizen revolt," the "Arab Awakening," or the "Arab Renaissance."

Half a year after the overthrow of the Tunisian and Egyptian regimes that launched this revolt, two important patterns have emerged. First, there is a common set of basic material and political grievances that citizens in most Arab countries share. Second, each regime's response to the protests has been determined by the intersection of two factors: the nature and legitimacy of the regime itself and the intensity of popular grievances. This is why the region is marked by such a variety of revolts and regime responses. There have been two regime changes to date, while active warfare and low-intensity violence continue in a few countries. In others, the national leaders, perhaps feeling themselves on firmer ground, are attempting to mute demands for change with a combination of massive cash handouts to the hard-pressed populace and negotiations, or at least dialogue, with those demanding changes in how power is exercised and citizens are treated.

Understanding what is happening now and how things might evolve requires, above all, grasping the nature of the grievances that have caused people to go into the streets, knowing they risk death. For decades, the average Arab citizen suffered multiple hardships and injustices. These included rampant corruption, poor wages, a lack of jobs, low-quality education, occupation by foreign powers, security service abuses, and curbs on personal freedoms. By the 1990s, the Arab order could be defined as one of continuous wars and internal violence, increasingly militaristic and corrupt security states, and burgeoning disparities in citizen well-being as a small, wealthy minority became increasingly distanced from masses of lower-income and poor Arabs. Average people were willing to endure as long as they felt that the future held out the hope of a better life for themselves or their children. From the 1930s to the late '80s, the future did indeed promise a better life for most Arabs. But the upward curve of promise flattened and in some cases reversed during the two decades before the current revolt erupted in Tunisia last December.

> *The Arabs who now challenge their governments share a common desire to achieve both personal and political goals.*

In Tunisia, Gallup surveys showed that the percentage of those who were "thriving" (a composite measure of well-being developed by the polling firm) fell by 10 points between 2008 and 2010. In Egypt, it fell by 17 points over a slightly longer period of time. (Last year, only 14 percent of Tunisians and 12 percent of Egyptians were classified as "thriving," compared with 43 percent of Saudis and somewhat higher percentages of those in other Persian Gulf states.) At the same time, both countries had growing economies, which created a wealthy elite even as the majority of citizens felt that their prospects were declining. Last year, Gallup found that more than a quarter of all young people in Arab states wanted to emigrate—and the proportion reached more than 40 percent in Tunisia, Yemen, and other countries. Arabs' confidence in the legitimacy of national elections was low. Dozens of other indicators affirm this picture of mass citizen discontent across the region, with the general exception of the wealthy Persian Gulf oil-producing states.

The Arabs who now challenge their governments share a common desire to achieve both personal and political goals. They want all the normal rights of citizenship, including meaningful voting rights, access to a credible judicial system, and freedom of the press. They want the ability to exercise their human faculties to read and write as they wish, enjoy arts and culture without draconian censorship, discuss public issues, travel and invest as they see fit, wear the clothes and listen to the music they prefer, and participate in the world of ideas that helps shape their society as well as define their public policies.

When Mohamed Bouazizi set himself on fire in Tunisia last December, inspiring the Arab revolt, he was driven to his desperate gesture by a terrible combination of material want and homegrown political humiliation felt by Arabs across the region. The intensity of the resulting demonstrations for serious change and the speed with which they spread throughout the Arab world suggest that these national rebellions, and the common regional trend they represent, will not wither away or be permanently suppressed by police actions.

This revolt is very different from the upsurge of Arab nationalism in the 1950s and '60s, when young Arab states still being born were caught up in a mass emotional and political response to a stultifying combination of what many saw as Israeli and Western aggression. That period of Arab nationalism was perhaps the last gasp of the anticolonial struggle that charismatic leaders such as Egypt's Gamal Abdel Nasser tapped into so effectively. The mere idea of Arabs with shared identities, rights, and interests fighting for their sovereignty and building new countries electrified masses across the region for a fleeting decade, until the debacle of the 1967 Arab-Israeli war revealed the structural weaknesses of Arab nationalist regimes.

The current revolt is anchored much more solidly in the fierce determination of millions of citizens to live decent and normal lives, free of material desperation and political indignity. The revolt's intensity and broad scope also reflect the fact that it did not emerge from a vacuum. It is, rather, the culmination of decades of activism by scores of groups small and large that have struggled unsuccessfully for civil and political rights. Those battles erupted in many countries but did not achieve regional momentum, and consequently received little attention abroad. The challenges to the Arab order came from a variety of civil society initiatives, democracy and human rights movements, more specialized campaigns to promote the rights of women and workers, and thousands of individual writers and academics. Professional associations of lawyers, engineers, and doctors in many Arab countries have long fought for greater rights anchored in the rule of law, and business associations in recent years have also pushed for change, especially in education and the judiciary.

The Arab region enjoyed a brief spell of liberalization beginning in the late 1980s as a result of fallout from the Soviet Union's collapse and a serious economic crisis that brought widespread hardship and forced bankrupt authoritarian states to open up their systems enough to allow citizens to air their frustrations and grievances. Roughly between 1986 and 1992, Arabs in the tens of millions embraced the possibilities of a more open press and the ability to create political parties and civil society organizations. Flocking to vote and speak their minds, they forcefully expressed their long-pent-up demand for real citizenship.

Islamist movements emerged in the 1980s as the most important challengers of Arab state power, and in most cases they were beaten down by the state's security forces, their members jailed en masse or forced into exile. The important thing about these movements—including the Muslim Brotherhood in Jordan, Egypt, and Syria; Al-Nahda in Tunisia; Amal and Hezbollah in Lebanon; and the Islamic Salvation Front in Algeria—is that in almost every case they grew primarily on the strength of their status as local groups demanding more citizen rights and empowerment, better government, and less corruption, rather than their criticisms of the United States and Israel. Today's revolt is built on the same foundation, with demands centered on citizen rights and constitutional changes, while foreign-policy issues take, at least for now, a back seat.

One American scholar who has long studied Arab political economy, former American University of Beirut president and Princeton University professor John Waterbury, noted in a private communication some months ago, "Quiescence has never been a consistent feature of the Arab world. Citing only from memory, I note the following: cost of living riots in Casablanca, 1965; food riots in Egypt, 1977; the Hama massacres of 1982 in Syria; cost of living riots in Jordan, Sudan, Algeria in the late 1980s; the Shia uprising in Iraq in 1991; the long-smoldering Islamist insurrection in Algeria after 1991; Houthis and others fighting the regime in Yemen; civil war continuously in the Sudan since the early '80s; the Lebanese civil war, 1976–89; the Palestinians against the Israelis seemingly forever, and so on.

"We should not confuse police states with political docility. There have been at least three other civilian-led protest movements that led to real change, but not to lasting change. In 1964 and again in 1985 civilian demonstrations led to the downfalls of General [Ibrahim] Abboud and Jaafar Numeiry of the Sudan, leading to years of civilian government, until 1989 when General Omar Bashir seized power and remains in power. In the spring of 2005 a million mostly young Lebanese went to Martyrs' Square in Beirut and brought about the downfall of the Karami government and the withdrawal of Syrian military forces from Lebanon."

Egypt alone in recent years has witnessed the rise of the Kefaya movement, which challenged Mubarak family rule in the years before the election of 2005; the judges' movement for the rule of law; human rights and voters' rights movements that included brave pioneers such as Saad Eddin Ibrahim and the Ibn Khaldoun Center; the April 6 Movement, which emerged from the 2008 labor strikes; the vibrant opposition press led by the start-up newspaper *Al-Masry Al-Youm* and others; and thousands of young bloggers who spoke on the Web when they were not allowed to speak in public. Such determined activism for freedom, democracy, and the rule of law has occurred in almost every Arab country over the past two generations.

Some Arab countries are now moving toward radical change, while in others, citizens' democratic aspirations are frozen by the heavy hand of a ruling security state. New actors are emerging or reasserting themselves, including youth groups, formerly exiled or banned political parties, labor unions, private-sector-led political parties, and reform-oriented civil society organizations. Other actors, notably the military, Islamists, and traditional political parties, are repositioning themselves. The Arab political stage has now been repopulated with a rich array of new and reinvigorated actors. It will be some time before they sort themselves out, determining which will lead and which will play niche roles. Most Arab countries have not engaged in public politics for half a century; they should not be expected to transform themselves instantly.

Even as they are experiencing these momentous changes, Arab countries must deal with four enormous and simultaneous challenges: maintaining security, rekindling economic growth, creating legitimate and participatory governance systems, and preventing mass discontent sparked by unfulfilled expectations from pushing countries back toward autocratic rule. The liberated Arab lands that are able to slowly establish more democratic political governance systems will each take on a different tone and color as they create their own formulas from the possibilities before them: tribal values, pan-Arab sentiment, narrow nationalism, corporate globalism, Islamist influences, and roles for the military. Arab democracies will look very different from Western ones, and the world should have the patience and composure to let the people of this region find their own sustainable balances between religiosity and secularism, state-centered and pan-Arab nationalism, and traditional and modern forms of governance.

The key to success will be the ability of reconfigured democratic Arab systems to institutionalize citizen rights and limits to state power in enforceable constitutional systems, with the rule of law protected by an independent judiciary. These are the common elements of the rallying cry across the region. In every single country where Arab citizens have revolted against their regime, the main demand is for constitutional changes that protect the rights of individuals.

Arab democratization will need time to succeed. It will take at least a decade to show if the change now under way is irreversible—as I believe it is.

The last of the line? Egypt's Hosni Mubarak was the third in a series of long-reigning "pharaohs" who have led the nation in modern times.

❖

Rami G. Khouri, a former public policy scholar at the Woodrow Wilson Center, is an internationally syndicated columnist and the director of the Issam Fares Institute for Public Policy and International Affairs at the American University of Beirut.

The Arab Autumn

By Stephen L. Carter
Newsweek, November 7, 2011

Tyrants have fallen. Elections have begun. Does America have the stomach to stand up for freedom once again?

It is autumn now in the Arab Spring. The protests that began last December when a Tunisian street vendor set himself afire have toppled three of the Arab world's seemingly eternal strongmen and show few signs of abating.

In Western hearts, the Arab Spring has excited admiration but also envy. Commentators have drawn labored and myopic comparisons with Occupy Wall Street, or the Tea Party. Only in America could we imagine a link between the passing spasms of our electoral politics and the greatest cultural upheaval of the young century, the demand for freedom and democracy by an entire people of whom experts said for decades that authoritarianism was a natural way of life.

Others choose as metaphor the collapse of the Communist bloc in 1989, another world-shaking political event that took the West by surprise. But the governing parties of the Arab world, although they claim to rule in the name of Islam, are not united by a central ideology. If the strongmen who have fallen and those who yet reign share a common belief, it is in the importance of their own power—and the ability to enrich their inner circles.

Should the passions of the Arab Spring continue unabated, America will face a conundrum. The Obama administration seemed ill at ease in the early days of the protests, undecided, for example, whether it was for Mubarak or against him. The United States seemed to be chasing the news, even though President Obama had declared in Cairo just two years earlier that "government of the people and by the people sets a single standard for all who hold power."

The president found his footing with the decision to go to war against Gaddafi. Across the region, other dictators, and other people yearning for freedom, are wondering whether America has the stomach to do it again, or whether our effort to help the Arab Spring along was one final gesture by a superpower pressed by more urgent matters at home.

The Libya intervention, contrary to the fears of its critics, may actually have enhanced America's reputation around the Mediterranean. In Syria, antiregime demonstrators are carrying signs lauding the death of Gaddafi and promising Assad that he is next. Dissenters in both Syria and Yemen are inviting the American military to take up their cause.

Ironically, the people spilling into the streets of Hama and Sanaa have seen clearly what the administration, for no good reason, continues to obscure. Libya was an American war in which NATO assisted—not the other way around. We provided the drones, the refueling planes,

> *The protests that began last December when a Tunisian street vendor set himself afire have toppled three of the Arab world's seemingly eternal strongmen and show few signs of abating.*

and the cruise missiles, to say nothing of surveillance and command-and-control facilities. Without the United States, Gaddafi would still be running the country. All the Arab world knows this, although the affection in which those demanding freedom now hold the United States may fade as the American presence wanes, especially if our withdrawal from Iraq leaves that struggling young democracy to devolve into a vassal of Iran.

What the Arab Spring has made clear is that slaughter is yesterday's tool of control. Heartened by the success of the revolutions in North Africa, the protesters in Syria seem less cowed than emboldened by the regime's violence. Even Assad by now must realize that the Baath Party's reign may be nearing its end.

In the nations where the mighty have already fallen, we do not know how matters will play out. Tunisia just held free elections. Libya's new leaders have frightened Westerners with talk of Sharia, but until we know the details, there is no reason for panic: in the abstract, at least, government based on principles of Sharia is analogous to government based on the Ten Commandments. Egypt is a more troubling case: the military remains in charge, and appears increasingly to view internecine violence not as a problem but as a tool.

Still, it is far too early for hand-wringing and second thoughts. Will Rogers once said that freedom works better in speeches than in practice. The Arab world is new to the practice of freedom and, like the rest of us, will make errors along the way. That is no reason not to cheer them on.

Neoconservatives and the Arab Spring

On the potential blessings and lurking hazards of a much-hoped-for revolution

By Joshua Muravchik
Commentary, September 2011

"Be careful what you wish for," it is said. Are neoconservatives soon to regret their wish for democratization in the Middle East? This was the very issue that thrust them into prominence in the early 2000s, and it gave neoconservatism a second lease on life after a decade of quiescence in the wake of the Cold War. It was said that President George W. Bush's strategy to defeat terrorism by ousting radical regimes and spreading freedom in the Middle East reflected the capture of his administration by "neocons." In truth, neoconservatives inside his government did not have their hands on the levers of policy, and the strategy seems to have been the president's own. But it was akin to things that had been advocated by some neocon writers, myself included, for many years. And neoconservative intellectuals outside the administration became highly visible spear-carriers for Bush's approach.

This precipitated a sharp split between neoconservatives and hard-headed Israeli analysts who had long been their allies and friends. While neocons saw democratization as a balm to soothe the fevered brow of the Arab world, Israeli strategists (with the notable exception of Natan Sharansky) thought this utterly naive. Their message in essence was this: you do not know the Arabs as we do. Difficult as their governments are to deal with, they are more reasonable than their populations. Democratization of the Arab world would lead to radicalization, which would be a bane to you and us. (This split was studiously ignored by the new wave of conspiracy-minded hate-mongers like Stephen Walt and John Mearsheimer and Andrew Sullivan, who claimed that neoconservatives were acting wholly in the interests of Israel. In fact they often said that neoconservatives were in particular devoted to the service of Israel's Likud Party—whose spokesmen, in contrast to some on the Israeli left, were especially adamant that spreading democracy among the Arabs was a fool's errand at best.)

The Israeli argument was akin to that of highly skeptical American and European conservatives. They said flatly that the problem with the Arabs went to the depths of their culture and could not be solved by political reform. More profound change would be required. Certainly a religious reformation within Islam might do the trick, but how could this be effectuated, especially from outside the faith? Others seemed resigned to a clash of civilizations, whatever that might mean. The neoconservative rejoinder did not deny that the problem lay deep but focused on what could be done about it. Perhaps Arab culture might be influenced in a way that would encourage its transformation. Democratization was less far-reaching than religious reformation or an anti-jihad jihad, but certainly it could influence a people's habits of thought. Witness how different Japan and Germany are today from the recent past.

That was the logic of the neoconservative position when it came to pushing for democratic change in the Arab world. The Bush administration adopted that position in the months after 9/11 and the president's 2002 National Security Strategy statement spelled it out. But 2005 and 2006 did not give democratization supporters much cause for hope. The victory of Hamas in Palestinian elections, the strong showing of the Muslim Brotherhood in Egyptian elections, and the failure of the political process inside Iraq to put an end to the spiraling violence there put Bush's democratization project on hold. The project was then utterly laid to rest by his successor, Barack Obama, who was determined above all to eschew anything that smacked of promoting Americanism. There it lay for two years until December 17, 2010. On that day, a policewoman in Sidi Bouzid, Tunisia, slapped an unlicensed fruit peddler, who proceeded to set himself on fire in protest. That ignited an explosion that has blown the status quo of the Arab world to kingdom come—to the surprise of neoconservatives and everybody else.

These events, while exciting and inspiring, are also frightening, even to some in the region who were staunchly opposed to the incumbent regimes. The revolutions have proclaimed the goal of democracy but might not achieve it, and they might inflame the conflict between the Arabs and Israel, and possibly other regional sore points.

Gradual transition would have been safer. In 2005, one of Egypt's leading liberals told me he would concede the point of regime apologists that Egypt might not be ready for democracy. But he believed it could be made ready in 10 years by starting with bona fide free elections at the local level.

Instead, we have had revolutions. And most revolutions end badly. The French, Russian, Chinese, and Iranian revolutions, to name a few, produced tyranny more awful than the regimes they had displaced. This, too, was the experience of the Arab world, which has had its share of revolutions, to disastrous effect. The first and modal one was the takeover of Egypt in 1952 by Gamal Abdel Nasser's Free Officers movement. That was followed by the Algerian uprising against France; upheavals in Iraq and Syria that ended in rule by the Baath parties; Muammar Qaddafi's seizure of power in Libya; and two turnovers in Sudan, one more leftist, the second more Islamist. The net effect was to make the region less free, more violent, and poorer than it would have been.

That history created this paradox: the Middle East's most liberal regimes are among the surviving monarchies of Morocco, Kuwait, and Jordan. The region as a whole is by far the least free in the world, but within it the variance is clear: on Freedom House's scale of freedom, where a score of 1 is best and 7 is worst, the Arab world's monarchies average a rating of 5—which is within the range, albeit barely, of what Freedom House calls "partly free." But its "republics" average 6, squarely defined as "not free." With the exception of Bahrain, all the revolutions of the Arab

Spring have taken place within these "republics." In other words, the region's various monarchies have managed to retain greater legitimacy than the heirs to the revolutions that overthrew their neighboring royals.

This in itself gives us real cause to worry about the outcomes of today's upheavals, and it is compounded by other worrisome signs. Democracy is widely saluted, but it is less widely understood. Public opinion polls in recent years throughout the Arab world have shown broad support for "democracy"... and for sharia, although none of the respondents explain how popular sovereignty and divine sovereignty can be practiced simultaneously.

This year's Egyptian protests were spearheaded by the inspiring April 6 Movement, a youth group that grew out of Kifaya ("Enough"), a coalition that crystallized in opposition to Mubarak's awarding himself yet another term of office in 2005. Those roots were, and are, problematic. Kifaya's spokesman, Abdel Halim Qandil, was a leading intellectual apologist in Egypt for the ideas of Egypt's most totalitarian former ruler, Gamel Abdel Nasser. And Kifaya's leader, George Ishaq, was a former Communist who gave scant sign of having rejected that creed.

"The liberals have failed to form a true ideological party that knows the street language of the people," lamented Shady Ghazali Harb, an Egyptian who has labored to create such a group. This plaint, true enough, is another way of saying that "the street" does not understand or fails to embrace the ideas of liberalism. The problem, however, is not only at the grass roots. The redoubtable blogger Sandmonkey recently described the current treatment of Mubarak in the Egyptian news media:

> [S]lowly but surely the perception of him as the traitor who helped assassinate Anwar Sadat in order to take power and neutralized Egypt for 30 years during which he kissed Israel's ass in every conceivable way in order to ensure his survival and U.S. support is being formed. Go to any newsstand any day and read the headlines. By the time he gets tried, and he will... he will be branded as the biggest traitor in the country's history.

In other words, the same papers and many of the same reporters who for decades identified Mubarak as the source of all good now depict him as the source of all evil. The former was not journalism suited to a democracy, but neither is the latter.

If even sophisticated and educated Arabs, such as those who work for newspapers, have an uncertain mastery of democracy, they know still less about economics—which bodes ill for the creation of the necessary adjunct to any democratic system, a relatively free market. Part of this is the result of the accident of Arab geography. How money is made and how private income is distributed are questions distorted in the Arab consciousness by the strange reality in their part of the world where great pools of wealth abound but very little of it is created through human labor or ingenuity. It just seeps from the ground.

As a result, the rulers of oil-rich states can do things that other governments cannot. When regional unrest began, the Saudi government drew $36 billion from its reserves to fund a basket of pay raises, housing subsidies, and other benefits for a citizenry already well cosseted by state subsidies. The king of Bahrain gave each

Bahraini family $3,000. Libya's Qaddafi promised every family $400 and doubled the pay of public employees. The emir of Kuwait bestowed each of his subjects with $3,500 in cash, plus free food for a year. And the sultan of Oman announced the creation of 50,000 new "jobs," with duties to be determined later.

It is difficult for non-oil-rich countries like Morocco, Tunisia, Egypt, Jordan, Syria, and Yemen to match that level of payoffs, but they have done what they could. They slashed taxes and duties and college tuition, raised subsidies on goods, and increased salaries—but without any resources to fund this largesse. One of the most perceptive Egyptians I know, a Copt, said to me recently, "I am not as afraid of Islamism as I am of populism."

Now polls in Egypt show a widespread expectation that standards of living will rise in the wake of the Arab Spring: 56 percent in a Pew poll expect the economy to improve this year; 80 percent expect their household income to rise, according to a poll commissioned by the International Republican Institute. Yet there is little sign of a corresponding appreciation that the country will have to become more productive in order for the real incomes of most citizens to rise. Instead, the body politic seems obsessed with searching out the ill-gotten wealth of Mubarak and his cronies. The sums bandied about in the Egyptian press, fueled by wholly speculative stories in the *Guardian* and on ABC News, are wildly fanciful—surely Mubarak didn't squirrel away $70 billion. (The *Guardian* attributed this estimate to "experts," then backed down claiming it relied on a single "expert," and then retracted even that.) But whatever Mubarak may have stolen, the restoration of that money would make no significant difference to Egypt's prospects and those of its 90 million people. Far more important is to reverse the flight of investment and the sharp reduction in tourism, the country's second largest industry.

Such mundane calculations, however, are drowned in the intoxication of "revolution," which is being invoked in the Arab lands like a talisman. Even Sandmonkey, whose métier is iconoclasm, posted this spring that he felt "nothing but optimism . . . the future is AWESOME." The other side of this same coin is an exaggerated fear of "counterrevolution." But it is hard to picture what model the people who express this fear have in mind.

They might do well to consider the sad history of the Mensheviks, those redoubtable Russian social democrats who spent 1917 so worried about a restoration of the czar that, much to their own detriment, they unwittingly abetted the Bolsheviks' seizure of power. The 2011 Middle Eastern analogue of the Bolsheviks is the Islamists. In June some 13 Egyptian political parties, including most of the country's liberal and leftist groups, announced an electoral bloc with the Muslim Brotherhood's Freedom and Justice Party. They agreed to work out a common slate of candidates in coming parliamentary elections.

"This coalition . . . will dictate the electoral outcome," crowed Brotherhood leader Essam al-Arian. Why did groups such as the Wafd Party, the traditional embodiment of liberalism, and Ayman Nour's al-Ghad tie their tail to the Brotherhood's kite? Apparently they feared a restoration of the power of the formerly ruling National Democratic Party. But the NDP was an administrative arm of the dictatorship rather than an electoral or ideological vehicle, and it is doubtful that there is much left of it.

Since Mubarak's fall, Egypt's Muslim Brotherhood has proclaimed ad nauseam its devotion to freedom and democracy (or, more precisely, "democracy based on Islamic reference," whatever that means). Its English-language website is thick with self-descriptions of its "moderation" and avowals of its opposition to "terrorism." But the organization has played bait and switch on these subjects before.

In 2004, the Brotherhood announced a new "initiative," expressing its support for democracy and the rights of women and nonbelievers. Cadres were even guided to substitute the slogan "freedom is the answer" for the group's traditional "Islam is the answer." But the slogan change lasted only a year. Then in 2007 the Brotherhood circulated a draft platform, the first ever made public, that proposed a Sunni equivalent of Iran's system of Shiite theocracy. It envisioned a Supreme Council of Clerics with plenary authority to overrule the president of the country. The Supreme Council would have to yield to the legislative branch of the government, but only in regard to issues "which are not unambiguously [settled] by sharia laws." In other words, whatever the clerics deemed to be covered by sharia—presumably most things, given that the constitution declares sharia to be the "main source of law"—would apparently be subject to the final authority of the holy men.

That draft platform seems never to have been approved. But neither was it superseded. Today, the Brotherhood's political actions call into doubt its commitment to democracy. Rather than seek office in its own name, it created the Freedom and Justice Party. The relationship between the two has been described by Middle East scholar Nathan Brown:

> The new Freedom and Justice Party will be free, says the parent Muslim Brotherhood, to make its own choices. But the Brotherhood [like a] helicopter parent cannot resist suggesting to its offspring who the new party's leaders will be, what it stands for, how it will be organized, who should join it, and who its candidates will be. The party is completely independent in decision-making so long as it does precisely what it is told. And actually, it is not only the party that is being told what to do; individual members of the Brotherhood movement have been told to join no other party and to obey movement discipline in the political realm.

The Brotherhood protests that it has no wish to take power, and originally Freedom and Justice was going to enter candidates for only 30 percent of the seats. That number has climbed to 50 percent and might go higher. If it wins anything near that, it will be able to dominate by bargaining for the adherence of marginal parties and independents, much as those groups did the NDP's bidding under the old regime.

The Brotherhood fought tooth and nail against postponing elections, which would give other parties time to organize. The Freedom and Justice Party's leader, Muhammad Morsi, denounced the advocates of electoral postponement as "Zionists and remnants of the former corrupt regime." It has fought, too, against the patently sensible proposal that a constitution be put in place before voters choose a new government. The Brotherhood hopes to win a quick election for a legislature and then to have that body write the constitution, allowing the Islamists to put their stamp on the new Egypt for a long time to come.

The Brotherhood is also slippery on the subject of violence and terrorism. It long ago renounced violence, and it decries "extremism"; its website features countless articles attacking al-Qaeda. Indeed, it has been outflanked on the extremist side by a movement of "Salafists," those who, following the radicals of Saudi Arabia, believe that everyone should live exactly as did the Prophet and his fellows. They have emerged from the shadows to form a political party and wage a campaign of violence against Egypt's Christians.

But in May, on a day when the Brotherhood declined to participate in a national conference of the various mostly secular protest groups, it instead held a joint gathering with the Salafists. And despite its polemics against al-Qaeda, it vociferously denounced America's assassination of Osama bin Laden. The Brotherhood did renounce violence in the 1970s, but only in exchange for the release of its leaders from prison. Since then, the Brotherhood has flourished in an ambiguous status, sometimes persecuted, sometimes winked at. Had the Brotherhood reprised its rich history of bloodshed, it would have faced ruthless repression.

In other words, the Brotherhood's embrace of peaceful methods is tactical, not philosophical. While it eschews violence within Egypt, it is full-throated in its encouragement of violence elsewhere. As Mehdi Akef, the immediate past "general guide" of the Brotherhood explained:

> The Muslim Brotherhood movement condemns all bombings in the independent Arab and Muslim countries. But the bombings in Palestine and Iraq are a [religious] obligation. This is because these two countries are occupied countries, and the occupier must be expelled in every way possible. Thus, the movement supports martyrdom operations in Palestine and Iraq in order to expel the Zionists and the Americans.

Akef was succeeded last year by Mohamed Badei, who expressed similar thoughts in sermons after taking office. Zionism, he declared in one sermon, "knows nothing but the language of force, so . . . improvement and change . . . can only be attained through jihad and sacrifice and by raising a generation that pursues death just as the enemies pursue life." In another sermon, he made clear this approach applied beyond Israel: "It is your obligation to stop the absurd negotiations," he urged the flock, "and to support all forms of resistance for the sake of liberating every occupied piece of land in Palestine, Iraq, Afghanistan, and all parts of our Muslim world."

Just as Islamism casts a cloud over the Egyptian revolution, so it does throughout the region. Tunisia is perhaps the most European-influenced of Arab countries, and its Islamist party, Ennahda, also makes a display of moderation. Yet its leader, Rashid al-Ghannushi, who returned from exile upon the overthrow of the government at the beginning of 2011, was named by a group of Arab and Muslim liberals in 2005 as one example of those who issue fatwas "encouraging the commission of terrorist acts in the name of . . . Islam." His fatwa, they explained, "permits killing all civilians in Israel, because 'there are no civilians in Israel. The population—males, females, and children—are the army reserve soldiers, and thus can be killed.'" Regarding its vision of Tunisia's future, "there are colossal suspicions about Ennahda," said Cambridge University regional specialist George Joffe. "No one believes their commitment to democracy and pluralism. Their discourse in Arabic is very different to their discourse in French."

In Libya, the role of Islamists has been tracked in a briefing paper and articles in the British press by No-man Benotman. Benotman, a veteran of jihad against the Soviet occupation of Afghanistan, was a senior leader of the Libyan Islamic Fighting Group, linked to al-Qaeda. He is today a leader of Quilliam, a courageous London-based organization of former Islamists who oppose Islamism. In the early days of the Libyan uprising, Benotman wrote that "jihadist groups . . . are nowhere near as powerful or as widespread as the Qaddafi regime has claimed." By summer 2011, he was warning that "jihadism . . . is now emerging as a problem in the liberated areas of the country." While both the early and later assessments contained qualifications and caveats, he clearly has grown more concerned.

> *In sum, there is danger that the Arab Spring could yield a deadly harvest.*

The possibility that Islamists could replace Arab governments overthrown this year is the most distressing but not the only alarming prospect in the Arab Spring. Even non-Islamist groups might opt for policies less cooperative with America and more hostile to Israel. Virtually every one of Egypt's declared presidential candidates, including the liberals, has called for either abrogating or "revising" the 1979 peace treaty with Israel. The common platform of the 14-party electoral alliance led by the Brotherhood calls for "a strategic dialogue with Iran and Turkey" and a "review of the settlement process with Israel on the basis that it is not a real peace in light of the unjust aggression and violation of the Palestinian right of self-determination."

In sum, there is danger that the Arab Spring could yield a deadly harvest. Yet there are substantial reasons to hope that it will instead produce something flourishing and beneficial. One such reason is the degree to which the protesters in Egypt, Tunisia, and notably Syria have maintained the discipline of nonviolence. Another is their focus on their own countries rather than foreign scapegoats. And even though the general Egyptian understanding of democracy is confused, there are quarters in which one can find surprising sophistication on this score. In July, 27 Egyptian advocacy groups issued "The Basic Constitutional Provisions Papyrus," a short but remarkably thoughtful document setting forth "basic principles" for a new constitution.

It calls for "sovereignty of the people"; "the separation, balance, and mutual oversight of the . . . executive . . . legislative, and the judicial" branches of government; and "diversity of the sources of legislation," in contrast to the current constitution which makes sharia the main source. It demands equal rights for "all Egyptians, women and men," it places strong emphasis on pluralism, asserting that the country's "multipl[icity of] religions, sects, confessions, ethnicities, and cultures . . . is the most significant source of the richness and distinction of Egyptian identity."

In addition, although only a few hundred words long, the Papyrus limns the equivalent of the U.S. Bill of Rights and also addresses issues specific to the region, such as the need to establish a school curriculum that will educate for democracy, the banning of private militias, a deep appreciation for balancing majority rule and minority rights, and the desirability of some transitional safeguards until "a democratic system is firmly established in Egypt, perhaps over the next 20 years."

A month before the release of the Papyrus, an overlapping coalition of eight groups issued a well-wrought statement setting forth the importance of devising a constitution before choosing a new government. The Cairo Institute for Human Rights Studies, a leader of such coalitions, also courageously warned against the current mania for retribution against the deposed authorities. In a June statement, the institute said:

> CIHRS believes that guarantees for a fair trial, which all defendants in all cases must enjoy, are particularly important in the cases involving the deposed president, regime figures, and security personnel. These guarantees, most important the presumption of innocence, are of the utmost importance for arriving at the facts and learning the lessons of the grave systematic and institutional abuses of the three decades of the Mubarak era.

The contrast between the stance of this group and the calls for Mubarak's head that continue to reverberate in Tahrir Square illustrates a nuance in the political picture often overlooked in analyses that posit two main camps, Islamists and "liberals." In truth many of the secularists who rallied to the revolution are not liberals, but socialists of various stripes or adherents of other ideologies or simply people of little political sophistication who were fed up with Mubarak's interminable rule and the prospect of a dynastic succession. The good news is that both of these elements—the fully fledged liberals and the broader constellation of secularists willing to come into the streets—turned out to be much larger than anyone had imagined before this year.

This points to an important difference between the revolutions of 2011 and those a half century or more ago in Egypt, Syria, and Iraq. The earlier events were military coups; these are popular uprisings. True, popular uprisings are frightening and the participants may believe foolish things. But it is hard to imagine that anyone could clamp new dictatorships on these countries, as Nasser and the Baathists did back then, without a fierce battle.

A source of fear on this score is the example of Iran's 1979 revolution. As an unnamed Israeli official told the *Washington Post*, Westerners looking at today's revolutions, "see Europe 1989, we see Iran 1979." True, Ayatollah Ruhollah Khomeini succeeded in imposing a new despotism on Iran more tyrannical than the reign of the shah, confounding many of the participants in Iran's uprising whose goal was freedom and democracy. But here is where the analogy breaks down. Khomeini established himself as the leader and icon of the revolution years before it triumphed. Iranian secularists and liberals misjudged badly in hitching their wagon to his star, thinking that once the shah was ousted, the Ayatollah would rest content as a figurehead. Instead, Khomeini exploited his charismatic appeal to crush his former allies and concentrate power in his own hands. In the Arab revolutions, however, no figures have emerged even roughly analogous to Khomeini in popular appeal.

It is also not certain that Islamists will score as well as expected in coming elections, despite being better organized than their opponents. In Egypt, the Brotherhood has been rocked by internal divisions. When it decided not to run a candidate for president, Abdel Moneim Abou el-Fotouh (perhaps its most popular leader and known for relatively moderate views) announced he would run as an independent. For this insubordination he was promptly expelled. Fotouh formed his own party, Renaissance, in opposition to the Brother's Freedom and Justice, and the other leading moderate of the Brotherhood's governing Guidance Council, Mohammed Habib, soon resigned to join him.

The Brotherhood's youth organization has been at odds with the parent body, for example, cosponsoring with secular groups a demonstration in Tahrir Square, vociferously opposed by the elders, in favor of postponing elections. One group of youth has formed its own political party, Egyptian Current, another rival to Freedom and Justice, and its leaders, too, were expelled from the Brotherhood. Some older reformers within the movement have left to form a third offshoot party, the Pioneers, and still others have formed a fourth.

Hisham Kassem, a leading Egyptian newspaper publisher and human-rights activist, notes that the Brotherhood's strong showing in the partially rigged and partially free 2005 elections may lead to the overestimation of its current level of strength. In 2005, it was the sole repository of protest votes, and the extremely low voter turnout magnified the strength of its loyal cadres. This year, turnout will be much higher, and Kassem believes the Brotherhood will capture no more than 10 to 20 percent of the seats, which corresponds with several voter polls.

Perhaps the most important of the region's hopeful signs is the rebellion in Syria. Who would have thought that Syrians, of all peoples, would have earned the world's admiration? Yet it is hard to think of many cases in which nonviolent protestors have exposed themselves to shoot-to-kill security forces for months on end without being cowed into surrender. If these brave people persevere and drive the Assad dynasty from power, that itself would go far toward making the Arab Spring a net benefit for the region and the world.

To be sure, the fall of the house of Assad would not guarantee democracy. But unlike in Egypt—where outcomes that are worse than the old regime (worse for America, for Israel, and for the Egyptians themselves) are not hard to picture—any successor government of Syria could scarcely be more malign than the present one. It is one of the 18 most repressive in the world, a category that Freedom House dubs "the worst of the worst." It keeps its own border with Israel quiet, but it is the patron of Hezbollah and the pipeline through which as many as 40,000 to 50,000 missiles have been shipped to Lebanon to be aimed at Israel. In addition, Syria is the linchpin of Iran's drive for regional hegemony, which is the source of the region's most dire problems. Remove that asset and Tehran's whole strategy crumbles. To indulge in a bit of perhaps wild optimism, it is even possible that the overthrow of the Syrian regime, which all Iranians know is their government's closest ally, could prove to be the spark that rekindles Iran's own Green Movement revolution.

Beyond Syria, there is reason to believe the outcome of the Arab Spring will be positive. Granted, the road to democracy will be bumpy. But to speak of democracy in the Arab world is not necessarily to speak of *liberal* democracy. While Freedom House currently counts 115 "electoral democracies"—that is, countries with governments chosen in free, competitive elections—it rates only 88 of them as "free." The other 27 are "partly free," meaning that the judiciary is not fully independent or the press is not fully free or corruption is rampant. It is not difficult to picture a country like Egypt joining the ranks of these partly free electoral democracies and remaining there for a long time. But that alone would be a big improvement and a big influence on the region, all the more so if Iraq were to settle into a similar status once American troops leave.

It is of course possible that the road will be worse than bumpy, that it will curve around to some other, awful destination in the manner of the Iranian or the Russian revolutions. Tragically, once regimes like those of Khomeini or Lenin seize power, they can hold it for generations however miserably they govern. Were that to happen in Libya or Syria, it could not be much worse than what has prevailed the last 40-odd years. In Egypt, however, it would be disastrous. But it seems unlikely that the Egyptians, aroused as they are and having lived through the Nasser experience, would succumb to a new despotism. The most likely force to impose it, the Muslim Brotherhood, has been having trouble keeping its own members in line, much less the rest of the country.

Israel will almost surely have to endure a less cooperative Egypt. And if the peace treaty is tampered with, that could be a terrible problem. But once this storm is weathered, there could be additional benefits. When a popularly elected Egyptian government faces this issue, the likelihood is that it will recognize that peace with Israel is in its own interests, which is of course what led Anwar Sadat to make peace in the first place. In that case, the Egyptian people might, however grudgingly, come to own the peace, rather than see it as something foisted on them, and this would make it all the more secure.

Finally, one must recall the original reason that neoconservatives and George W. Bush embraced the cause of democracy in the Middle East. It was a way of addressing the toxicity of Arab political culture, in which despotism is the norm even while democracy has become predominant in much of the rest of the world. This political sickness has deep roots, in the metastasized sense of pride and twisted idea of honor that prompts Arabs to kill their daughters and sisters and consider the existence of a single non-Arab sovereignty in their midst unbearable; in the perverted religious sensibility that has led numerous Arab spokesmen to intone in recent years, "you love life, but we love death"; in the stagnation and misguided energies that have made airport scanners the principle Arab contribution to modern life.

How to change this? It cannot be through mass therapy or religious conversion or a war of civilizations. Politics may reflect deeper levels of human experience—psychological, cultural, religious—but it also can influence those strata. Democracy is not only a way of choosing governments. It is also a practice that socializes citizens and fosters beneficent habits of thought. Even partial and imperfect democratization could strongly affect the Arab world in ways beneficial not only to the Arabs themselves but also to the world as a whole.

❖

Joshua Muravchik, a fellow at the Johns Hopkins University School of Advanced International Studies, is the author, most recently, of The Next Founders: Voices of Democracy in the Middle East (Encounter). *He is completing a book on the demonization of Israel.*

World Citizen: Don't Call It the 'Arab Spring' Just Yet

By Frida Ghitis
World Politics Review, September 22, 2011

When Mohamed Bouazizi set himself on fire in his Tunisian village last December, nobody knew he would electrify the entire Arab world and send the existing political order in the region into a long period of turmoil. Very quickly, however, there were signs that the success of Tunisian demonstrators in toppling their long-ruling dictator had sparked something important—something with probably lasting, although unclear consequences. As the first signs emerged that the movement might catch on elsewhere in the region, a catchy label derived from Czechoslovakia's brief Cold War–era uprising against Soviet rule quickly engraved itself in the Western lexicon. Today, the uprisings that have engulfed a dozen Arab countries are collectively known in the West as the Arab Spring. The label, apt or not, has taken hold for now.

Despite some disagreement about what the term suggests, most people would agree it evokes a Hollywood-esque outcome, one where the moral force and sheer courage of the people sends a series of dictators to their ignominious end, bringing freedom at last to the region.

We hope for a happy ending, of course. But the future, especially in the Middle East, tends to lay traps and hidden surprises. And not everyone thinks that such a sunny, hopeful label is the best way to characterize the revolts. In fact, the expression is for the most part not used in the countries where the uprisings are unfolding.

The tumult of the last eight months will unquestionably go down as a noteworthy moment in history, but the name used by future generations to describe these extraordinary times will depend on the shape of events to come. If the Arab Spring gives way to a wholesale defeat of democratic ideals, historians may prefer to call it something else altogether, perhaps the Arab Winter or the Arab Storm, perhaps even the Islamic Revival. If the final outcome of the disturbances ends up resembling a new version of the tyranny that was there before, future historians might speak of the Arab Interlude or the Great Popular Disappointment.

The first reference to an "Arab Spring" goes back to 2003, as the war in Iraq was just starting. In an article titled "Dreaming of Democracy," George Packard wrote pessimistically in the *New York Times* about the chances that the U.S.-led war would "ventilate the region with an Arab Spring." In the years that followed, many analysts, but particularly conservatives, used the expression in connection with the potential for democratic change in the Middle East in the wake of America's introduction of democracy in Iraq.

The term was revived this January in a *Christian Science Monitor* editorial after Tunisia's dictator Zine el Abidine Ben Ali fled his country. Pointing to the growing nervousness in the region, the editors wondered whether an "Arab Spring or Arab winter" lay ahead.

> *We hope for a happy ending, of course. But the future, especially in the Middle East, tends to lay traps and hidden surprises.*

The term caught on, and with it the inevitable extensions of the metaphor.

For a moment, after Ben Ali quickly left power, it looked as if peaceful democratic change might quickly sweep away a spate of dictatorships. But now it has become evident that much blood must be shed to dislodge entrenched tyrants and that some of the rulers may manage to hold on to power despite the brave and persistent efforts of their opponents.

With spring and summer now over, it looks as though the premature seasonal allusion, with its images of bright flowers and renewal, may well be the wrong name for what is taking place.

Some are openly rejecting the term, but for very different reasons.

Most of those who dislike it contend that its non-threatening overtones assume a Western-friendly outcome. The name implies that the upheaval is part of "the relentless march of progress and liberal democracy," wrote Ed Rooksby. By calling it an Arab Spring, he reasoned, we implicitly try to assert the "superiority of the Western model."

That association between the term Arab Spring and a positive outcome is apparently shared in Washington, where high-level analysts are reportedly saying that we should use a more neutral word, such as "Arab transition," to underline the fact that we don't know where the uprisings will lead.

But not everyone finds positive connotations in the term Arab Spring. Lebanon's Rami Khouri sees it as another derogatory expression of Western Orientalism. Spring, he says, "is a passive term. It just happens to people—helpless people who have no power and no say in the process." He also dislikes it because it evokes the temporary nature of the Prague Spring in 1968, when Czechs briefly rose up against the Soviets, only to see their dreams quickly dashed by Russian tanks in the streets, followed by a hardening of Communist rule.

Khouri prefers "Arab Citizens' Revolt." And Rooksby says we should dispense with metaphor and simply call it a revolution. But not everyone agrees that what we're seeing is, in fact, a revolution. George Friedman of Stratfor has been arguing for months that what happened in Egypt cannot be called a revolution because, in fact, there was no regime change. Mubarak, he says, headed the regime, but then the regime turned on him. Under Mubarak, a former general, Egypt was ruled by the military. Mubarak may be gone, he says, but the military regime has not relinquished power.

In Arabic, the most commonly used term to describe what is happening in the Arab Middle East is "thawra" (revolution). Khouri lists other terms, including "intifada" (uprising), "sahwa" (awakening) and "nahda" (renaissance.) The word "intifada" seems appropriate, since there is no question that a series of uprisings is taking place. But that term, at least in the West, has already been irrevocably associated with the Israeli-Palestinian conflict. The Arabic words sahwa and nahda have more aspirational than descriptive qualities. An awakening or a renaissance is what many protesters would like to see emerge from their efforts, just as they would like to see a successful revolution overturn the political system.

Because we are still in the early stages of what will undoubtedly be a lengthy process, it is impossible to know what these uprisings will accomplish. The debate over what to call them reflects the wishes, fears and ideologies of those arguing against the use of Arab Spring. Regardless of the negative connotations ascribed to it by Khouri, it seems clear that the label became the term of choice in the West because those living in Western democracies optimistically hope they are watching a bright, heart-warming story that will lead to a happy ending.

The coming months and years will reveal whether the events themselves, set in motion by a Tunisian fruit vendor and the forceful actions of millions of Arabs, will produce results that warrant such a cinematically promising label. But the fact is, we have not seen this movie before. We should wait to see how it ends before we choose its name. For now, we can hope for the best and give it a more accurate description: the "Arab uprisings."

❖

Frida Ghitis is an independent commentator on world affairs and a World Politics Review contributing editor. Her weekly column, World Citizen, appears every Thursday.

The Dark Side of the Arab Spring

By Jonathan Aitken
American Spectator, June 2011

The Arab Spring is fast becoming a winter of discontent for Christians and other religious minorities in the Middle East. In Washington the first stirrings of protest were hailed as a breakthrough for democracy. But the second phase of the uprising has brought fear, discrimination, and violent pressure against Christians in countries rebelling against incumbent regimes across the region.

This is particularly disappointing because the early signs of tolerance were hopeful. One of the most moving aspects of the crowds in Tahrir Square was that Christians and Muslims protested alongside each other in unity. Such was their solidarity that at prayer time on Friday the Christians formed a human shield to protect their kneeling fellow demonstrators from police baton charges. The cooperation was reciprocated but it was too good to last.

Egypt's 8 million Coptic Christians are now having a rough time. The vacuum left by Mubarak is being filled by the Muslim Brotherhood and the Salafists. Both are extreme in their Islamism. They campaigned for their followers to vote "yes" to the new and flawed constitutional proposals that will result in discrimination against religious minorities, women, secular organizations, and progressive youth groups. Small wonder that when the "yes" vote was confirmed to have won, the ultra-conservative Salafist leader Sheikh Mohammed Hussein Yacoub was quoted as saying, "That's it. The country is ours."

There are sinister signs of the anti-Christian direction in which the Islamic extremists want to take Egypt. On New Year's Day, 21 Christians were killed and another 70 injured by a bomb that exploded as worshippers were leaving midnight mass at Al Qidissin (The Saints) church in Alexandria. On March 8, 13 Christians died and another 70 were injured when Salafists attacked Copts who were demonstrating against the tearing down of their church in Sool village and the murder of a priest in Assait. On March 20, Salafists in the town of Qena cut off the ears of 45-year-old Coptic Christian Ayman Anwar Mitri after accusing him of having had an affair with a Muslim woman. These episodes are part of a continuing pattern of outrages, including lynchings and beatings of Copts. In a lecture given in London on April 8, the Anglican leader in Egypt, Bishop Mouneer Hanna Anis, said, "The plight of the Coptic Christians is getting worse. They are living in a climate of uncertainty, fear, and apprehension."

Bishop Mouneer's words apply to minority religious communities all across the region that some Washington commentators have far too optimistically hailed as "the new Middle East." If the Salafists, jihadists, and Muslim Brothers have their way it will become the medieval Middle East, notorious for its intolerance and persecution of Christians. Who is going to prevent this?

Until recently it was a strange paradox that some of the most repressive political regimes were protective of religious minorities. In Syria, the beleaguered Bashar al-Assad has a good record of safeguarding the rights of the Druze, the Christians,

> **One of the most moving aspects of the crowds in Tahrir Square was that Christians and Muslims protested alongside each other in unity.**

and the Jews. As a traveler to Damascus in 2008, I was moved by visiting the well-preserved Christian churches and holy places of the city, including those on Straight Street. They are not much changed since the blinded Saul of Tarsus had his sight restored there by Ananias and was lowered down the wall in a basket to escape his pursuers. I also saw the tomb of John the Baptist that President Assad visits once a year to lead a Christian prayer ceremony. Such tolerance is unlikely to last. The regime, even if it survives, will have to dilute its secularism by further concessions to its Islamist partners like Iran, Hezbollah, and Hamas.

If you want to understand how grim the future looks for Christians in the Middle East, go to Baghdad, where the continuing sectarian violence has driven most of them out of the city and the country. Once they worshipped peacefully under Saddam Hussein. Now 80 percent of Iraqi Christians have emigrated. Those that remain are mainly elderly, although there are heroic younger congregations who literally have to fight the good fight to remain churchgoers.

One of the bravest men I know is Canon Andrew White, Vicar of St. George's, Baghdad and author of *Faith Under Fire* (Monarch Books, 2011). I recently shared a platform with him at a Christian Solidarity Worldwide event in London. As we discussed the situation in the Arab world, I was moved to tears by his description of what he and his flock have to endure.

"Christianity in Iraq is under very vicious attack," says White. "It is a question of abduction, bombing, torture, rape, and murder. Christians are forced to pay jizya, the tax historically imposed by Islamic states on non-Muslims—in effect, protection money. So things are very difficult. Last year alone 93 members of my congregations were killed. The threat is particularly great for those who convert to Christianity. I baptized 13 adults secretly last year. Eleven of them were dead within a week."

Occasionally the deaths of persecuted Christians send shock waves in the right direction. One of the first casualities of the Tunisian revolution was a Polish priest, murdered for his faith by jihadists. His martyrdom caused protests in the streets that produced clear statements in favor of religious diversity by the new regime. Would that this example might prevail in other countries. Unfortunately all the signs point to greater intolerance.

Away from the dramatic episodes of bombings, assassinations, and ear or limb amputations by Islamist extremists, the everyday reality of life for Christians in the Middle East is that they face increasingly uncomfortable experiences of discrimination. Thanks to subtle or often unsubtle Islamist pressures, Christians have far less chance of employment in such organizations as the police, the military, the universities, the teaching professions, and the government bureaucracy. They also find themselves at a disadvantage in matters like housing or the issuing of driving licenses. One of their many problems is that they are suspected of being pro-Western. This is odd since more than 70 percent of Middle East Christians are from the Oriental Orthodox Churches—Armenian, Syrian, and Coptic—while an Eastern Catholic Church with the Maronites and the Chaldeans forms the second-largest group in the region. The doctrinal differences between these elements go back to the historic ecumenical Councils of Nicaea, Constantinople, and Ephesus, held respectively in AD 325, 381, and 431. It has taken the Arab Spring of 2011 to put them on the front line of hostility and persecution.

When the popular demonstrations against unpopular Arab rulers began earlier this year, the Christian churches in the region saw the movement with mixed emotions of hope and fear. Sadly, fear is now in the ascendant. The Christian community's hope of equality in freedom of speech and freedom of worship within pluralist democracies is being brutally obstructed by the Islamic extremists. Yet it is too early to despair. These revolutions have some way to go and many of their younger and more moderate Muslim supporters know that intolerant Islamism is not the answer to the problem of how to change society for the better. We Westerners should watch and pray!

❖

Jonathan Aitken is most recently the author of Nazarbayev and the Making of Kazakhstan: From Communism to Capitalism *(Continuum). His biographies include* Nixon: A Life *(Regnery),* Charles W. Colson: A Life Redeemed *(Doubleday), and* John Newton: From Disgrace to Amazing Grace *(Crossway).*

Arab Spring Transforms North Africa's Media Landscape

By Peter Feuilherade
The Middle East, July 2011

Arab journalists at the dawn of the 21st century, far from being defenders of the status quo, see their mission as driving political and social change.

The rapid transformations in North African media during the Arab Spring show they are embracing that mission with enthusiasm, replacing the formerly state-dominated media.

Fighting in Libya and political upheavals in Tunisia and Egypt have brought unprecedented changes to the media landscape, as new broadcasters, publications and websites have emerged.

Pundits differ over the role played by online media and social networking sites in fuelling the unrest, and the media revolution that has ensued.

The New York–based Committee to Protect Journalists (CPJ) described the blogging, video sharing, text messaging and live streaming from mobile phones of the demonstrations in Tahrir Square and Tunis as a "seismic shift" in how journalists rely on the internet and other digital tools. But the CPJ warned that oppressive regimes were also showing increasing sophistication in using the tools of new technology to suppress information.

For established broadcasters, the Arab uprisings have brought a surge in viewing figures, but with no corresponding economic benefit.

Audiences for satellite TV news channels, primarily the leading pan-Arab stations *Al Jazeera* and *Al Arabiya*, have doubled in key markets such as Saudi Arabia, the Dubai-based Pan Arab Research Centre (PARC) reports.

However, spending on TV advertising across the Arab world has slumped. In Egypt, it was down by 97% in February and 78% in March 2011, compared with the same months a year ago, PARC added.

Since the 17 February 2011 uprising, various opposition groups in rebel-held areas in eastern Libya, as well as abroad, launched their own affiliated newspapers, websites, radio and satellite TV stations to counter what they termed the "propaganda" of the state-controlled broadcaster.

Voice of Free Libya radio stations went on air in Benghazi and Al Bayda, as well as the besieged rebel-held port of Misrata in the west. The rebel-linked stations reflect a mix of Islamist and Libyan nationalist views in their programmes. In the town of

Nalut in the mountains of western Libya, journalists who had formerly broadcast pro-Gaddafi material on the local radio station switched sides, relaunching it as *Radio Free Nalut*.

Of the new opposition satellite TV channels, the slickest is *Libya TV*, launched at the end of March. It is based for the time being in Qatar, the first Arab country to recognise the Transitional National Council, the opposition shadow government.

After more than 40 years of state control over the media, apart from a short-lived period when Gaddafi's son Saif Al Islam operated the country's first privately owned media outlets, it is no surprise that most journalists in Libya fall short on production and technical skills.

But they make up for this in creativity and enthusiasm. The *Voice of Free Libya* broadcasts include revolutionary music, popular songs by Arab divas such as Fairuz, poetry with rebel themes, and phone-in programmes allowing citizens to air their views and grievances.

State-run *Al Jamahiriyah TV* went on the counter-offensive, launching an English-language TV channel to convey the Gaddafi regime's views to international audiences. The channel took the line that the uprising in Libya was fomented by Al Qaeda and "foreign elements".

Libyan state TV says its external service has been deliberately jammed. Air strikes on Tripoli by NATO-led forces have also intermittently disrupted state-controlled TV broadcasts.

The media in Egypt were already cowed by the severe crackdown that preceded the November 2010 parliamentary elections. Now media outlets are moving cautiously, after being given mixed signals.

> *For established broadcasters, the Arab uprisings have brought a surge in viewing figures, but with no corresponding economic benefit.*

The Supreme Council of the Armed Forces warned in March that it would carry out prior vetting of all reporting on topics covering Egypt's military establishment. In late April, it said that it would not interfere in media policy. But in May, the Council warned against websites and Facebook pages which could, in its words, "incite sectarianism and violence, and spread rumours that could destabilise the country."

Many laws impeding media freedom are still to be abolished. When a military court sentenced an Egyptian blogger to three years in jail in April for defaming the army and "disseminating false information," journalists got the message that limits on free speech still apply, particularly where the armed forces are concerned.

The new heads of state newspapers, TV and radio appointed by the government after President Mubarak was ousted in February have been accused of having close links with the former regime.

On the plus side, the new government has brought in new rules making it easier for privately owned TV channels to launch, and 16 new channels have already been approved.

A debate is under way about whether foreign models for media reform are compatible with Egypt's still-evolving political reality. But the vast majority of the tens of thousands of mainstream journalists still operate in a culture of self-censorship.

Aspiring media entrepreneurs in Tunisia are already accusing the interim government of using outdated bureaucratic procedures to block private broadcasting.

More than 40 applicants have sought approval to launch new radio and TV stations, but the authorities claim the number of "frequencies" is limited.

In mid-May, activists reported cases of resumed internet censorship. And journalists also complain they are still not free to do their jobs because of attacks and threats by security police, party activists and demonstrators.

With government institutions in North Africa accustomed to decades of state control over the media, not everyone regards western-style media pluralism as the highest priority, so significant reform could take years to consolidate.

As happened in Iraq after the overthrow of Saddam Hussein in 2003, many new broadcasters and publications have been launched, but not all will survive.

Some will go under for financial reasons such as high printing and production costs or lack of advertising; because they have fulfilled their short-term political objectives of spreading a particular group's message; or because the market simply cannot sustain too many competitors. Others, especially web-based media which are cheaper to operate, may enjoy a longer existence.

Arab Spring and the Mukhabarat Moment

By Ed Blanche
The Middle East, November 1, 2011

The fight back against repressive Arab regimes whose intelligence services and secret police once seemed invincible is well under way, but the 'democratic dawn' is not going down too well with western agencies fighting terrorism.

The downfall of the pro-western rulers of Egypt and Tunisia in the Arab Spring up-heavals, and the prospect that other authoritarian regimes in the Middle East may tumble has alarmed western intelligence services that depended on their Arab allies to help combat terrorism.

Given Washington's deteriorating relations with Pakistan, a vital partner in the war against Al Qaeda, any sustained reduction in intelligence cooperation with key Arab states could be potentially disastrous for the West.

Jordan, a vital US ally in the intelligence war, remains steadfast under King Abdullah II, as does Saudi Arabia under King Abdullah, whose wide-ranging but opaque intelligence establishment has often been challenging to deal with over the years.

But western sources say there has been a marked drop in the flow of intelligence from key Arab allies in recent months, as the region has been swept by unprecedented turmoil, particularly in Egypt, Tunisia, Yemen and even one-time adversary Libya.

This is particularly troublesome for the Europeans, who dislike the idea of hostile forces close by on their southern flank. "It's fair to say that we're concerned that further instability could affect intelligence exchanges," one source observed amid fears that large numbers of weapons, including shoulder-fired anti-aircraft missiles, looted from Libyan arsenals are finding their way to Al Qaeda groups and their allies across the region.

With the fall of Tunisian President Zine El Abidine Ben Ali in January and President Hosni Mubarak of Egypt a month later, and even the collapse in August of Libyan dictator Muammar Gaddafi, who had ruled since 1969, western agencies have found themselves cut off from a flow of vital intelligence concerning a global foe.

For Central Intelligence Agency veteran Michael Scheuer, who once headed the US spy organisation's unit tasked with hunting down Osama bin Laden, the Arab Spring has been "an intelligence disaster for the United States, for Britain and other European intelligence services" because of the fall of Middle Eastern leaders who had worked with them for decades.

"The help we were getting from the Egyptian intelligence service, less so from the Tunisians but certainly from the Libyans and Lebanese, has dried up—either because of resentment at our governments stabbing their political leaders in the back, or because those who worked for the services have taken off in fear of being incarcerated or worse," he lamented.

First and foremost, he says, is the loss of the so-called "black rendition" system the CIA launched after 9/11. That involved the agency secretly flying captured terrorist suspects to Egypt, Jordan, Morocco and other Arab states for interrogation by their intelligence services, which frequently involved torture.

But in the end, of course, even the Americans, self-styled guardians of democracy and the moral high ground, resorted to waterboarding and other harsh interrogation that the rest of world classifies as torture.

Meantime, the murky rendition operation allowed western agencies, under scrutiny to one degree or another by their countries' legislatures, to claim they were not involved in nefarious or illegal activities while attempting to secure the "product" necessary for them to be able to counter terrorism.

Avalanche of anger

Scores, probably hundreds, of suspects were thrust into the hands of Arab intelligence services that human rights organisations accuse of using systematic torture against political prisoners.

Western intelligence agencies, particularly the CIA and Britain's Secret Intelligence Service, MI6, garnered much invaluable information on Al Qaeda, its allies, and what they were plotting, through the cooperation of friendly regimes across the Middle East.

Scheuer, author of several books, including *Imperial Hubris: Why the West is Losing the War on Terror* in 2004, spent 22 years in the CIA and headed Alec Station, the unit tasked with tracking bin Laden, in 1996–99. He currently teaches peace and security affairs at the University of Georgetown in Washington.

"The amount of work that has devolved on US and British services is enormous, and the result is blindness in our ability to watch what's going on among militants," he said.

"The rendition programme must come back—the people we have in custody now are pretty long in the tooth in terms of the information they can provide in interrogations."

"The imperative now is to end our condition of collective captivity to military orders and liberate the Arab spirit and mind," Jordanian commentator and academic Rami Khouri wrote back in May 2006.

"Bringing Arab military and security establishments under the oversight and control of civilian institutions is critical to this goal," said Khouri, a longtime advocate of breaking the power of the Mukhabarat, the generic Arab word for secret police, that has dominated Arab political life for decades.

Across the Arab world, citizens have turned on the once-powerful intelligence and security services that tormented them for decades under authoritarian rulers who have been brought down or are scrambling to hold on to power in the face of this unprecedented avalanche of anger, reminiscent of how Eastern Europeans threw off the Soviet yoke in the 1990s.

In other Arab states such as Jordan, Bahrain and Oman, protesters have put kings and presidents on notice that they must democratise or fall. Saudi Arabia, Kuwait, Morocco and Sudan have also felt the stirrings of the winds of change.

Egypt's hated security services are supposedly being reorganised and made to conform to legal constraints. Tunisia's new prime minister has scrapped the reviled State Security Department, whose secret police tortured dissidents under the ousted Ben Ali.

In a move to placate protesters, Algerian President Abdelaziz Bouteflika has announced he will revoke a state of emergency in effect since 1992, which gave carte blanche to the country's fearsome security services. Oman's ruler, Sultan Qaboos, has replaced one of his security chiefs in a bid to quell street protests.

Tunisia's new government is weeding out personnel in its security and intelligence apparatus that were loyal to the ousted Ben Ali, most notably Abdessatar Bennour, head of the National Security Directorate. But dismantling a security establishment as vast as the one Hosni Mubarak built up during his 30 years of authoritarian rule will be no small undertaking.

> *Any sustained reduction in intelligence cooperation with key Arab states could be potentially disastrous for the West.*

Other Arab rulers did the same, but Mubarak's build-up was extraordinary, comparable only to the multi-tentacled instruments of repression created by Saddam Hussein of Iraq and Hafez Al Assad of Syria in the 1960s and 70s.

Mubarak, a former air force commander, steadily expanded the size of Egypt's security apparatus, particularly the much-hated State Security Investigations Sector (SSIS), the secret police, during his 30-year rule.

Now it is supposedly being dismantled and replaced by a more accountable organisation "in accordance with the constitution and human rights principles".

In 1974, the Interior Ministry commanded 150,000 personnel. By 2009, the strength was an estimated 1.7 million, including 400,000 SSIS officers, 850,000 policemen and associated staff, and 450,000 Central Security Force troops.

They outnumbered the army 3–1, and in 2002 accounted for one fifth of all government employees. No Arab security apparatus has ever been dismantled and been made accountable before.

President Hafez Assad of Syria, a Soviet-trained air force general who ruled with an iron grip from 1970 until his death in June 2000, built up an extraordinary network of intelligence and security services whose primary function was keeping his regime in power.

His son Bashar, who inherited power when Assad died in June 2000, has retained that vast apparatus and is now using it to crush the insurgency that began on 15 March and has already taken the lives of 3,000 people, largely unarmed protesters.

Assad's minority Alawite sect dominates Syria's vast security apparatus, which in the immediate aftermath of 9/11 was actually cooperating with the CIA against Al Qaeda. It massacred thousands of Muslim Brotherhood members and their families in a 1982 revolt and now it is mowing down dissidents as Bashar Assad fights for survival.

Democratic dawn

His security apparatus embraces 15 separate branches headed by Military Intelligence, and employs upwards of 50,000 people—an average of one Syrian in every 240. Some estimates run three times higher.

As much as one third of the military budget, of around $3 billion, is devoted to intelligence and internal security. The chiefs of these services are exclusively from Assad's Alawites and form one of the most important pillars of the regime in Sunni-majority Syria.

For 20 years, US intelligence relied on Hosni Mubarak's massive intelligence apparatus to help combat Islamist terrorism. The Cairo regime fought and crushed Muslim militants for two decades, but released hundreds of jihadist prisoners when Mubarak fell.

Mubarak's longtime intelligence chief, General Omar Suleiman, was cut out of the loop after the president was forced from office after three decades in power. CIA sources say Suleiman's successors are not as enthusiastic about helping Washington as he was.

In part, that is because US President Barack Obama abandoned Mubarak to the mob, a fear that now pervades amongst other Arab allies. That is particularly true in Saudi Arabia, which along with Jordan has one of the most effective intelligence services in the Middle East.

It is still not clear how changes in Egypt's General Intelligence and Security Service (GISS), which was the main link to Washington, will affect US counter-terrorism operations. But the military caretaker government that has emerged since Mubarak was toppled has distanced itself from Israel and its foreign intelligence service, the Mossad, with which Mubarak's regime had worked closely since Egypt's historic 1979 peace treaty with the Jewish state.

Despite the dramatic changes sweeping the Arab world, it's too early to say with any confidence that the brutal years of repression are over, or are even truly ending. The military in Egypt and Tunisia still call the shots.

But Arab scholar and historian Fawaz Gerges believes that for the Arabs, the corner has been turned. "Regardless of whether the oppressive Arab regimes weather the violent storm, their ruling order is no longer sustainable," he observed.

"Ordinary Arabs feel empowered, on the verge of a new democratic dawn. They have shed political apathy and joined the political space. The genie is out of the bottle."

2

The Awakening of Revolution in Tunisia

Mohamed Bouazizi, a twnty-six-year-old university graduate, sparked massive demonstrations and set the course for the subsequent Arab Spring after his self-immolation to protest harassment by municipal officials and unemployment in Tunisia.

Why Tunisia?

Muhammad Bouazizi and the Birth of the Arab Spring

By Paul McCaffrey

The outbreak of the Arab Spring uprisings can be traced back to a single act in the town of Sidi Bouzid, Tunisia. On December 17, 2010, twenty-six-year-old produce vendor Mohamed Bouazizi doused himself in gasoline and set himself alight in front of the offices of the municipal government. The desperate young man was driven to such straits after high-handed local officials confiscated his cart and all his wares earlier that day and repeatedly humiliated him as he sought redress. In the hours after his immolation, demonstrators gathered at the scene, and the Jasmine Revolution, the first mass protest of the Arab Spring movement, was under way. The unrest in Tunisia catalyzed similar displays throughout the Arab world, spreading to Egypt, Bahrain, Yemen, Libya, and Syria, in particular.

Bouazizi died several weeks later, on January 4, 2011, but not after receiving a visit from Tunisia's president, Zine El Abidine Ben Ali. Ben Ali's bedside vigil did little to quell the disorder in his country. Bouazizi's suicidal act came to be interpreted not only as a protest against official corruption and economic stagnation, but also against an overwhelming lack of political freedom. The problem was not with local officials, in other words, but with the ruling regime itself. Ben Ali could not survive the challenge, and on January 14, 2011, he stepped down after twenty-three years in power, fleeing with his family to exile in Saudi Arabia. Subsequently, elections for a constituent assembly were held. Once installed, this constituent assembly chose a new president, the long-time dissident and human rights activist Moncef Marzouki.

Ben Ali was not the only autocrat to fall in the Arab Spring. Thus far, Egypt's Hosni Mubarak and Libya's Muammar Qaddafi have each been overthrown. Mubarak was imprisoned, while Qaddafi was killed by rebel forces. Elsewhere, the regimes of Syria's Bashar Assad and Yemen's Ali Abdullah Saleh remain under threat in the face of violent resistance. In Bahrain, the ruling Ali Khalifa monarchy has apparently weathered the challenge to its reign, brutally cracking down on protesters.

Though the full effects of the Arab Spring are still playing out, Tunisia, the birthplace of the movement, remains its most hopeful success story. In Tunisia, unrest did not descend into sustained bloodshed or civil war, as it did in Libya, and the toppling of Ben Ali led in quick succession to democratic elections and a new government. In Egypt, Mubarak, too, was overthrown without excessive violence, but the transition to democracy has been more fitful and the overall outcome not quite so positive. The best-case scenario that developed in Tunisia is not an accident, nor is it an accident that Arab Spring agitation broke out in Tunisia and not elsewhere. Thanks largely to its history and demographics, Tunisia, more than the other nations affected by the recent turmoil, had the tools and structures in place to endure and adapt to the tumult.

One of the key assets Tunisia possessed, unlike Syria, Yemen, or Bahrain, is a largely homogeneous population. Around 98 percent of Tunisian citizens are Arab by ethnicity. A roughly equal proportion subscribes to the Sunni branch of the Islamic faith. As the experiences in Syria and Bahrain demonstrate, in times of civil unrest, divisions often break down along sectarian lines, whether religious or ethnic. By not having any major sectarian divides, Tunisia had little to fear from internal conflict.

Of course, neighboring Libya has similar demographics but experienced a prolonged and bloody civil war during the Arab Spring. What accounts for the discrepancy? Unlike Ben Ali in Tunisia, Qaddafi had Libya's massive oil wealth to bankroll his regime. Having control of essentially unlimited funds and bearing a deluded sense of his historical importance, Qaddafi was not the type to go quietly.

Tunisia's history, too, demonstrates a noteworthy pattern for the region of both national unity and political moderation. Long ruled by the Ottoman Empire, Tunisia was the first Arab nation to outlaw slavery, banning the practice in 1846. Thirty-five years later, Tunisia became a French colony, but the transition from Ottoman to French administration did not involve internal upheaval. When Tunisia achieved its independence in 1956, the end of the colonial era came about in a relatively peaceful fashion as well. This stands in marked contrast to neighboring Algeria, which endured a vicious eight-year civil war before gaining sovereignty. In 1957, the Tunisian republic was declared, and Habib Bourguiba, the major figure in the independence movement, became its first president.

Over the next two years, a constitution based on the French model was developed and officially adopted in 1959. The constitution mandated an entirely defensive role for the Tunisian armed forces, which served to keep the military out of the political process. Bourguiba, who ruled until 1987, aligned his nation with the West during the Cold War and maintained a moderate stance in the Arab world, becoming an early advocate of a two-state solution to the Israeli-Palestinian conflict. He promoted development, instituting programs that increased literacy rates through compulsory education, and protected the rights of women. The country's Personal Status Code, adopted not long after independence, safeguarded workers' rights as well as private property. Bourguiba embraced a secular approach to governing, outlawing polygamy and taking a strong stand against Islamic fundamentalism. By virtue of his policies, Tunisia developed one of the region's most diverse and prosperous economies with a vital middle class. Broadly popular, Bourguiba won reelection several times and was declared president for life by constitutional amendment in 1975.

Despite this apparent moderation, Tunisia remained largely a one-party state and Bourguiba gradually acquired dictatorial powers and an attendant cult of personality as his reign endured. Yet the trappings of dictatorship were not enough to preserve his regime indefinitely. Thirty years into his presidency, Bourguiba was overthrown in a peaceful coup d'état engineered by Ben Ali, a former policeman and at that time

Bourguiba's prime minister. A team of physicians charged with caring for Bourguiba declared the president incapable of carrying out his duties. Based on this, Ben Ali ascended to the office and Bourguiba was forced into a supervised retirement.

As president, Ben Ali continued the moderate approach of his predecessor in terms of economics and international affairs. Despite pledges to open up Tunisia's political system, Ben Ali maintained the dictatorial one-party template he inherited from Bourguiba. He often ran for reelection unopposed and never received less than 89 percent of the vote and sometimes captured more than 99 percent.

As time wore on, the Ben Ali regime turned Tunisia into a family business, with various relatives holding lucrative stakes in national industries. Ben Ali's in-laws especially leveraged their familial connections into vast wealth. One of Ben Ali's brothers-in-law is said to have acquired enormous real estate holdings, an airline, a radio station, and an auto-assembly plant, among other assets. Global Financial Integrity, an international monitoring organization, estimates that in a country with an annual gross national product of $80 billion, "[t]he amount of illegal money lost from Tunisia due to corruption, bribery, kickbacks, trade mispricing and criminal activity between 2000 and 2008 was, on average, over $1 billion a year." There have also been suggestions that the family was involved in criminal activities.

Not only did corruption increase under Ben Ali, so did political repression. An opponent of political Islam, Ben Ali staged show trials and executions to intimidate potential adversaries, targeting the Ennahda party, a moderate Islamist group with ties to Egypt's Muslim Brotherhood. Even nonviolent activists like Marzouki were forced into exile. One of the means employed to control the population was Ben Ali's ruling party, the Constitutional Democratic Rally (RCD), or Rally. With around two million members in a country of ten million, the Rally had a presence in all sectors of public life, whether in the mosque or the workplace. Informers were everywhere and dissent was forbidden. A massive police force helped further support the prevailing order.

Though a corrupt police state, on the spectrum of modern dictatorships the Ben Ali regime was far from the worst. Motivated largely by venality, it sought, above all, to enrich itself. It served no established constituency and lacked an underlying ideological basis. Thus it had few defenders when a concerted opposition developed. When confronted by a popular uprising, Ben Ali offered only token resistance before fleeing the country, with much of his ill-gotten plunder in tow. Ben Ali lacked the stomach for violence demonstrated by Qaddafi in neighboring Libya, and though the shortcomings of his rule are many and profound, he still left a national community largely intact upon his departure.

Unlike neighboring Libya and other Arab Spring nations, and despite the trauma of decades of dictatorship, Tunisia possessed elements of civil society. Labor unions, though infiltrated to some extent by agents of the regime, maintained a degree of independence, and when demonstrations broke out, they added their voices to the chorus through sit-ins and sympathy strikes. The Tunisian League for Human Rights also contributed to Ben Ali's expulsion. Founded in 1977 and once headed by Marzouki, the League advocates and monitors human rights and is the first indigenous organization of its kind in the Arab world. Of equal import was the degree to which women were integrated into Tunisian society. Women's groups were frequently at the forefront of the resistance to the regime and played a central role in its downfall.

But there were other components to the uprising that were not particular to Tunisia. Despite its strong education system and robust economic growth, Tunisia, like much of the Arab world, has high rates of unemployment, especially among young people. Its population—like that of the Middle East as a whole—also exhibits a distinctive "youth bulge," meaning that a high percentage is under thirty years of age. Historically, such statistics correlate with greater rates of political unrest and social turmoil and, no doubt, influenced the upheaval in Tunisia and throughout the region.

Meanwhile, the same internet technologies that propelled the Jasmine Revolution were used to similar effect in other Arab Spring uprisings. To hold on to power, the Ben Ali regime, like most dictatorships, had to control the media. Ruling the airwaves was tantamount to ruling the nation. Fawning press coverage and state censorship all contributed to the construction of the cult of personality and the maintenance of the regime. But controlling the internet is not like controlling a newspaper, radio, or television station, and the Tunisian authorities could not silence the websites and social media applications that were used to organize protests and disseminate the message of the demonstrators. Neighboring regimes have been similarly outflanked in the communications battle.

Though the chain of events it set in motion lacks few parallels in recent history, Mohamed Bouazizi's final act of protest was far from unique. Over the past few years, around a dozen Tunisian men have set themselves on fire in a similar fashion. According to analysts, what set Bouazizi apart, what gave his act its transcendent resonance, was that it happened in Sidi Bouzid. One of the central trends of modern history is the process of urbanization. Throughout the globe, people have left the rural enclaves that supported their ancestors for generations to pursue jobs and opportunity in larger cities. This migration has dissolved many of the extended familial and tribal connections, the ties of community that bound people together for centuries. The Tunisian men who set themselves on fire prior to Bouazizi did so in the major cities; their alienation did not come as such a shock. Sidi Bouzid, however, was a provincial town in Tunisia's rural heartland. Communal ties should have been stronger and shielded Bouazizi from the humiliation he endured. "In a little place like Sidi Bouzid," the American political scientist Christopher Alexander observed, "half the town or more is likely a cousin of Mohamed Bouazizi." That such connections failed him suggested that the corruption of the regime had tainted Tunisia to its core. In turn, the demonstrations that broke out in the hours after Bouazizi set himself alight—which over the next month swept away a half-century of dictatorship—stood as a powerful corrective: The system that abandoned and abused Bouazizi had itself been uprooted and destroyed.

That Other Tunisia

Without social justice for unemployed youth, revolutionary hopes may descend into class war.

By Graham Usher
The Nation, September 12, 2011

This past May Farhat Rajhi, one of several former interior ministers in postrevolutionary Tunisia, mused on Facebook about what could happen if the country's Islamist Nahda (Renaissance) movement came out on top in the October elections for a new Constituent Assembly.

"Since independence, political life has been dominated by people from the Sahel [coast]," he said. The class included the country's founder and first president, Habib Bourguiba, and his successor, Zine el-Abidine Ben Ali, whose ouster in January announced the Tunisian Revolution and the Arab Spring.

"They are not ready to give up ruling," he warned. Elements of Ben Ali's ancien régime were, in fact, plotting with the army to prevent the coming to power of Nahda or any other party not of their ilk. "If the results of the forthcoming elections go against their interests, there will be a military coup," he predicted.

Fired across Tunisia's blogosphere, Rajhi's comments ignited four days of protest in the capital of Tunis. Banks were burned, police stations stoned, shops looted. The country's still mostly hated police force (a crucial prop of the Ben Ali dictatorship) beat back protesters with batons and tear gas. Two hundred people were arrested. After four days of rioting, a night curfew was imposed.

It brought only a lull. In July antigovernment riots flared again in the capital after police fired tear gas inside a mosque. In solidarity, hundreds fought the police in Sidi Bouzid, leaving a 14-year-old boy dead from stray gunfire. Adrift in Tunisia's impoverished interior, Sidi Bouzid is the fly-blown town where the revolution began when an unlicensed street vendor set himself ablaze.

Prime Minister Beji Caid Essebsi blamed "religious extremist parties" for the latest violence. Rachid Ghannouchi, Nahda's septuagenarian president, spoke darkly of plots to tarnish his movement.

The violence was the worst since mass demonstrations rocked Tunis's Avenue Habib Bourguiba and Casbah Square in January, scuttling Ben Ali and his family onto a one-way plane to Saudi Arabia. It also told us what had changed in postrevolutionary Tunisia.

"The police are the same," one man told Reuters, his mobile phone relaying pictures of cops trashing young men off Casbah Square. The rapid inflammation of the protests showed how parties like Nahda and politicians like Essebsi can still be goaded to confrontation by dubious theories long on conspiracy but short on fact: how rapidly, in other words, the unity forged by the struggle against Ben Ali has been rent by differences among those who would claim his mantle.

The events also reaffirmed Tunisia's status as regional bellwether. With its small and homogeneous population, educated workforce and vibrant civil society, Tunisia remains the best hope of an Arab revolution minting a durable constitutional democracy out of the debris of dictatorship. Yet success is hardly assured. Tunisia will have to negotiate three rapids if it is to reach any kind of settled shore. First, it will have to make certain the transition to democracy is owned not only by a new clique but by entire social classes in what remains a deeply unequal society. Second, it will have to integrate an Islamist movement deemed anathema by important parts of Tunisia's existing political elite. Third—and most important—Tunisia will have to satisfy a sullen mass of jobless young who believe they have sacrificed the most for the revolution, which has so far brought them little except penury. It was they who did the burning and looting.

> *There were two Tunisian revolutions over the winter of 2011. Whether there will be a third depends on the second realizing at least some of the hopes of the first.*

From Coalition to Conflict

There were two Tunisian revolutions over the winter of 2011. Whether there will be a third depends on the second realizing at least some of the hopes of the first.

The first has become folklore. Twenty-six-year-old Mohamed Bouazizi, in an act of outraged despair over the indignity of not being allowed to work, enveloped himself in flames and released a contagion among his peers that went from Sidi Bouzid to the coast and thence to the region, toppling dictators of twenty-three years (Tunisia) and thirty years (Egypt) on the way.

The second was as remarkable, even if eclipsed by upheavals in Egypt, Libya, Yemen, Bahrain and, somewhat later, Syria. From January 14, when Ben Ali fled, to March 3 a grassroots national/popular coalition of trade unions, leftists, lawyers associations, human rights organizations and Islamists mainly but not only from Nahda laid siege to Casbah Square and other sites in the capital to protest any and all attempts by the ancien régime to steal back the revolution. Having refused to open fire on demonstrators in the first revolution, Tunisia's 30,000-strong army kept to its constitutional role in the second: it guarded public spaces but allowed the struggle to play out between serial interim governments and what became known as the Casbah coalition.

Play out it did. Rolling campaigns of civil disobedience swept away two cabinets, forcing the resignation of Ben Ali–appointed governors in the provinces; the dissolution of his ruling Constitutional Democratic Rally (RCD); and the disbanding of the state security apparatus, including the hated political police. Banned parties like Nahda were legalized, and amnestied political prisoners were allowed to run for office.

The coup de grâce came on March 3. After avalanching sit-ins in Casbah Square, Essebsi bowed to the coalition's core demand: elections for a Constituent Assembly that would be empowered to draft a new Constitution and convene parliamentary and presidential elections. In a speech broadcast live on Tunisian TV that day, President Fouad Mebazaa vowed that there would be "a new political system that definitively breaks with the old regime."

The scale of Tunisia's achievement can be contrasted with what has happened elsewhere. In Egypt voters approved the kind of regime-steered transition that the masses in Casbah Square fought so hard to prevent: Egypt is now paying the price for having an army midwife a democracy. In Syria and Yemen dictators turned bloodily on their people. In Libya there was civil war and foreign intervention. In Bahrain, occupation and show trials.

Yet no sooner had "the people brought down the regime" (to echo the revolution's most infectious slogan) than the national alliance that enabled it fell apart: the Casbah coalition devolved into discrete, fractious and antagonistic parties.

The rupture was apparently over the pace of elections. Nahda and the centrist Progressive Democratic Party (PDP) wanted to keep the original polling date of July 24: the longer Tunisia goes without the legitimacy of an elected authority, they said, the likelier outbreaks of lawlessness. But most of the ninety or so parties wanted a deferral. Overwhelmingly neophyte, they said a July date would give undue advantage to parties with an established base and national organization—like the PDP and Nahda.

The country's new electoral commission agreed: it ruled that the vote should wait until October so that Tunisia's 3 million voters could register. All parties bowed to the decision, the Islamists through gritted teeth. They charged that the spat over tempo masked a deeper one over politics.

Despite Nahda's avowed commitment to multiparty democracy, much of Tunisia's liberal and secular elite (the "people from the Sahel," in Rajhi's phrase) view any kind of Islamism with paranoia: once in power, they say, Nahda will impose Sharia law, ban alcohol, enforce the veil and destroy tourism, on which one in five jobs in Tunisia rely.

Women especially fear for Tunisia's personal status code, the most liberal in the region: this bans polygamy, grants equal pay and permits the legal right to abortion. Ghannouchi has vowed to keep the code, but few secular women believe him. "He says one thing to you and another to his people," said a woman who works with an international NGO specializing in "democratic transitions." "To his people Ghannouchi says one way to reduce unemployment among Tunisian men is to keep Tunisian women at home."

A new "modern democratic alliance" has been formed—made up of social democratic and ex-communist parties as well as women's groups—with the aim of keeping Nahda from power. In response, Nahda has resigned from a government committee in charge of the transition to elections, protesting its "takeover" by the left. The new secular bloc is "possibly aimed at postponing the elections" out of fear that Nahda will do well, charged Ghannouchi (polls show the Islamists are the most popular party in Tunisia, with 14–20 percent support).

The acrimony not only shadowed the violence in Tunis and Sidi Bouzid; it revived old feuds. Nahda cadre remind all that it was an alliance of Ben Ali's RCD, certain professional syndicates and women's organizations that backed his dictatorship, including his ruthless persecution of their movement in the 1990s, when thousands were killed, tortured, exiled and jailed. Ben Ali justified what he called "eradication" as necessary to stop Tunisia from going the way of Algeria, where a savage civil war between Islamist insurgents and the army left hundreds of thousands dead. It was a spurious charge, but it can still be heard among Tunisia's Westernized elite.

The fear of Nahda is exaggerated, says a PDP leader. So too are Nahda's charges of conspiracy against the left. The real threat facing Tunisia's fledgling democracy is not that the Islamists could emerge as the biggest party in the Constituent Assembly or that the left is a surrogate for counterrevolution. It's that 67 percent of Tunisians have little trust in any politician, Islamist, secular or liberal.

The Sahel and the Lumpen-Intelligentsia

Joblessness is Tunisia's most incendiary issue. Unemployment is said to be 15 percent, but the figure masks large regional and generational discrepancies. In coastal cities like Tunis it may be as low as 7 percent. In Sidi Bouzid it may be as high as 30 percent. In the interior's Gafsa district, where strikes in phosphate mines in 2008 are deemed the real harbinger of the 2011 revolution, it is said to be 40 percent, with perhaps one in four families in poverty. Among Tunisians under 30 (54 percent of the population, according to the National Institute of Statistics), it is 26 percent, with 170,000 out of 400,000 university graduates without work. Again, the deprivation is harsher in the interior and south.

By common assent, this was the class and age cohort that brought down Ben Ali. You see them everywhere: killing time in Sidi Bouzid, packed into slums in Tunis's grim northern estates, milling on street corners near the Casbah. After "the revolution of the youth," they remain all fired up but with nothing to do. Most are poor and rural in origin. They become proletarianized after their drift to the coast in search of work. They are mostly religious in outlook and conservative in habit, embodying the anomie of a generation that is overschooled, underemployed and with little hope of a job except the menial, unskilled and dead-end. They are "a kind of lumpen-intelligentsia," said one pollster. And they are Nahda's natural constituency, the reason he thinks the party will do well in the elections.

But for the coastal elite they represent another, suddenly visible and enfranchised Tunisia, one with which it has never had to share power. This is not to say the rich were all allied with Ben Ali. By the 2000s they, like most Tunisians, were disgusted by the kleptocracy of his clan and the mafia rule of his regime. But after independence the elite had struck a pact with the state: minimal political rights in return for relatively high rates of growth, uneven development in favor of the coast and a national identity that was homogeneous, modern, Francophile and secular. Nahda embodies the antithesis of all this, and so do the people who support it. The elite's fear of the Islamists is thus not really about religion; it is about culture and class.

And it could become class war. For many Tunisians the only way this can be averted is if the national unity among parties and civil society groups initially achieved in the Casbah over the transition to democracy can be resurrected over issues of social justice.

This will mean moving away from an economy in which cheap labor and tourism are the main draws for European investment to one where jobs are created, factories built and resources redistributed from the coast to the interior. Otherwise, the violence seen in Tunis and Sidi Bouzid may not be the last throes of the old Tunisia but dire omens of the new.

In such a future, it seems odd to cast Nahda as the problem. The party's espousal of democratic politics, its willingness to work in alliances, its preference for "a government of national unity" and base in the interior suggests, rather, that it is a necessary part of the solution—if that young, poor, other Tunisia is not to turn as violently against democracy as it did against dictatorship.

❖

Graham Usher is a writer and journalist who has written extensively about the Arab world and South Asia.

From People to Citizens in Tunisia

By Nadia Marzouki
Middle East Report, Summer 2011

While Mohamed Bouazizi's self-immolation will undoubtedly remain the iconic image of the 2011 Tunisian revolution, another set of pictures has also stuck in the minds of Tunisians. On the evening of January 14, despite an army curfew, a man staggered across Avenue Habib Bourguiba, shouting, "Ben Ali fled—the Tunisian people is free! The Tunisian people will not die! The Tunisian people is sacred!"

The scene, captured on camera by Al Jazeera, deeply moved many Tunisians. Throughout the spring into April, the pan-Arab satellite channel ran the clip over and over as filler for the minutes between the news hour and the preceding programs. Along with other slogans disseminated by Al Jazeera, like the famous, "The people want the fall of the regime," this evocation illustrates that "the people" (*al-sha'b al-tunisi*) has come to be the decisive category of identity in the country. The concept of *sha'b* is hardly new, of course, but it was the revolution, as broadcast into Tunisian and Arab living rooms by Al Jazeera, that made it effective for the first time.

Indeed, from the beginning of protests in December 2010 to the resignation of interim Prime Minister Mohammed Ghannouchi on February 28, 2011, a love affair of sorts grew between Tunisian demonstrators and Al Jazeera. A robust interaction developed whereby the network used images of Tunisians to promote its coverage and the protesters carried signs reading, "Thank you, Al Jazeera." Tunisians were perfectly aware of how their revolt was misperceived. The numerous demonstrators who brandished loaves of bread, chanting "Bread, yes—Ben Ali, no," were objecting to analysis of their discontent in the Western press as purely economic, another "bread riot" to be quelled with minor subsidy adjustments. No, Tunisians argued, they represented not the hungry and downtrodden, but the entirety of the Tunisian people claiming their dignity. The emergence of the term *sha'b* was part and parcel of this collective *cri de coeur* and thus of the success of the revolution.

Rulers and Ruled

The normative dimension of the category of "the people" is novel in post-colonial Tunisia. Previous social movements, while often quite militant, did not take on an overtly political thrust. During the bread riots of 1983–1984, for example, the notion of *sha'b* ironically appeared mainly in the patronizing rhetoric of the regime, as when President Habib Bourguiba announced his decision to reverse planned increases in the prices of bread, sugar and pasta. "O Tunisian people," said Bourguiba in his televised address, "I have decided that we are going back to the former situation." Neither these disturbances nor earlier ones were able to transform the relationship between ruler and ruled so that "the people" had agency as well as needs. After independence in 1956, Bourguiba promulgated an ideology based on the ideal of a homogeneous, united, modern, Francophile and secular national body.[1] In the name of this ideal, he crushed his main rival Salah Ben Youssef, a proponent of pan-Arabism close to Nasserism, and methodically constructed the image of a leader (*za'im*) who was the sole legitimate benefactor and protector of the people.[2] While Bourguiba's era saw significant achievements in literacy, public health and women's rights, the paternalistic relationship that developed between the *za'im* and Tunisians left little room for participatory politics. After Zine El Abidine Ben Ali seized power in 1987, this form of governance turned into a pervasive police state that restricted the space available for collective action even further. Abiding by the "pact of obedience"[3] or open resistance were the only two alternatives.

In January 2008, violent protests took place in the town of Redayef, a town of 26,000 located near the mining basin of Gafsa. The workers of this economically abandoned area took to the streets to express their anger at the fraudulent results of a hiring competition launched by the state-owned phosphate company. Most of the 81 positions opened by the company were given to workers with friends in high places, and not, as per an agreement between the company and the labor federation, to sons of workers who had died or been injured in work accidents and other inhabitants of the region. Despite its intensity and determination, which spread to the neighboring towns of Metlaoui and Moulares, and included a large number of women and unemployed graduates, the movement remained essentially about advocating the rights of mine workers of the Gafsa area. It did not translate into a wider mobilization demanding the comprehensive rights of the Tunisian people. Most Tunisians, again, chose the option of the "pact of obedience." On December 17, 2010, the day that Mohamed Bouazizi set himself on fire, all that began to change.

As the revolutionary moment of 2011 gives way to uncertainty and anxiety over security and the outcome of the democratic transition, it might be tempting to dismiss the power of the category of *sha'b* as illusory. To do so, however, would be to miss two important aspects of what the notion of *sha'b* has achieved.

Consensus and Justice

"The people," like the nation, is what the scholar Benedict Anderson called an imagined community. One might point to various discrepancies between this imagined community and the real sociology of the Tunisian population—divisions of class, for example, or ideological affiliation. It is nonetheless important that the category of *sha'b*, and not Islam or workers or unemployed graduates, emerged as the rallying cry of the Tunisian revolution.

"The people" has subsequently become the reference point that political projects must adopt to be accepted as legitimate. This fact has the effect of making the projects more inclusive and, one may hope, broadening minds. On March 10, in an interview on Al Jazeera, Abdelfatah Mourou, second-in-command of the Islamist

Nahda party, referred to the *sha'b*, not Islam or Muslims, as the central category of the Tunisian polity. When asked about Nahda's position toward partisan politics, often considered to contradict Islamists' ideal of unity, Mourou insisted on "the right of the people to its self" (*haqq al-sha'b li-nafsihi*). "The people may have different feelings," he granted, going on to contend, "the only parties that will win will be those chosen by the people." The concept of *sha'b* seems to compel Mourou to acknowledge pluralism. The necessity of framing decisions in terms of the interests of the Tunisian people has equally become apparent in a number of declarations by Prime Minister Beji Caid Essebsi, as well as members of the League for Defense of the Revolution, party and association leaders. Every protest or strike—whether of journalists, railway workers or janitors—invokes not only the name of the demonstrating group, but also of the "Tunisian people." Within the Arabic and Francophone media, there has been major transformation, though the habits of the old regime are far from fully uprooted. Articles, op-eds and forums about the expectations and needs of the Tunisian people proliferate. The notion of *sha'b* has established itself as the relevant signifier of consensus.

One may fear that the newfound hegemony of this term will lead to anti-democratic consequences. Reference to "the people" is no guarantee of democratic intent; a particular group or party could try to hijack the revolution, presenting itself as a manifestation of the popular will. But it is unlikely that Tunisians will be so credulous, precisely because of the absence of leadership in the Tunisian revolution that has been so extensively remarked upon. The explosion in the number of political parties (more than 70) is regarded as a sign of fragmentation. But it could just as well be argued that the plurality of voices is clear evidence that the normative power of the category of people cannot be coopted by an opportunistic new *za'im*. The attitude of *dégage* or *irhal*—directed at Ben Ali and then two interim cabinets—has been criticized as capricious and unconstructive, but it clearly shows that Tunisians are not ready to abandon their recovered rights to free expression to any pretender to the throne. The self-immolation of Mohammed Bouazizi indeed manifested the tremendous suffering of people living in depressed towns like Sidi Bouzid, Casserine and Tataouine. But the movement that occurred between December 2010 and February 2011 was about dignity and justice, not collective self-pity. It is very unlikely that a *za'im* claiming to have miraculous healing powers will be able to seduce Tunisians, who are advocating a politics of justice, not compassion.

Terms of Debate

While the revolution has made the supposedly amorphous Arab "street" into a self-conscious people, many challenges lie ahead in the formation of democratic citizenship. The revolution has made apparent a plurality of voices, but also important divisions. In the face of these divides, simply calling for unity is vain at best. Bridging the gaps seems particularly urgent in three areas: regional, generational and cultural.

Bouazizi's desperate act has revealed dramatic disparities between the poorer interior and the economically and politically more powerful coast. During the Ben

> *While the revolution has made the supposedly amorphous Arab "street" into a self-conscious people, many challenges lie ahead in the formation of democratic citizenship.*

Ali era, the relationship between the coast and interior was often described as pure center-periphery exploitation. Now, at a time when revolution fatigue is setting in, some political leaders might be tempted to play the provincial card and stir up regional antagonisms. Already, in the empty cafés of Sousse and Monastir, it is not uncommon to hear the people of Sidi Bouzid blamed for the absence of tourists. Conversely, the inhabitants of rural areas do not seem to trust the commitment of the coast dwellers to achieving true change. While party leaders and Prime Minister Essebsi seem aware of the dangers of regionalism, others have not hesitated to start down this slippery slope. In May, Farhat Rajhi, who was dismissed from his post as interior minister in March, triggered a nationwide scandal after contending, in an interview broadcast on Facebook, that coastal leaders were fomenting counterrevolutionary plots. This declaration, though it lacked evidence, helped to spark a new wave of demonstrations that were violently repressed by the police. While Rajhi's freedom of expression should be protected, such provincial sentiments are completely unproductive.

Most of the participants in the Tunisian revolution are under 35. If their call for respect has been heard, their sense of hopelessness about the job market has not disappeared. A significant minority of the country's youth still dreams of only one thing—escaping to Europe. As for others, they organize in associations and shop for ideas among the new political parties. Yet a huge gap remains between the youth activism and the response of the government. The *irhal* attitude of the young demonstrators can be defined as a libertarian stance toward authority, derived from a mixture of distrust for the government, ignorance of older political activists, interest in a strong, active civil society and skepticism toward projects and ideals that seem to contradict an individualist, utilitarian approach to politics. The youth are increasingly anxious about their immediate future: How will they complete their studies? How will they find employment? Will they be able to marry and raise a family? They are struggling with how to contribute constructively to the national debate on these questions. In view of this disposition, it was worrisome that on May 4 Essebsi told the nation that his main priority is to reestablish the "prestige of the state." The police then quashed demonstrations on May 6–7 in Tunis and Siliana, leading to the decision to reinstate the curfew on May 9. The interim government shows little understanding of the type of political participation that youth are interested in and capable of.

Last but not least, there is the debate between Islam and secularism. In light of the unquestionable popularity of Nahda, many have fallen into the trap of the "Islamist threat" paradigm. The secular left is frightening itself by imagining a scenario, in which a landslide Islamist victory leads to a military coup, as in Algeria in 1992. Declarations made by Nahda leaders Rachid Ghannouchi and Mourou about their respect for the rules of democracy and their commitment not to alter the personal status code or establish *shari'a* are derided as doublespeak. No matter how justified these fears are, exclusion of Islamists has proven a bad idea, both in Algeria and Tunisia. Inclusion in the political game, as in Morocco, has led to more positive results. The problem with political Islam, in Tunisia and elsewhere, is not that it is too political but that is not political enough. It is not integrated into a transparent and competitive political sphere, where, instead of one "Islamist threat," there are many parties within the Islamist nebula. Although there is no extensive survey, it is far from clear that the pious Tunisian middle class embraces the project of Nahda. Many of these middle-class Tunisians want to express piety in the public sphere, but do not trust Nahda leaders and are very attached to gender equality. Some other parties, such as the newly founded Islamist party Alliance Nationale pour la Paix et la Prospérité (that includes Kamel Omrane, former minister of religious affairs under Ben Ali), the secular, center-left Congrès pour la République or the center-right Afeq, as well as new unions, have understood the complexity of the supposedly homogeneous Islamist electorate. They refuse to resort to the old tool of sowing antagonism between Islamists and secularists. As Tarek Masoud has shown, it is pointless to speculate about whether Islamists are truly democratic.[4] What matters is to establish solid institutions that safeguard the possibility of robust public debate. Proportional representation is a good method whereby Islamists can be included in electoral competition while guaranteeing significant pluralities for other political trends within a national assembly.

The continuing dominance of the category of "the people" in the public sphere raises hopes that neither Islamists nor secularists will be able set the terms of debate and that other, more immediately compelling issues will stay on the agenda. It is necessary to maintain a focus on the people's practical problems to prevent the Tunisian revolution from sliding back into the false dilemmas of the 1990s.

Notes

1. See Mounira Charrad, *States and Women's Rights: The Making of Post-Colonial Tunisia, Algeria and Morocco* (Berkeley, CA: University of California Press, 2001).
2. See Michel Camau and Vincent Geisser, *Habib Bourguiba, la trace et l'héritage* (Paris: Karthala, 2004).
3. See Béatrice Hibou, *La Force de l'obéissance: Economie politique de la répression en Tunisie* (Paris: La Découverte, 2006).
4. Tarek Masoud, "Are They Democrats? Does It Matter?" *Journal of Democracy* 19/3 (July 2008).

What Future for Tunisia's Economy?

The Middle East, October 1, 2011

The political and economic situation in Tunisia is in a state of transition, yet the interim government urgently needs to restore foreign and private investment, trade and tourism. Crucial elections are scheduled for later this month.

In a round table discussion, a group of businessmen from the Tunisian-British Chamber of Commerce in Tunis explained to Pamela Ann Smith the challenges that lie ahead and how a democratic future will help the economy to develop and become more transparent. They also discussed their efforts to diversify Tunisia's trade and investment partners, to include more European countries.

The delegation was led by Hassine Doghri, President of the Chamber who is also President of the Compagnie d'Assurances et de Réassurances Tuniso-Européenne (Carte), and by its Interim Director, Hafidh Chaibi, who is the owner of a business development consultancy in Tunisia, Maghreb Frontiers. They were joined by Noureddine Hajji, Managing Partner, Ernst & Young in Tunis; Mehdi Ben Abdallah, Vice-President of BG Tunisia and Naoufel Aissa, Country Chairman of Shell Tunisia.

The Political Transition

Doghri

Realistically, the situation in Tunisia is going well. Firstly, because we had institutions before the revolution. We have a strong administration. We have highly educated people. And strong laws. The transition was very smooth and very secure.

Now we are moving to a new system which is more democratic, with more transparency and more visibility. The rules will be much clearer. Investment will be much easier, both for the foreign business community and the local one. This is why we are going through the democratic and political process. The next step . . . will be to promote a new constitution to meet the expectations of the people.

We are very confident about the future. The economy is also moving in the right direction. Of course, after a revolution there is a transition period. And there are some social and economic costs during this period. That's normal. That's what happened in Spain, in Portugal, in the ex-Soviet countries and in some areas of Asia, such as Malaysia and Indonesia. They have experienced both revolution and post-revolution. I think Tunisia has the capacity to succeed and to offer to the Tunisian citizen a better chance and better instruments to be one of the most modern countries in the Mediterranean region. If we carry out this transition successfully, we can ensure that the long-term future is right.

Today there are some 100 parties, and many new media outlets. Of course, we need strong reforms. We expect more transparency, more courage. We need a positive way to add value. Our culture and the way we work has to have full transparency.

Some of the countries that experienced a revolution took two years, maybe even six, to reach full democracy. We hope we won't need six years, or even two years. We are moving rapidly ahead. Today the priority is political reform. After the new constitution, a new government will be appointed which will propose the real reforms for the medium and long term. We have to be patient.

In the meantime, we have to secure our country. We have to move ahead. We cannot allow ourselves to wait for the new government, because if you wait a long time, it will cost a lot. It will cost jobs. Remember, the revolution started because of unemployment among young people. We have to secure this transition period in the right way.

Ben Abdallah

We are positive about how Tunisia operated during the difficult two or three months [of the revolution]. Today, we are in a completely different world. We are back on track with a government that is getting more credibility. Security is coming back, and the economy is getting back on track. Today we have a government that is very accessible, listening to us, helping us, working alongside foreign investors to help find a solution for these difficult times.

Hajji

We are completely confident about the potential of our country. We are confident that international companies will come. But we do have a couple of concerns. We need time. We are dealing with a situation that just after the revolution was quite unstable, but things are getting better now. We have the feeling that the government is in control of the situation. There is a consensus about the political agenda and about how it will be run. So business will be better.

I don't expect the demonstrations to stop. This is democracy. This means that people have to voice their opinions. We will never get a 100% solution. We are progressing on consultations. A high commission of 150 people, composed of all existing parties, of representatives from civil society and from the regions has been formed. It is like a Parliament and it is discussing the way the coming elections will take place. They have reached agreement on monitoring the elections and on the electoral model.

It's not just the new government that's on the agenda. It's also civil society and the solidarity which was revealed by this revolution. Civil society is now represented by more associations and some include young leaders and entrepreneurs. The private sector is helping to support the creation of new businesses all over Tunisia. We expect these to succeed.

The Economy and Investment

Hajji

Tunisia has many strong fundamentals. These are still there. In terms of sustainable GDP growth, Tunisia has had an average of 5% in the past years. Tunisia has always had a very balanced economy. We have no dominant sector. Agriculture, depending on the weather, tends to account for about 10 to 15% of GDP.

Tunisians are experts in exporting. The country is a base for exporting. Fifty per cent of our GDP is derived from exports. Now we are exporting the revolution!

We also have a large number of international businesses—about 3,000. In international benchmarking exercises, Tunisia has perhaps one of the best rankings in the region, according to the World Economic Forum. In terms of ease of doing business, Tunisia has the best ranking in Africa and in the Arab world and is also one of the best in terms of competitiveness, in foreign direct investment, and in the regulation of business.

Aissa

Employing our graduates is a top priority. This means creating growth, but after the revolution it will not be there. GDP growth will probably fall from 5% to 1 or 1.5% this year. The interim government is looking for interim solutions. It is looking at technology to add value to exports. It is looking to create jobs immediately.

Tourism is being affected by what is happening in Libya. Tunisia is working with its traditional tourism markets in the EU, such as France and the UK, to find ways to communicate and share observations with them. The security situation has improved tremendously. In the coastal parts of the country, which are the main tourism areas, it is almost back to normal.

Doghri

You cannot say that there is no change at all. There is fundamental change. The real changes on the economic side are going to happen, but they need to happen in the right way.

Speaking from the business community, from the private sector, we need more transparency and clearer rules. We are expecting new laws, and we are confident that these will be democratic. The new government, which will be elected by the citizens, has to decide which economic policy the country needs. This is democracy. When we have a clear economic policy, we can allow the investor to invest with total liberty, and we can open the market to all foreign investors. This is what we are working for.

Chaibi

Britain was the first to lift the ban on tourists going to Tunisia, and they did it throughout the country. France took time to lift the ban, and then they did that just for the coastal areas. This is bound to help Tunisian's view of Britain.

Industry is also very important, particularly the electro-mechanical sector. Companies like Airbus have chosen Tunisia as a site to sub-contract the assembly of some of their very complicated parts. Even the design process has been outsourced to Tunisia.

Textiles is a traditional industry but it has been less and less focused on, due a perception that China will take over in a new environment. But British companies have decided to stay in Tunisia because of its competitiveness. Tunisians are very capable of producing high quality small batches, something that is not reliable in Far East markets or where it is less profitable, or less economic.

Ben Abdallah

Of course, there are no magical solutions for what is happening, but it is very important, as a foreign investor, to feel that we have the right support, and the right ear, to work with us.

BG has been a partner of Tunisia for more than 20 years. We are pleased with our investment in the country and we are definitely looking to stay a long-term partner and investor. We are the biggest investor in the country, with more than $3.5 billion invested.

> *"We are talking about the young people, the ones who made the revolution happen . . . The young people are the most valuable asset that we have." —Noureddine Hajji*

We account for about 50% of Tunisia's consumption of natural gas. When you realise that about 90% of its electricity comes from gas, it gives you an idea about the importance of BG's production in the country.

During the three most challenging months, we never stopped production. We always worked to deliver our commitment to the country and we had the leadership to do that. This gives us confidence about business in the future and about investment.

Banking and Finance

Chaibi

The financial sector is very important. Tunisia aims to become a financial hub for the region. The Tunisian British Chamber of Commerce is very active in this, given the expertise that you can find in the UK.

Hajji

We haven't got a good banking sector. This is a reality. We need to restructure our banking system. I understand from certain members of the government, including the new governor of the central bank, that they are aware of that and that they know there is a big job to do on the banking side, including the re-capitalisation of banks and the consolidation of banks. We have too many.

There really isn't much ability to finance because of the limited capital base and because of the lack of risk management procedures, etc. So I do not expect specific things to come from the financial sector to support the economy other than what we already have.

But the government is planning to start microfinance immediately, through BF-PME [Banque de Financement des Petites et Moyennes Entreprises], the bank which was set up to help small- and medium-sized companies.

The interim government has also announced new initiatives in the field of private equity to support the creation of big investments with venture capital, which is more focused on smaller projects, many in IT. Civil society organisations have agreed to support that.

This is the best we can do during this period. We do recognise that it is not enough to address the needs of our young people, but in the medium-term, after the new government is appointed, we will see better changes.

Education and Employment

Hajji

Up to now, we didn't talk enough about the strongest asset of Tunisia. The revolution revealed it to the world, and that is the quality of our people. Our youth offer a competitive advantage for international companies.

We have a very young population, which is highly educated. Today we have a literacy rate of 80%. Fifty-six per cent of our university students are female. Thirty per cent of today's students are taking courses in computer sciences and in engineering.

In early April, the interim government announced a programme which has a major part dealing with unemployment. Today, if the official figure is 80,000 unemployed graduates, the actual one may be as much as 120,000 to 140,000. If the economy achieves 5% growth, we may be able to create 50,000 jobs. So we may need growth between 7 and 8% to create enough jobs.

This year, the government's programme includes the creation of roughly 60,000 jobs for graduates: 20,000 in the public sector, including education and health care; 20,000 in the private sector and the other 20,000 through the creation of the "smart" economy. The government has also set up a dedicated programme to provide educational opportunities and financial support for more than 100,000 graduates during this period.

IT and Start-Ups

Hajji

I would really like to underline that we are talking about the young people, the ones who made the revolution happen. You have seen what technology means with Facebook, Twitter, etc. This demonstrates a high commitment, courage, solidarity, enthusiasm, creativity and leadership. This, for me, is what will create the difference in the future. The young people are the most valuable asset that we have. International businesses can also benefit from this.

Chaibi

One IT company identified talented Tunisians who had both excellent English skills and strong skills in medicine or nursing. That's where Tunisians can help, in software and technical support platforms. Even in the poorer areas of Tunisia, like Gabes, new startups are being created with small business incubators, the support of entrepreneurs, training and financing programmes. The cyberparks are playing the role of incubator but they also have a regional development role whereby they take on an investor and do promotional work.

Assessing Tunisia's Elections

By Dale Sprusansky
Washington Report on Middle East Affairs, January 2012

George Washington University's Project on Middle East Political Science hosted a Nov. 2 panel discussion titled "After Tunisia's Elections" at the university's Elliott School of International Affairs in Washington, DC. The panel, which featured three experts on Tunisian politics, dissected and analyzed the results of Tunisia's Oct. 23 parliamentary elections. Marc Lynch, a professor at George Washington University, moderated the discussion.

In his introductory remarks, Lynch commented that Tunisia "beat the odds" by conducting "astonishingly successful elections." Melani Cammett, a professor at Brown University, pointed out that the voting process was carried out in an overwhelmingly orderly manner.

Turning to the election results, Prof. Cammett noted that, as expected, the Muslim Ennahda Party won the most votes, gaining 89 of the Tunisian parliament's 217 seats. Nevertheless, she pointed out, Ennahda received only 30 percent of the popular vote and did not gain enough seats to form a majority in parliament. The presence of more than 100 political parties on the ballot resulted in an extreme fragmentation of the votes, Cammett explained.

The party that finished closest to Ennahda was The Congress for the Republic (CPR), she said, which won 29 parliamentary seats. The Democratic Modernist Pole, the most secular party running, won only 5 seats. Fellow panelist Chris Alexander, a professor at Davidson College, noted that the Progressive Democratic Party (PDP), which was expected to have a decent showing, performed rather poorly, winning only 16 seats.

Cammett attributed Ennahda's success to its strong grassroots presence and well-established informal social networks. Alexander added that Ennahda was by far the party with the greatest monetary resources. Parties that demonstrated a willingness to enter into a coalition with Ennahda performed better than parties that expressed an unwillingness to do so, Cammet observed. Alexander agreed that Tunisians "share a commitment to working together in coalition," and blamed the PDP's poor showing on the party's highly polarized politics. Fordham University Prof. John P. Entelis concurred, commenting that the PDP "went totally over the top in [its attacks] against Ennahda."

While Cammett and Alexander focused on Tunisia's political institutions, Entelis stressed the importance of people and personalities, emphasizing that parties cannot substitute for individuals. Despite the popular image of Tunisia as a homogeneous nation, he added, the country is home to a wide array of cultural, religious and ideological views.

Addressing Tunisia's challenges as it moves forward with its democratic experiment, Entelis noted that the country's political parties must work to capture the interest of its youth. Many currently view political parties as being "boring and useless," Lynch elaborated.

> *Despite the popular image of Tunisia as a homogeneous nation, the country is home to a wide array of cultural, religious and ideological views.*

While emphasizing that no accurate analysis on the strength of Tunisia's democracy can be given until at least after the next parliamentary elections, Alexander did state that he believes Ennahda is genuine.

3

Egypt:
Tahrir Square and After

(AFP/Getty Images)

An Egyptian antigovernment demonstrator holds his national flag with an anti-Mubarak slogan at Cairo's Tahrir Square. He and other protestors are preparing on the eleventh day for sweeping "departure day" demonstrations to force President Hosni Mubarak to quit.

Egyptian Politics: Nasserism and the Muslim Brotherhood

By Paul McCaffrey

The Arab Spring uprising in Egypt that ended the thirty-year reign of President Hosni Mubarak illuminated underlying conflicts in Egyptian politics and society that are representative of those throughout the Arab world. The divide between the secular and the religious, pan-Arabism and pan-Islamism, finds its most vivid manifestation in the Egyptian example. Indeed, the two chief strands of modern political thought in the Arab world, Gamal Abdel Nasser's pan-Arab socialism and the Islamism of the Muslim Brotherhood, both originated in Egypt and continue to influence the nation and the region.

The effective birth of modern Egypt occurred on July 23, 1952, when a collection of disaffected soldiers from the Egyptian armed forces, the Free Officers, staged a coup d'état overthrowing the country's ruler, the ineffective British-backed King Farouk. Though the titular head of the new regime was General Muhammad Naguib, the real power rested with Colonel Gamal Abdel Nasser. Over the next few years, Nasser gradually exerted his control, assuming the office of prime minister in 1954 and being elected president in 1956, a post he held until his death in 1970.

The son of a postal worker, Gamal Abdel Nasser was born into a lower-middle-class family on January 15, 1918, in the Egyptian city of Alexandria. A British colony since 1882, Egypt achieved its nominal independence in 1922, when Nasser was four years old. Despite this apparent milestone, the British, through the rickety monarchy they had installed, continued to exercise a strong influence on Egyptian affairs. This resulted in widespread resentment among native Egyptians. As a teenager, Nasser joined the Young Egypt Society, an independence movement that sought to free the country from de facto British rule. At one of many street demonstrations, he was struck on the forehead during a melee with police, causing a scar that he would bear for the rest of his life.

As Nasser grew into his nationalism, other currents were circulating in Egyptian society. In 1928, Sheikh Hassan al-Banna founded the Muslim Brotherhood, an Islamist organization that envisioned a religious state based on sharia law. The organization grew rapidly, becoming such a threat to the monarchy that in early 1949, al-Banna was assassinated by the Egyptian police.

Upon completing secondary school, Nasser took up legal studies for a few months but soon opted for another vocation. Admitted to Egypt's Royal Military Academy in Cairo, he embarked on a career in the armed forces. In 1938, Nasser graduated with the rank of second lieutenant. After his first posting, near his father's hometown in Upper Egypt, he volunteered for duty in the Sudan. Nasser made some valuable connections in his early years of service, befriending Abdel Hakim Amer and Anwar Sadat, fellow officers who would serve as important advisors in the years ahead. During World War II, he became an instructing officer at the Royal Military Academy. In this new capacity, Nasser cultivated relationships with the next generation of Egyptian military leaders, continuing to build the network that would later help him seize power.

His army service only strengthened Nasser's earlier nationalist inclinations, and he dedicated himself to ridding Egypt of colonial influence. In 1948, Nasser, who by then had been promoted to major, served in the first Arab-Israeli War. Though the united Arab armies outnumbered their adversaries, they suffered a humiliating rout. Nasser's unit was surrounded and besieged by the Israelis, and Nasser himself was wounded by a sniper's bullet. Incensed at the incompetence of his superiors, he blamed the debacle on the corruption of the ruling Arab regimes, especially the British-supported Egyptian monarchy. In response, he formed the Free Officers movement and started conspiring to overthrow King Farouk. On July 23, 1952, the Free Officers seized strategic locations in Cairo and ordered the king to either abdicate or face execution. King Farouk offered no resistance and fled the country.

During the initial stages of the revolution, Nasser kept himself in the background, ruling anonymously through his control of the Revolutionary Command Council, comprised of about a dozen members. When he emerged from behind the scenes in 1954 and declared himself prime minister, he also placed Naguib under house arrest. That same year, after surviving an assassination attempt allegedly sponsored by the Muslim Brotherhood, he suppressed the organization, imprisoning or exiling its leaders. The brutal repression marked the beginning of a long-running war between the Brotherhood and the government, first Nasser and then his successors.

In 1956, Nasser unveiled a new constitution that declared Egypt a socialist Arab state. In a plebiscite held that June, the constitution was approved by more than 99 percent of the vote, while Nasser, the only nominee, was elected president, also with over 99 percent of the vote.

A key aspect of Nasser's domestic program was land reform. Land distribution in Egypt was heavily skewed toward the wealthy and was almost feudal in its degree of inequality. Among his initiatives, Nasser reduced the cap on landownership, established in 1952, from two hundred acres per household to one hundred, and confiscated vast tracts from major landowners to redistribute to the poor. He also nationalized much of Egyptian industry, creating a huge public sector.

One of Nasser's more ambitious domestic projects was the massive Aswan High Dam, which would generate electricity for much of the country and benefit Egyptian agriculture. The United States and Great Britain both offered loans to begin building the dam but soon withdrew them over concerns about Egypt's stance in the Cold War; though Nasser had outlawed the Communist Party, as well as all other parties besides his, he nevertheless turned to the Soviets for military aid. In fact, in attempting to modernize his armed forces, he had first sought to purchase arms from the Americans. The United States agreed—provided the weapons were defensive and were accompanied by supervisory American personnel. Faced with such conditions, Nasser instead accepted an offer from the Soviet bloc.

After the British and American loans for his Aswan project fell through, Nasser announced the nationalization of the Suez Canal on July 26, 1956. With the money raised by operating the canal, Nasser declared, Egypt would fund the Aswan High Dam. The nationalization effort also fit into his larger political mission of removing foreign and colonial influence from Egypt. With financial stakes in the Suez Canal Company, not to mention a strategic interest in keeping the canal out of Nasser's hands, the British and French joined the Israelis in beginning to develop counter-measures. In October, the combined armed forces of the three nations commenced their attack, seeking to wrest control of the canal away from Egypt. The Egyptian military could not withstand the onslaught and, at first, suffered heavy losses. But diplomatic intervention by the Americans and Soviets forced the French, British, and Israelis to withdraw and handed Nasser his greatest victory. The canal stayed in Egyptian hands and Nasser became a galvanizing hero throughout the Arab world.

With his victory in the Suez Crisis, Nasser looked to export his revolution and unite the Arab world under his leadership. He supported Algerian revolutionaries in their struggle against French colonial rule. He singled out the monarchies of Iraq, Saudi Arabia, Jordan, and Yemen, dismissing them as "regressive" regimes that stifled the pan-Arab aspirations of their people. Not long after Suez, Syrian politicians proposed union with Egypt under Nasser's leadership, and the United Arab Republic (UAR) was established in 1958. The UAR proved short-lived, however, when Syrian forces, resenting Egyptian authority, staged a coup d'état three years later that ended the union.

Nasser's international agenda wasn't strictly pan-Arab, nor did his purchase of arms from the Soviets and their allies indicate a preference in the Cold War. In September 1961, along with Jawaharlal Nehru of India and Josip Broz Tito of Yugoslavia, among other leaders, Nasser established the Non-Aligned Movement (NAM) of nations. Countries in this informal alliance sought to chart a middle course between the Eastern bloc and the West in both foreign and domestic policy.

The failure of the UAR did not diminish Nasser's pan-Arab aspirations. In 1962, he sent tens of thousands of Egyptian troops to North Yemen to support an insurgency against the ruling imam. The conflict in North Yemen turned into a proxy war, as the Saudi and Jordanian monarchies both supported the royalist faction. North Yemen developed into a quagmire for Egypt and in later years became known as Nasser's Vietnam. Egypt suffered heavy casualties as well as major financial losses, and there were incidents of Egyptian forces using chemical weapons against their opponents. Following the shattering defeat in the Six-Day War of 1967, Nasser withdrew Egyptian forces.

The Six-Day War with Israeli nearly dealt a fatal blow to Nasser's rule. Responding to Egyptian provocations, Israel launched a surprise attack, destroying most of Egypt's air force while it was still on the ground and crashing through Egyptian defenses to capture the Sinai Peninsula. Humiliated by the defeat, Nasser tendered his resignation, but popular demonstrations in his favor persuaded him to reconsider, and he remained in office until his death on September 28, 1970. With Nasser's passing, much of the Arab world went into mourning. His funeral drew crowds of over five million.

Whatever his achievements, Nasser did not accomplish what he set out to do. His leadership during the Suez Crisis gave the Arab world a resounding victory, but he could not build on it. Meanwhile, his failures in Syria and North Yemen, and in his confrontations with Israel, overshadow his early coups. Nasser's land reform in Egypt and his Aswan High Dam won him the enduring loyalty of the Egyptian underclass and of Arab masses throughout the world, but his policies did not bring about sustained prosperity. Politically, Nasser failed to construct viable institutions; instead, he built a repressive one-party police state. To this day, that police state is perhaps his most enduring actual legacy, and it has been employed to great effect by his successors.

But in the Arab world, Nasser always represented something much more consequential than his record. After centuries of foreign rule, the Arab people did not find the unity they longed for in the postcolonial era. Their new nations were drawn up by their former colonizers, and foreign influences still permeated society. The postcolonial governments were either corrupt kingdoms or tottering republics, torn by factionalism and sectarianism. Most galling of all for many Arabs, the state of Israel had been constructed in the heart of the Middle East, and Arab attempts to confront it had met only with humiliation and defeat. For a time, Nasser countered this losing narrative and restored dignity to the Arab people.

"Within the Arab circle, there is a role wandering aimlessly in search of a hero," Nasser observed. "This role is beckoning to us—to move, to take up its lines, to put on its costume and give it life." More than anyone in the modern era, Nasser came closest to fulfilling this unifying role. He stood as the archetype of the Arab nation and personified the aspirations of the Arab masses. The Arabist Elie Salem commented that twelfth-century Muslim hero Saladin "achieved success through his political and diplomatic skill, but there was no question of identifying with the masses. Since the time of the Prophet, Nasser was the first leader to address himself to the *shaab*, the forgotten masses." A powerful speaker who could couch his appeals in both classical Arabic and the colloquial Egyptian dialect, Nasser built his following largely on the strength of his personality. But the resources he had at his disposal were not equal to his ambition or the hopes he came to symbolize.

Nasser's exalted status in the Arab world did not help his successors, nor did his actual policies. Anwar Sadat, who took over leadership of Egypt following Nasser's death, opened up the Egyptian economy, undoing much of Nasser's socialist program. He also rebuilt the Egyptian military and steered it toward a renewed confrontation with Israel. During the Yom Kippur War, Egypt and its allies took Israel by surprise, scoring early victories. Soon, however, the Israeli armed forces counterattacked. By the time hostilities ended in a cease-fire, the Israelis had the strategic advantage, but by virtue of their initial successes, the Arab forces, and Egypt's in particular, had scored something of a symbolic victory.

After the war, Sadat pursued peace with the Israelis, eventually signing the Camp David Accords in 1979. The treaty with Israel cost Egypt much of its standing in the Arab world and led to Sadat's assassination by Islamic extremists on October 6, 1981. During his reign as president, Sadat had taken a less secular approach than Nasser, easing the repression of Islamists and releasing thousands of Muslim Brotherhood members from prison. But the treaty with Israel antagonized the Islamists.

Following Sadat's assassination, Hosni Mubarak was elected president and ruled for the next thirty years. He instituted further market reforms to the Egyptian economy, but the nation stagnated. Corruption and repression were endemic, while Mubarak positioned himself as a bulwark against the growing Islamist influence in Egypt. Faced with the uprising in Tahrir Square, Mubarak resigned on February 11, 2011. The following month, the Egyptian public voted to approve changes to the constitution and to establish a constituent assembly. Presidential elections are expected to be held before June 30, 2012. In the initial rounds of voting for the legislative assembly, Islamist political parties, particularly the Muslim Brotherhood, have garnered the most votes and will likely form the majority of the new parliament. Such developments suggest that the era of pan-Arab Nasserism is giving way to a more Islamist approach in Egyptian politics.

Egypt's Islamists: A Cautionary Tale

The Muslim Brotherhood's patience and prudence should not be mistaken for moderation.

By Hillel Fradkin and Lewis Libby
Commentary, April 2011

On February 18, crowds gathered in Cairo's Tahrir Square to celebrate the ouster of Egyptian strongman Hosni Mubarak—but also to pray, since it was a Friday, and Friday is the Muslim Sabbath. As it had on every Friday since the uprising began the month before, the Muslim Brotherhood took a leading role. But on this Friday, the subject was no longer Mubarak but rather Egypt's future and the place the Brotherhood—the venerable Islamist organization—would have in it. Would the Muslim Brotherhood ultimately support a turn toward democratic governance, or would it revert to its oft-cited goal of installing a theocracy? How that question might be answered arose in the person of Wael Ghonim, the young Google executive whose secret work on Facebook and elsewhere on the Web had been so crucial to organizing the protests.

Would Ghonim speak?

He would not. Despite his centrality to all that had happened, this undeniable hero of the revolution was denied access to the podium by the Muslim Brotherhood. Ghonim's parting gesture, as he left the square, was to wrap himself in the Egyptian flag. In his stead was Sheikh Yusuf al-Qaradawi, an Egyptian who had lived in exile for more than 30 years, had had no apparent role in recent events, and had just flown in from Qatar. Qaradawi is known to millions in the Muslim world through his weekly TV show on Al Jazeera and through his founding and direction of Islamist institutions, many of them in Europe. He is the chief ideologue and spiritual guide of the Muslim Brotherhood worldwide.

And so February 18 turned out not to be a celebration of the "agenda" of Egyptian reform for all Egyptians but rather of the agenda of the Muslim Brotherhood. What is that agenda? That is the question. The Muslim Brotherhood is the largest and most organized Egyptian entity apart from the Egyptian military and the state itself. The institutions that the Brotherhood manages or dominates—schools, clinics, and loose affiliations of lawyers, doctors, and students—constitute something like a parallel state. And the Brotherhood has shown its strength with the Egyptian public in recent years. In 2005, in the only semi-free legislative elections in decades, the Brotherhood managed to win 20 percent of the seats. The Brotherhood seems well positioned to benefit from the protests and the departure of Mubarak, and that fact has cast a shadow over the extraordinary events in Cairo—the peaceful ouster of a sclerotic autocrat.

Some observers have expressed the hope that the Brotherhood might actually play a benign role as Egypt moves forward. They cite the soothing words of one of the members of its Supreme Council, Essam el-Errian: "We come with no special agenda of our own—our agenda is that of the Egyptian people. We aim to achieve reform and rights for all, not just for the Muslim Brotherhood, not just for Muslims, but for all Egyptians." This and other pronouncements have been taken as evidence that the Brotherhood is not the radical organization of old—the organization from whose ranks the assassins of Mubarak's predecessor, Anwar el-Sadat, emerged, and from whose theoretical seedlings al-Qaeda sprouted.

But even if the Brotherhood hasn't changed, say, others, we shouldn't worry too much. It won't have the legitimacy necessary to dominate the political life of the new Egypt. Common estimates of its public support range between 20 and 30 percent, which suggests to optimists that the Brotherhood would lack the capacity to overpower the pro-democracy elements of the movement. After all, the senior leadership of the Brotherhood was not initially involved in instigating the protests, and once the organization got involved, it supposedly played at best a subordinate role. The public knows this. And the Brotherhood knows it too, they say, which explains why it has announced it will not field a candidate for Egypt's presidency, nor run a candidate slate sufficiently large to win a majority in the new parliament. Indeed, in offering their hopes for a new Egypt, Brotherhood leaders have invoked the relatively reassuring model of Turkey—present-day Turkey, that is, under the governance of the AKP, a party that grew out of the Turkish branch of the Muslim Brotherhood.

But as the sobering treatment of Ghonim and appearance of Qaradawi on February 18 both suggest, democracy advocates need to keep their wits about them when considering the composition of the new Egypt. The passions that stoked these remarkable events are very fresh and very raw and very powerful. But they will abate over time, and time is the Muslim Brotherhood's friend. The organization is nearly 80 years old, and it has learned the benefits of both patience and prudence.

It is proceeding with caution, and so, in relation to the Muslim Brotherhood, should we.

Far too many analysts seem to confuse the caution the Muslim Brotherhood has displayed thus far with moderation. There is no conflict between being immoderate and acting with discretion. We know very well from historical experience that successful radical movements and organizations often proceed carefully in pursuit of a violent revolutionary aim.

The Brotherhood's difficult eight-decade history in Egypt has schooled its leaders in the need for caution. During those 80 years, the Brotherhood has sometimes enjoyed some freedom and even favor, only to see them replaced by hardship. In the 1930s and early 40s, the Brotherhood's founder, Hassan al-Banna, enjoyed influence—sometimes considerable—under the Egyptian monarchy. But in 1948, Banna was murdered by King Farouk's police. Subsequently, the Brotherhood became friendly and complicit with the group of young officers who overthrew the monarchy in 1952 and established the regime that persisted through the reign of the three generals—Gamal Abdel Nasser, Anwar Sadat, and Hosni Mubarak (it persists today, in spite of the latter's ouster).

But in two years' time, the Brotherhood had fallen out with the regime and found itself subjected to ferocious persecution far worse than anything it had endured under the monarchy. For a time, Nasser relented, but he turned on them yet again and launched another cycle of attacks in the 1960s. This campaign culminated in the 1966 execution of Sayyid Qutb, the anti-Western thinker who was the Brotherhood's most popular figure.

> *Far too many analysts seem to confuse the caution the Muslim Brotherhood has displayed thus far with moderation.*

After Nasser's death in 1970, the Brotherhood enjoyed a period of relative freedom under his successor Anwar Sadat, who was more pious than Nasser and needed the group to combat the influence on Egypt of the Soviet Union and its Communist allies. But that second honeymoon, too, soon faded, and ended altogether under Mubarak, in the wake of Sadat's assassination by Islamist radicals who had broken from the Brotherhood.

So we can see how and why the Brotherhood was forced to learn the virtues of caution. At the same time, its vision of Egypt's future, and the Muslim future as a whole, is anything but moderate. From its very beginnings in 1928, the Brotherhood has been explicit about its ultimate goal: the radical transformation of contemporary Muslim society and its political order. Its central pronouncement, authored by its founder, Banna, remains authoritative to this day: "Allah is our objective; the Prophet is our leader; the Koran is our law; Jihad is our way; dying in the way of Allah is our highest hope."

The Brotherhood's strategy for realizing its vision was long term, to put it mildly, and thus has been mistaken for a legitimate effort to effect gradual change from the bottom up through the construction of institutions separate from the government—like providers of social services and communities of like-minded professionals. But these organizational efforts in no way have led to the abandonment of its radical vision in its most comprehensive and ultimately political form.

The Brotherhood's "gradualism" arose from a belief that such an approach was the best way to achieve its comprehensive and radical political vision of a fully Islamic society and way of life. Of course, this strategy posed problematic tactical questions: How would the Brotherhood determine the right moment for the transition to genuinely political activity and the acquisition of genuine rule? Did it need to wait until society was Islamically homogenous by Brotherhood standards? Or should it proceed at a moment somewhat short of this goal, if adversity or the right circumstances presented themselves?

The inherent uncertainty and difficulty of answering these questions could and did lead to divisions within the Brotherhood's leadership. It even led to defections from the Brotherhood and the founding of alternative groups. One such group assassinated Sadat. As later interviews with the conspirators revealed, they undertook their plot not only or even primarily because of the Israeli-Egyptian peace treaty, which had been signed two years earlier. Rather, they considered work on women's rights championed by Sadat's wife, Jihan, an existential threat to true Muslim society.

The main body of the Muslim Brotherhood demurred on using violence in that instance. But that was a tactical difference of opinion; it did not represent an alteration in the essential character of the group's overall objective. One of the anti-Sadat conspirators, Ayman al-Zawahiri, shouted from his jail cell, "Islam is our religion and our ideology." Released, he later became al-Qaeda's second-in-command.

Might the new opening of Egyptian politics lead the Brotherhood to shed its bruised history and adopt a new, participatory, or democratic notion of its role? Or, even if it does not yet deserve to be called "moderate," might it come to be so through the give-and-take of future Egyptian electoral politics? Perhaps. But even the evidence suggesting that the Brotherhood is evolving in this way is subject to a far less reassuring interpretation.

It is true that senior leaders of the Brotherhood were not members of the committee of youth who first organized the protests. But that committee included a leader of the youth arm of the Brotherhood, so the senior leadership knew what was happening. Other members of the youth committee, moreover, included the Brotherhood precisely because they believed they might need their ranks swelled by Brotherhood members. The Brotherhood supplied that need on the first occasion that suited its own institutional requirements: January 28, the first Friday of the revolt. The weekly Friday prayers permitted the Brotherhood to mass its forces easily in the mosques and with the protective cover of religious duty. Large groups of people who emerged from the mosques were led to Tahrir Square under the supervision of Brotherhood monitors. This pattern was repeated on all subsequent Fridays, and the Brotherhood declined to participate in a mass demonstration in March that did not fall on a Friday.

None of this suggests that the Brotherhood had simply a subordinate role in the Egyptian events. But it does exemplify the Brotherhood's characteristic caution. When Mubarak was still on the scene, and even following his fall with the military in charge, there was—and there still is—a substantial risk in being too conspicuous.

Nor should one take too much comfort from the analyses that say that the Brotherhood has the support of only about a quarter of the electorate. That is a shaky estimate and may be too low. To get that 20–30 percent number, analysts are relying on the results of that 2005 election, but given the extent to which those elections were limited, controlled, and stolen, those results may well understate the degree to which the ordinary Egyptian is in sympathy with the Brotherhood. Indeed, some polls show that a high percentage of the public holds extreme views on key issues, views that should make Brotherhood candidates attractive to them. In truth, we do not know reliably what the Brotherhood's strength might be, and the Brotherhood may not either. Only the senior Brotherhood leadership is privy to their strategy going forward. Indeed, that strategy is necessarily a work in progress, since they, like all Egyptians, cannot foresee how events will unfold or what crises or turning points might lie ahead. Thus it has ever been in revolutions, and the Brotherhood has been through several.

Westerners have little cause for comfort in the pronouncements of the Brotherhood that it is attracted to the "Turkish model." That may seem like a course we can welcome, given that the Brotherhood has also praised the bravery of Iran's leaders and their model for governance. But Turkey should give us pause. Yes, Turkey's Islamist AKP was democratically elected, then re-elected, and may win yet a third term this spring. But its leader, Recep Tayyip Erdogan, knows to play his own cautious game, skillfully using state power to weaken the army and other institutions, like the press and judiciary, whose independence could check his ambitions. The Turkish model is characterized by growing authoritarianism through intimidation, questionable detentions of opponents, and diversion of public assets to friendly hands. That may be more congenial than the "Iranian model," but that ought to be cold comfort, given the speed with which Erdogan is effecting Islamist changes in what was the most secular country in the Muslim world.

Indeed, perhaps what the Brotherhood likes most of all about the AKP's success in Turkey is the way it has succeeded in bringing that country's formerly powerful, secular military to heel. That might be the "Turkish model" it really seeks to pursue in Egypt.

The Brotherhood might also want to bide its time when it comes to taking power. For whenever the newly elected civilian government comes to power in Egypt, it may not be able to wield broad powers to effect change, either because the Egyptian military (acting with caution) might act to limit them or because too many parties will win seats and governing authority will be diffuse. The result could be a first government too fractious or enfeebled to tackle Egypt's enormous problems. Indeed, if the history of Central Europe in the 1990s is any guide, even empowered governments with international support will probably be unable to satisfy the pent-up demands of a long-suffering public, especially one unused to democratic ways.

Those who attempt to take on the overwhelming job of governing the country in this atmosphere face the specter of a body politic that comes to view them with hostility and contempt. If the Brotherhood is among the governing number, it might find itself on the knife's edge. The roiling dissatisfaction created by these circumstances might produce calls for a national savior to redeem the revolution. That savior might arise from the military's ranks, or be the military itself. In that event, the Brotherhood might find itself suppressed yet again, its goal of a wholly Islamic society defeated once more.

Thus the Brotherhood has good reason not to seek a majority too soon. It might serve its own purposes best by taking a role as a junior partner in the new government, with particular interest in certain ministries like education or social services that it can use to make the case that the Brotherhood is the only force in Egypt working to provide a better life for the people.

All in all, it might regard the downside risk of tarnishing its reputation or endangering its goals as substantially greater than the upside rewards of a major role in the early going. This might have the effect of making the Brotherhood seem as though it has chosen a far more moderate course than fearful Westerners expect, because it will have chosen caution over a risky attempt to seize the revolutionary moment. And, to be fair, one cannot rule out the possibility that a "new" Muslim Brotherhood more genuinely moderate than cautious, one opting for a departure from its radical past, might be emerging. We know that a cohort of new and younger leaders exists, and some are said to disagree with the senior leadership.

But for the time being, the old Muslim Brotherhood is still in charge, and its tradition was well in evidence on February 18 in the decision to invite Qaradawi—regarded as the highest authority and bearer of that tradition—to dominate the day. In his sermon, Qaradawi celebrated the demise of Mubarak—the Pharaoh, the Koranic exemplar of tyranny—and urged the consolidation of that victory. But in so doing, he darkly warned of the "hypocrites," a Koranic term denoting those who apparently supported Muhammad's "revolution" but secretly conspired against it. It was not obvious who such hypocrites might be. Were they the remnants of Mubarak's regime, or people like Wael Ghonim, who ostensibly had been comrades in arms but might resist an Islamic state?

Qaradawi was not there simply to celebrate the new Egypt and the new national agenda of "reform and rights" for "all Egyptians," as el-Errian had put it. Rather, he urged his audience to look beyond Egypt and its reform not as Egyptians but as Muslims and Muslim Brothers. He offered an impassioned "message to our brothers in Palestine." "I have hope," he declared, "that Almighty Allah, as I have been pleased with the victory in Egypt, that he will also please me with the conquest of the Al-Aqsa Mosque [in Jerusalem]."

As the many millions who have heard Qaradawi know all too well, his words in Tahrir Square reflect his hope to participate in the extermination of the world's Jews—Jews, not merely Israelis. He has applauded Hitler's work and seen Allah's hand in it. Indeed, he has expressed gratitude that the final work has been left to Muslims, a task, he claims, that goes to the roots of Islam. This is neither "moderation," nor a contribution to the pressing task of building a new democratic and healthy Egyptian polity. Nonetheless, Qaradawi's message received thunderous applause. We don't know if there is a "new" Brotherhood aborning, but we certainly do know that the old Muslim Brotherhood is not only surviving, but thriving.

In this sense, the future course of Egypt presents a very great risk—for Egyptians most of all, and for others. This ancient nation has begun its liberation from oppression, but the high hopes raised by the astonishing results of its winter revolt cannot obscure the cold facts. The nation's direction is uncertain and the structures necessary for true democracy are barely in evidence. Outsiders may yet have a role to play in this, but that role will be limited; and early elections, which may now be in the cards, leave little time for newly liberated democratic forces to adjust.

We should not delude ourselves. There is a great possibility that a state either under the direction of the Muslim Brotherhood or deeply influenced by it will adversely affect our position in a crucial part of the world. Secular forces would recede. More radicals would be schooled. Islamists would dominate the most populous and most developed countries in the Middle East—Iran, Turkey, and Egypt. The dire straits in which Israel would find itself would not be limited to the Jewish state alone. At long last, and to the world's great peril, the Muslim Brotherhood would have no more need of caution.

❖

Hillel Fradkin is senior fellow at the Hudson Institute, where Lewis Libby serves as senior vice president.

Bloody Democracy

Fears of violence as Egypt races toward its first free elections

By Mike Giglio
Newsweek, November 28, 2011

One evening last week, Azza Soliman and her husband, Mazen Mostafa, sat beside the croquet pitch at the Heliopolis Club, one of Cairo's oldest private sporting clubs, which the British founded in 1910. Soliman once ran a small liberal political party, and Mostafa is a well-to-do businessman. As they listened to the hard taps of croquet mallets, the couple made a surprising admission: they were thinking of buying a gun.

In the nine months since Egypt's revolution, a pervasive unease has seeped into the country's initial sense of optimism. That anxiety is on full display when people discuss the status of their streets, where a once smothering security force has seemed to fade eerily into the background. Mostafa and Soliman ticked through the safety concerns weighing on Cairenes these days: a rumored raft of weapons flowing in from Libya, on top of the ones looted from police stations after the fall of the regime; a wave of press reports of kidnappings and violent crime. And with the police now noticeably thinned out, even things like the snarled traffic on Cairo's chaotic streets are taking on an ominous tone. "Life in Egypt is sliding to intended chaos," Mostafa said.

Tension has been rising as Egypt heads into its first round of parliamentary elections, which begin next week. Conspiracy theories abound about whether the cops will intervene to suppress political violence, or even perhaps instigate violence themselves. Soliman, who ran as an independent in the 2010 elections, planned to run again this time around. But as Egypt's mood darkened, she decided against it. "I think maybe it will be a bloody election," she said. She worried that authorities have been pulled back to bring about that very scenario: "Maybe this is why the police are hiding."

Egyptian elections were long seen as dangerous affairs, where hired thugs descended on polling stations to help muscle regime candidates into power. Now, with the implosion of former president Hosni Mubarak's old political party, a wealth of new ones have mushroomed into existence. Turnout is expected to be far greater than in previous years—24 million expected voters, versus 6 million in the last elections. With the police pulling back, some Egyptians fear they have an explosive cocktail on

> *Egyptian elections were long seen as dangerous affairs, where hired thugs descended on polling stations to help muscle regime candidates into power.*

their hands. "The atmosphere in Egypt is much more tense now than it was several months ago," says Brookings analyst Shadi Hamid. "You have so many factors that make for a combustible mix . . . Violence is almost inevitable."

Mohamed Mahfouz, a former police official who is now spearheading reform efforts, worries that the violence could take a different shape than in the past, when it was mainly used to ensure that certain candidates prevailed. Now, Mahfouz says, disruptive elements could be aiming to make the entire election fail. "There is nothing to lose."

Dalia Ziada, a liberal activist turned candidate, has had an uneasy time in the electoral spotlight. Earlier this month she received a death threat via text. "Your end is near, sweet girl," it read. She has yet to decide whether to even head out to the polls. "The other plan: just stay at home," she says.

The Muslim Brotherhood, which stands to make big electoral gains, is warily watching the situation in the run-up to the vote. One Brotherhood organizer worries that the elections might not happen at all. Instability could be used as an excuse to put off the vote, he says. In an attempt to fill the security gap, the Brotherhood has set up its own office to field complaints that would normally go to police.

Signs of turmoil bubbled up last Thursday, when Coptic Christians marched in commemoration of a previous attack on their brethren. One cabdriver witnessed people throwing Molotov cocktails and glass bottles at the marchers, and officials reported that 29 people were injured in the melee. Hours later, a small demonstration made its way toward Tahrir Square in preparation for a Friday protest. Some teens in the crowd began harassing one of the few policemen in sight on the route. An activist ran over and shooed the kids away. "I'm sorry," he said to the cop, "but you should really get out of here."

Mahfouz, who is in regular touch with former colleagues in the force, thinks that police have holed up in their stations to avoid their duties: "They're not picking up the [emergency] calls," he says. Many Egyptians think that the police may be absenting themselves because they feel the revolution tarnished their status. Hussein Hammouda, a former brigadier at Egypt's Interior Ministry who joined the revolution in January, points out that the protests that toppled Mubarak started as a response to police brutality—the date of the first big demonstration was planned to coincide with national Police Day. "They're humiliated," Hammouda says. "Some of them hate the revolution."

Speculation over the police disappearing act plays into a deeper confusion over what exactly the military council wants. When the Supreme Council of the Armed Forces took charge in the wake of Mubarak's exit, it initially seemed open to accommodating some of the revolution's demands and promised a quick transition to democracy. But it has since made a series of worrying moves: instituting emergency law, erecting military courts, and proposing to stay in power until Parliament elects a president, which could be more than a year away. Ziad Sami, a student who attended Friday's protest, summed up the sense of confusion this is creating for many Egyptians: "There are some strange things happening. Maybe they don't want us to be convinced that it's safe to do elections."

Gamal Eid is one of Egypt's most respected human-rights defenders, with a long record of fighting against the old regime. He warns that while press reports and word-of-mouth spread concerns over insecurity, reliable analysis has been in short supply—and that talk of violence and chaos might be a destabilizing force in itself.

On Friday night in Shoubra, one of Cairo's most notorious neighborhoods, colored lights were strung across a busy street to celebrate the expansion of a local grocery store, which bustled with customers, and rickshaws buzzed past election posters for Islamic politicians. Residents spoke of guns and thefts, and one man showed off the fresh cuts on his face from an attempted carjacking. But one taxi driver insisted that life in Cairo hadn't changed all that much. "The same problems have always been here," he said. "We've always protected ourselves."

Revolution Returns to Tahrir Square

By Bel Trew
New Statesman, November 28, 2011

Tahrir Square has once again become a makeshift community of tents, field hospitals and wounded protesters. "We are exhausted but morale is high," says Omar Marsafy, 24, who has gunshot wounds to his legs, arms and head. Many have been sleeping there since Saturday 19 November, when the state security forces attacked the south-eastern side of the square with tear gas and rubber bullets.

The square hosts a mix of ages, genders, background and religious persuasions. "On the front line it's mostly young men from the poorer and more disaffected areas," explains Omar—although, he adds, not exclusively. This becomes abundantly clear when you visit the morgue and speak to bereaved families. The official body count is 23, and many news agencies are reporting 33.

The front line, next to the American University in Cairo library, is a constant battle for ground. The protesters face lines of the Egyptian Central Security Forces (CSF) and a handful of plain-clothed officers. "They shoot directly at the people, some aiming at our faces," says Ahmed Fathi, 23, a student. These fighters rarely leave the battlefield, Fathi explains—only if they are hurt.

There is a continuous stream of men on scooters and pick-up trucks bringing the injured back to the square. Women with bottles of vinegar and men with saline solution, anti-acid solution and eye drops to alleviate the effects of tear gas are scattered along Mahomed Mahmoud Street, helping protesters as they stagger from the attacks. Street children as young as six run through the centre of the fighting where, it is now confirmed, live ammunition has been used.

There are now more than seven makeshift medical centres on and around the square. Men and women link arms around these areas to give the doctors, who have been working 18-hour shifts, room to treat the wounded.

At approximately 5:30 p.m. on Sunday 20 November, the army stormed Tahrir. I witnessed officers beating protesters. One activist told me: "They shouted, 'You deserve it!'" as they hit them. I saw a heap of bodies and at least one death at the hands of the army—a soldier dragged the corpse of a young man and left him on a pile of rubbish.

United demand

The presence of the army was an important development. Since the beginning, the resounding chants on the square have been "Down, down with the military regime" even though, aside from Sunday's attack, most of the battles have been with the Egyptian police, who are controlled by the national ministry of interior. When you talk to people on the square, there is one united demand: for a civilian-led government and the removal of the Supreme Council of the Armed Forces (SCAF), which has ruled since the fall of Hosni Mubarak in February.

> *I saw a heap of bodies and at least one death at the hands of the army—a soldier dragged the corpse of a young man and left him on a pile of rubbish.*

Why now? "It's accumulation and escalation of tension and violence between state and the people," says Salma Shukrallah, a journalist for Ahram Online.

"Like Mubarak, the SCAF has been creating enemies with everyone—with the workers, the Salafis, the Muslim Brotherhood and the protesters making social demands."

On 18 November, hundreds of thousands came to the square protesting against the military junta and their attempt to expand the army's powers. With one eye on the forthcoming elections, Salafists and the Muslim Brotherhood were in full force on Friday, while liberal and revolutionary groups focused on the military trials for civilians and the detention of the internationally renowned blogger Alaa Abd el-Fattah and thousands like him. By the next morning only a few hundred remained. The forced clearing of that tiny sit-in by the CSF is what sparked the clashes.

"The SCAF is incapable of governing," says Ghada Shabender, of the Egyptian Organisation for Human Rights. "This is a national crisis." The constitutional declaration, which in effect is the constitution until an assembly is appointed to write a new one, is vague and allows the SCAF final say over legislation. "We have a puppet government right now," Ghada says.

In addition, the supraconstitutional declaration that the SCAF is trying to push through would give the military powers over the new president. Many important political groupings, such as the Muslim Brotherhood, have rejected it.

There are also grass-roots grievances. I asked one boy, 15-year-old Mohammed Abdalla, who had a rubber bullet injury to his forehead, why he was on the square. "The revolution has not been fulfilled," he says. "The financial situation is worse than when Mubarak was in power."

While the fate of what people are calling the Second Revolution remains in the balance, the driving force behind it is clear. As a young field doctor, Ahmed Saber, tells me: "I'm here for Egypt, for freedom, for our future, not just mine."

❖

Bel Trew is based in Cairo.

With Eye on Political Power, Egypt's Muslim Brotherhood Treads Carefully After Election Win

By Hamza Hendawi
The Associated Press, January 9, 2012

The Muslim Brotherhood has emerged as the biggest winner in parliamentary elections, but the fundamentalist group that has long dreamed of ruling Egypt is likely to be cautious about flexing its newfound muscle.

The Brotherhood has been crushed by the military before and will likely tread carefully to avoid spooking the ruling generals or the country's Western supporters, who provide generous amounts of badly needed foreign aid.

That may be the best tactic for the Brotherhood as it seeks to translate its impressive electoral victory into political power while reassuring this turbulent nation of 85 million people that it has no intention of monopolizing power.

So far, the Brotherhood's political arm, the Freedom and Justice party, is insisting it has no immediate desire to push through Islamic legislation or form a new government to replace one led by a prime minister named by the military only days before the staggered elections began on Nov. 28.

Additionally, it has distanced itself from more militant Islamic groups, including the ultraconservative Salafis, who won a quarter of seats, and has gone to great lengths to avoid a clash with the powerful generals who took over from Hosni Mubarak 11 months ago.

The Brotherhood has spent most of the 84 years since its inception in 1928 as an outlawed organization. At times, it enjoyed a level of relative tolerance by authorities that allowed it to function as a religious charity and political body, running a huge network of social services and fielding parliamentary candidates as independents.

But for most of those eight decades, Brotherhood leaders and supporters have been targeted in harsh government crackdowns that saw hundreds jailed, tortured and convicted, often on drummed up charges.

The Feb. 11 ouster of Mubarak heralded the empowerment of the Brotherhood. The group responded with astonishing speed, quickly organizing its ranks to contest the elections and emerging as the nation's most dominant political force. Its Freedom and Justice party is now the largest bloc in the next legislature, though final results of the staggered election have yet to be announced.

The Brotherhood's show of flexibility is typical of an organization that has honed to perfection survival tactics developed during decades of functioning underground to escape crackdowns by successive governments. It also emanates from the series of setbacks it has suffered over the years whenever it flaunted its power.

For example, Brotherhood leaders forged close ties with the army officers who seized power in a 1952 coup, acting as their political and spiritual patrons until the same officers cracked down on the group two years later.

The group enjoyed something of a revival during the 11-year rule of President Anwar Sadat, who used it to counter the weight of militant Islamic groups. Mubarak, who succeeded Sadat in 1981, initially tolerated the group, but subjected it to wave after wave of arrests starting in the 1990s on the grounds that it offered militant groups tacit support.

Some in Egypt, however, believe the Brotherhood's desire for power is what may prove its undoing.

"The Muslim Brotherhood has a rich history of failures," cautioned Amir al-Mallah, a leader of the protest movement that toppled Mubarak. "It is not after the creation of a civilian or a religious state—all it ever wanted is power."

The Brotherhood did not take a leadership role in the 18-day uprising that forced Mubarak to step down, only joining the uprising when it felt confident the protest movement had gained irreversible momentum. Its supporters also stayed away from recent protests demanding the military immediately step down, arguing that it was time to focus on the political process and not demonstrations.

"We have acted out of concern that we should work to rebuild the nation and not destroy what is left of it," Brotherhood leader Subhi Saleh told The Associated Press.

> *The Brotherhood's show of flexibility is typical of an organization that has honed to perfection survival tactics developed during decades of functioning underground to escape crackdowns by successive governments.*

The rise of the Brotherhood in post-Mubarak Egypt has become a serious source of concern to liberal and left-leaning groups, as well as women and the nation's large Christian minority, all of whom fear the group's long-term goal of implementing Islamic Sharia law will relegate them to the sidelines and stoke sectarian tensions.

While it has repeatedly stated its desire to maintain Egypt's close relations with the United States, the Brotherhood has sent conflicting signals on Israel, with whom Egypt has a 1979 peace treaty. Brotherhood leaders have said they will put the treaty to a nationwide referendum and have pledged to never recognize the Jewish state.

However, the Freedom and Justice party has said it will respect the nation's international commitments, a reference to the treaty.

"No not at all," said Saleh when asked whether the party intended to push legislation to bring the mainly Muslim nation more in line with Islamic teachings. "Our priority is economic and political reform."

Many of the Brotherhood's detractors see such assurances as a smoke screen to conceal the Brotherhood's Islamic agenda and calm nerves at home and abroad about whether it intends to put into practice its longtime slogan of "Islam is the solution."

The Freedom and Justice party's political manifesto, posted on the group's website, does not speak of the prohibition of alcohol and the segregation of the sexes, but there is enough there to suggest it may just be a matter of time.

The section devoted to the media, art and culture says the party will work for "clean film production" along with television programs sensitive to "the needs, values and customs of Egyptian citizens." It also says it will create a network of Internet sites that "bolsters constructive culture, and the social and religious values of Arab and Islamic societies."

Going on the defensive, Saad el-Katatni, the party's secretary general, said fear of the Islamists was "exaggerated" and amounted to scare mongering.

"The people have spoken. If you respect democracy then you must respect the new political map," he told reporters in comments carried by the official news agency, MENA.

Subhi and Brotherhood spokesman Mahmoud Ghazlan emphatically deny the Brotherhood has struck a deal with the generals. Both argue that, like all other political groups, the Brotherhood just wants the generals to make good on their promise to step down.

Activists and antimilitary protest leaders, however, say the Brotherhood has promised a safe exit for the generals when they leave power, protecting them against prosecution for killing protesters. That, say the activists, would be in return for giving the Brotherhood-dominated legislature a mandate to appoint a 100-member panel to draft a new constitution.

Writing in the Monday edition of the independent *al-Tahrir* newspaper, columnist Ibrahim Issa summed up the predicament of the Brotherhood—winning Egypt's freest and fairest election only to be reluctant to realize its longtime dream of ruling the country.

"The Brotherhood waited for 84 years for this moment: to rule Egypt," he wrote. "But when the moment has finally arrived, the Brotherhood seems to believe in the saying that one must be careful what one wishes for."

4

Libya: Qaddafi's Downfall

A Libyan National Transitional Council (NTC) fighter fires at loyalists troops on October 19, 2011, during a battle in Sirte's neighborhood Number 2, one of the last two bastions of ousted leader Muammar Qaddafi's gunmen.

The Strange Odyssey of Muammar Qaddafi

By Paul McCaffrey

Dictators tend to be defined by two traits in particular: brutality and eccentricity. In his forty-two years as the ruler of Libya, Muammar Qaddafi embodied the latter characteristic with aplomb. He bestowed grandiose titles upon himself and regularly appeared in unusual attire. Qaddafi espoused a bizarre and opaque ideology of his creation. The four decades he spent as ruler of Libya helped to make him a defining archetype of the modern dictator. In August 2011, Qaddafi's regime came to a brutal and chaotic end, with his last moments filmed on cell phone cameras.

Muammar Qaddafi was born outside the Libyan coastal city of Surt (sometimes spelled Sirte) in 1942. Some sources record his birth date as June 7. A member of the al-Qadhadhfa tribe, he belonged to a family of Bedouin nomads and in later years, went to great lengths to preserve the traditions of his birth, often pitching his traditional tent while on official visits in foreign capitals. Qaddafi did not receive any formal schooling until the age of ten, but what he learned as a child about his family history and the history of his country left an indelible imprint on him that lasted his entire life. Parts of Libya were colonized by Italy in 1911, but the country was never fully subjugated to Italian rule. Qaddafi's grandfather was killed fighting the Italians, and his father was wounded in battle against Italian forces. The Italians responded to Libyan recalcitrance by establishing labor camps that resulted in the deaths of as many as one in three Libyans. The memory of colonization and its excesses bred in Qaddafi a suspicion of the West and a fierce pride in the cause of Libyan nationalism and resistance.

Not long after Qaddafi's birth, during World War II, Allied forces seized control of Libya from Italy and its German allies. For the next eight years, British and French authorities administered the country. On December 24, 1951, under the auspices of the United Nations (UN), Libya finally achieved official independence when the United Kingdom of Libya was established under King Idris I. Idris I attained the throne thanks in part to British political maneuvering, and Great Britain continued to influence Libyan affairs in the years following independence.

Though he had studied under a local cleric as a child, Qaddafi embarked on his formal education soon after the United Kingdom of Libya was established, attending grammar school in Surt. Too poor to rent a room in town, Qaddafi slept in a mosque during the week and traveled home to his family's encampment on weekends.

Qaddafi grew up during a tumultuous period in Middle Eastern history. The post–World War II era saw the dismantling of colonial regimes in Libya and throughout North Africa. Various independent Arab states were established, many with arbitrary, ahistorical borders and unstable, unreliable governments. The era also saw the founding of the state of Israel and the beginning of the Israeli-Palestinian conflict. Oil was discovered and exploited in many countries. Among the forces unleashed during the era was that of pan-Arabism and pan-Arab socialism.

During the early days of the new monarchy in Libya in 1952, the Free Officers, a faction within the Egyptian armed forces, overthrew their ruler, King Farouk. Over the next few years, Gamal Abdel Nasser consolidated his leadership of the new Egypt. Nasser was a committed pan-Arabist. He supported the unification of Arab people in North Africa and the Middle East. Nasser issued appeals to Arabs of all nations and took a confrontational stance with the Western powers, circumventing them to acquire arms from the Soviet Union for the Egyptian military in its conflict with Israel and nationalizing the Suez Canal in 1956. Nasser became a hero throughout the Arab world. His vision of pan-Arab socialism, known as Nasserism, became a galvanizing force throughout the Middle East.

As a high-school student in the town of Sabha, the young Muammar Qaddafi drew inspiration from Nasserism. He would hold up Nasser's picture in class and organize political demonstrations. School administrators eventually asked him to leave. Qaddafi gained admittance to the Royal Military Academy in Benghazi, Libya, in 1963. His support for pan-Arabism attending the academy did not sit well with his British instructors.

In 1966, Qaddafi was sent to Great Britain with other Libyan officers for additional training. On his first trip to London, he wore traditional Libyan attire and strolled proudly through the streets "prompted by," in his own words, "a feeling of challenge and a desire to assert myself." He had no interest in exploring Great Britain. He pretended not to speak English so he wouldn't have to communicate with British officers, whom he found insulting, and sequestered himself with other Arabs.

In Libya, vast reserves of oil had been discovered in 1959, and money had flooded into the country, resulting in simmering political resentment over how the new wealth was being distributed by the country's rulers.

Upon his return to Libya, Qaddafi began plotting a coup with like-minded members of the Libyan military. Following Nasser's model, they styled themselves as Libyan Free Officers. On September 1, 1969, with King Idris out of the country, Qaddafi and his colleagues staged a bloodless coup d'etat and took control of Libya. Following the coup, they established the twelve-member Revolutionary Command Council (RCC) and declared a new Libyan Arab Republic.

Far from the caricatured figure of his later years, Qaddafi, only twenty-eight in 1969, possessed undeniable charisma and quickly rose to the forefront of the RCC. In time, he became Libya's unofficial head of state. He took the title "Brother Leader and Guide of the Revolution," a post he would effectively hold until 2011. Patterning himself after Nasser, Qaddafi embraced pan-Arabism and the Palestinian cause; he evicted British and American forces from Libyan military bases. Thousands of Italian residents left over from the colonial period were deported, and their property was seized. The remains of Italian colonists were dug up from cemeteries and returned to Italy. Libya's minority Jewish community suffered similar treatment.

Qaddafi renegotiated Libya's contracts with oil companies, quadrupling the amount of revenue going to the state and setting an example that many oil-producing states in the region would follow. With these funds, Qaddafi sought to modernize the country, building roads, hospitals, and schools and launching ambitious infrastructure projects—all the while cementing his status as the nation's unrivaled leader.

As his control of Libya became more dictatorial, Qaddafi morphed into a political philosopher. In his three-volume *The Green Book*, he presented his "third universal theory," which he claimed would reconcile the conflicts between capitalism and communism. Central to his vision was the Jamahiriya, a term he invented and defined as the "state of the masses." According to this theory, leaders would disappear as power was disseminated to the people. Although Qaddafi's ideas were seen as mere ramblings and propaganda by many international officials and analysts, the *Green Book* became an essential component of Libyan life and education.

Qaddafi used Libya's oil revenues to support his increasingly lavish lifestyle, building numerous mansions and providing homes and cars for loyalists. However, he left much of the population in a state of near-poverty and unemployment. As with other oil states, much of the Libyan labor force was composed of foreign workers, while native Libyans collected government checks and remained largely idle. Private industry was forbidden in the Jamahiriya and shortages of certain goods were common despite the country's oil wealth. The Qaddafi regime did not tolerate political dissent and relied on common tools of dictatorship—secret police, show trials, public executions, and torture—to keep the Libyan people in line.

Bizarre government decrees became a staple of Libyan life under Qaddafi. He once determined that all Libyans should raise chickens, and had the money for cages deducted from state stipends. Another time, Qaddafi ordered all of Libya's tea shops be closed, claiming that men sitting in tea shops during the day gave the false impression that Libyans lack industriousness.

Donning flowing robes and unusual headdresses, as well as elaborate military uniforms, Qaddafi became an icon of dictatorial excesses. His entourage reflected his unusual tastes. He had a team of machine-gun bearing female bodyguards—the Revolutionary Nuns—outfitted in combat fatigues and fashionable shoes.

Given his ambition and sense of destiny, Qaddafi was not content to limit his designs just to Libya. He sought unsuccessfully to unite Libya with other Arab countries. Frustrated in these schemes, Qaddafi became a pan-Africanist and pan-Islamist and started using Libya's oil wealth to influence affairs in Africa. He also sent Libyan troops to Chad in a dispute over a strip of territory. His forces were routed. Most of Qaddafi's machinations generated little in the way of concrete results, but oddities were abundant. In one ceremony in 2008, a group of traditional African leaders crowned Qaddafi "King of Kings."

Qaddafi also embraced international terrorism. He funded and offered sanctuary to pro-Palestinian terrorist organizations, the Provisional Irish Republican Army (IRA), and other factions. His decision to purchase arms from the Soviet Union drew the ire of the United States and the West. In the early 1980s, a bid by

Qaddafi to expand Libya's territorial waters resulted in the shooting down of two Libyan fighter planes by the United States. In 1986, Qaddafi was incriminated in the bombing of a West Berlin disco frequented by American military personnel. In response, the United States unleashed a series of airstrikes on Libya in a failed attempt to kill Qaddafi.

Libyan agents were next implicated in the 1988 bombing of Pan Am Flight 103 over Lockerbie, Scotland, which killed 270 people. Many suspected Qaddafi was behind the destruction of a French airliner that killed 170 people in the skies over Niger in 1989. As a result of Qaddafi's involvement with terrorism, Libya endured a series of economic sanctions instituted by the international community over several decades. Isolated throughout the 1990s, Libya made some concessions beginning in 1999, turning over suspects in the Lockerbie bombing. In 2003, Qaddafi agreed to pay a $2.7 billion settlement to the survivors of the Flight 103 victims, which resulted in the end of imposed economic sanctions. That same year, Qaddafi revealed that Libya had been pursuing nuclear arms but would renounce weapons of mass destruction, and began to collaborate with the United States in its war on terror.

Following improved relations between Libya and the global community, Qaddafi addressed the United Nations General Assembly in August 2009. Although he had been allotted fifteen minutes, he spoke for over an hour on subjects ranging from Western imperialism to political theory. At one point during his speech, he tore up a copy of the UN charter.

In February 2011, anti-Qaddafi elements within Libya began to organize themselves and conduct demonstrations. The rebels were inspired to act after witnessing the Tunisian revolution of December 2010. Following the beginning of the Libyan uprising in February 2011, Qaddafi vowed to fight critics of his regime, dismissing the rebels as drug-addled teenagers who had been influenced by terrorists. After Qaddafi threatened the use of violence against Libyans who supported the revolution, the UN passed a resolution in March 2011 authorizing the use of NATO airstrikes to support the Libyan uprising. As fighting between rebels and Qaddafi loyalists continued, supporters of the revolution organized Libya's National Transitional Council (NTC). After a prolonged stalemate, the NTC forces gained control of Libya's major cities and Qaddafi went into hiding.

The last days of Qaddafi's story played out where his story began, on the outskirts of Surt. Attempting to break out of rebel encirclement on October 20, Qaddafi's convoy was hit by NATO airstrikes. Wounded and desperate, the dictator took refuge in a drainage pipe with a handful of his surviving loyalists. Cornered by NTC forces, he was captured, beaten, and executed. Footage of Qaddafi's capture was recorded by cell phones and broadcast worldwide on the internet.

What the future holds for post-Qaddafi Libya is a question unlikely to be settled anytime soon. After forty-two years of brutal and erratic dictatorship, the nation has few functioning civil institutions. Nonetheless, the country's oil reserves have the potential to provide a strong foundation for prosperity, but the risks of corruption and in-fighting loom large. How quickly Libya emerges from the dark age of Qaddafi may be determined by the depth and insidiousness of his legacy. Since Qaddafi's death, some outbursts of violence between rival militias have occurred in Libya. Meanwhile, Qaddafi's son, Saif al-Islam Qaddafi, was captured and put on trial for conducting crimes against humanity at the International Criminal Court. US Secretary of State Hillary Clinton visited Libya in October 2011 to pledge American support to the country's rebuilding efforts.

"Qaddafi Gave Us No Choice"*

By Anjali Kamat
The Progressive, December 2011

Early this February, an underground group of Libyan activists and intellectuals across the country—some of whom knew each other only by the pseudonyms they used in online forums—announced a call for a nationwide protest on February 17. Inspired by the changes sweeping across neighboring Tunisia and Egypt, their demands focused on ending four decades of political repression and unrepresentative rule. Soon after the call, many well-known dissidents were arrested in an apparent attempt to suppress a possible uprising. "The crackdown on our revolution began even before we started coming out onto the streets," recalled Ghaidaa al-Tawati, one of a small number of politically active Libyan women bloggers. Based on her posts on Facebook, the outspoken thirty-three-year-old from Tripoli was charged with incitement against Colonel Muammar Qaddafi and taken to Abu Salim prison, notorious for the 1996 mass execution of more than 1,200 political prisoners.

Another man who was arrested in this period was Fathy Terbil, a well-known Benghazi-based lawyer working for years with the families of the Abu Salim victims. Spontaneous demonstrations broke out immediately after his arrest, and he was quickly released early the next morning. But it was too late; the spark had been lit. After a week of protests and bloody clashes, Benghazi and cities further east suddenly found themselves free of Qaddafi's iron grip. When I met Fathy in a dusty back room of the Benghazi courthouse a few days later, he had just been elected to the newly formed city council. Unassuming in his worn-down leather jacket and kuffiyeh, and still in a bit of shock over the speed of the unfolding events, Fathy laughed and acknowledged that his arrest had backfired on the regime. At the time, in late February, foreign intervention was nowhere in the cards. "The West and the so-called international community, they always wait to see who will emerge the winner before declaring their alliances," he said when I asked him about the response of the United States and Europe. "They have never supported democracy or freedom, just the strongest party. I hope the international community reassesses its political strategies and supports people and not regimes. But I doubt that will happen," he added.

Like its counterparts in Tunisia and Egypt, the Libyan uprising began as a largely peaceful and leaderless popular struggle, with the aim of toppling a dictator and establishing a democratic political order. The decision to take up arms and then to ask for international military support was not easy, but from the perspective of almost everyone in eastern Libya, it was born out of necessity. Suleiman, a civil engineer and longtime activist with the Abu Salim families, told me that if Qaddafi had not used lethal force on peaceful demonstrators, the Libyan uprising could have had a very different trajectory.

"When we began, we didn't want this to be violent, and we never dreamt of asking for outside intervention," he said, with a hint of regret in his voice. "We wanted to do it ourselves. But Qaddafi went too far; he gave us no choice."

For many anti-war observers abroad, this history is eclipsed by the fact of Western intervention and the role of the United States, particularly President Barack Obama's decision—without Congressional approval—to involve the U.S. military in enforcing a no-fly zone over Libya, to covertly arm and train Qaddafi's opposition fighters, and to support NATO's bombing campaign. This has led some observers to question the credibility of the Libyan revolutionaries who not only called for external military support, but also welcomed it. But from the perspective of most Libyans, what has happened since February is an unprecedented popular revolt firmly embedded in the same electrifying mix of hope, fearlessness, and a desire to reclaim and transform their country that drove the uprisings across the Arab world.

> *"We didn't go through this bloody revolution to hand over this country to a foreign power or let any foreign power determine our future . . . "*
> —Hassan al-Amin

For Habib al-Amin, a poet and writer who was arrested from Misrata on February 18 and spent the next six months in Abu Salim prison, the fall of Tripoli was nothing short of a miracle. "With Qaddafi gone from Tripoli, it's as if our most impossible fantasy has been realized," he gushed. His name was on a list of a thousand people to be executed on September 1, the forty-second anniversary of Qaddafi's revolutionary coup. Then, without warning, on August 24, fighters burst open the prison doors and, suddenly liberated, Habib walked into freedom and a dramatically different country.

Despite the widespread euphoria over Qaddafi's fall, hardly anyone, especially former prisoners like Habib, is naïve about the political choices that were made during the revolution and the challenges that lie ahead. In fact, the most scathing critiques of the forces jostling for power in the new Libya come from people like Habib and the scores of former dissidents who were systematically tortured and imprisoned under Qaddafi, and in some cases forced into exile. Their worries, it's worth noting, differ significantly from the main Western preoccupations about Libya—imperial domination, civil war, tribalism, and Islamism.

"We didn't go through this bloody revolution to hand over this country to a foreign power or let any foreign power determine our future and involve itself heavily in our affairs," said Hassan al-Amin, Habib's older brother, who spent twenty-three years in exile. The hostility to international troops extends not just to overt intervention or military bases, but also to private security companies. Some young fighters were familiar with Blackwater's bloodstained history in Iraq and warned that security companies would not be tolerated, either.

One of the biggest controversies in the new Libya is over the presence of Qaddafi-era officials and technocrats who are now prominent figures on the National Transitional Council, which was formed in March and has been significantly reconstituted since then. "The victims of Qaddafi over the past forty-two years don't want a reminder of this painful experience," Hassan noted.

The National Transitional Council has publicly promised to investigate and try all former Qaddafi-era officials who were involved in murder, torture, and corruption. But the continued presence of individuals from the old regime, many of whom were affiliated with the Western-backed reform efforts led by Qaddafi's son Saif al-Islam, is a source of contention. They are seen to have jumped ship only after the start of the revolt and have spent most of the past eight months negotiating a political transition with Western politicians, the same ones who had become Qaddafi's most powerful friends over the past decade. Many Libyans initially welcomed their efforts to win international support, but now they are increasingly questioning the political credibility and representativeness of these high-level figures.

"The new leadership of Libya isn't here yet; these are just transitional authorities," said Ibrahim, an oil-engineer-turned-fighter I spoke to near the front line in September. "We don't trust them," he added firmly.

While the fate of high-level officials from the former regime hangs in the balance, on the ground it's those perceived to be Qaddafi's foot soldiers who have felt the brunt of popular anger and the desire for revenge. To the dismay of the activists who struggled for years against Qaddafi's security state, makeshift detention centers run by bands of opposition fighters are filling up with anyone suspected of having been sympathetic to Qaddafi or having fought for him. Among the worst affected are dark-skinned Libyans and sub-Saharan African migrant workers, partly as a result of persistent claims about Qaddafi's use of African mercenaries to attack civilian protesters as well as rebel fighters.

"They kept calling me a mercenary and one of Qaddafi's African dogs," said one prisoner I met at a detention center in Misrata, describing how anti-Qaddafi fighters captured him. The slight twenty-five-year-old from the southern Libyan town of Sabha used to play in one of Qaddafi's military bands. "If your skin is black, you are not considered Libyan; this is the problem of the revolution. Don't you think this is racism?" he asked bitterly.

Apprehensions about Libya's political future are only compounded by the militarization of the civilian population and a growing fear that people have gotten accustomed to settling disputes with arms. When Qaddafi's apparatus crumbled in city after city in the east, the first sites to be abandoned were the warehouses storing vast stockpiles of weapons. And as opposition fighters closed in on Tripoli and other cities still under his control, Qaddafi opened his supplies of arms to loyalist volunteers. Human Rights Watch estimates that thousands of weapons, including powerful surface-to-air missiles, have gone missing.

Ghaidaa Tawati, who lives half a mile from Bab al-Aziziya, Qaddafi's former compound in Tripoli, witnessed hundreds of people raiding the barracks for arms the day it was liberated. As much as she cheered the brigades fighting Qaddafi's forces, she said the proliferation of armed units in every town and city across the country terrified her. In a context of simmering regional rivalries, many worry that the lack of a clear structure of accountability and the poor coordination and communication between these various militias can be lethal.

"What will happen to these militias?" asks Zahi Mogherbi, an avuncular political science professor in Benghazi who advises the Council. "The situation is extremely volatile."

After months of war and countless lives lost on all sides, most Libyans are simply trying to rebuild their lives and their country amidst the mounting challenges of reconciliation and disarmament. In the broadest sense, many feel that the coming struggle is over constructing an open democratic political culture and a strong independent civil society that is unafraid to hold those in power accountable. There are some hopeful signs: Dozens of new newspapers are in circulation, political parties are being formed, and workers are organizing themselves and staging strikes. But activists like Ghaidaa, Habib, Hassan, and hundreds of others are monitoring every misstep of the National Transitional Council and speaking out against even the smallest hint of authoritarianism from newly emerging political powers. "This revolution is very clear in its principles; it's about real change in every aspect of this country," Hassan says.

"The revolution will continue," he adds, "until we make sure that its aims are totally and completely realized."

"When we began, we didn't want this to be violent, and we never dreamt of asking for outside intervention."

❖

Anjali Kamat is an independent journalist and a correspondent for Democracy Now. She traveled to Libya four times in 2011.

Libya: Where Will the Chips Fall?

By Adel Darwish
The Middle East, October 2011

As the Libyan revolutionaries surprised even themselves by their speedy advance into Tripoli, toppling the regime of Colonel Muammar Gaddafi vintage 1969, too many Cassandras to count were shouting from left-wing rooftops 'We can see another Iraq.'

The dissimilarities between Iraq and Libya are too many to list, but the two main linked factors indicating a happier conclusion for the Libyans are Gaddafi himself and the structure of the NATO operation under UN Security Council Resolution 1973.

Gaddafi saw himself a philosopher, inspired by the stars. He dismissed capitalism and rubbished Marxist-Leninism as a primitive irrelevant system. He minted his own Third Way theories of governance, as described in his *Green Book.*

Those, like this writer, who encountered Gaddafi and followed his career over decades, doubt his ability to organise an Iraqi-style insurgency. Still nowhere to be seen at the time of going to print, Gaddafi's 'resistance' remained on the battlefield of rhetoric. In defiant audiotapes transmitted by Syria-based television, the Colonel calls upon imaginary forces from among the 'heroic Libyan masses' to resist a non-existent NATO invasion.

In truth, Gaddafi in his paranoia deliberately weakened Libya's army to remove the possibility of any other officer copying his 1969 coup. He ensured the absence of serious institutions or even a strong ruling political party, making it simpler for the Libyan National Transition Council (NTC) to design a new system on a clean slate.

International input

More importantly, there is no American governor like Paul Bremer in Libya. Bremer misguidedly disbanded Iraq's army and dismantled a strong ruling party, creating a power vacuum, soon filled by pro-Iran militia, terror groups and gangs manipulated by Iraq's neighbours.

Although providing logistics, reconnaissance, ammunitions and intelligence, America has taken a back seat in Libya, letting Britain and France steer the campaign.

As Gaddafi fled and the world recognised the 'new' rulers of Libya, Britain led a UN drive to unfreeze Libyan assets (frozen by UNSC resolution 1970 when Gaddafi took to butchering those among his people who took to the street demanding their human rights).

At a conference in Paris last month, the world agreed to release billions to the NTC. South Africa's President Jacob Zuma objected to the move, refusing to recognise the NTC's legitimacy, alongside Algeria, which has become host to the largest gathering of Gaddafi's fleeing family.

Regional influence

With the error of Iraq on everyone's mind, all agreed on the urgency to restore law and order in post-Gaddafi Libya. The NTC finds itself in a catch-22 situation. It remains based in Benghazi, as the capital is not yet entirely safe. Tripoli was swiftly taken on the night of 21/22 August by Berber rebels from the western mountains. Their Amazigh language and ethnic identity being long suppressed by Gaddafi in his pursuit of a pan-Arab ideology was one factor in sparking the revolution. Despite a facade of unity, a political accommodation between the disparate groups is required before the NTC can move to Tripoli to govern all of Libya.

Since the spirit of revolution swept the MENA region starting in early January, only Tunisian dictator Zein El Abidine Ben Ali has shown any survival instinct. He packed his money, his wife's jewelry and all the gold he could carry and fled to a luxurious retirement. A move his fellow members of the MENA despots club failed to make, preferring to remain entrenched in a make-believe bubble of vanity.

> *Gaddafi's bubble was made of vanity and self deluding rhetoric, impregnable either by logic or advice . . .*

Egypt's disgraced Hosni Mubarak refused to see the writing on the wall and woke up to find himself horizontal on a stretcher in the dock, charged with corruption and conspiracy to murder.

Saddam was picked dishevelled and confused from a rat hole, a mere 10 months after turning down an offer from the late Sheikh Zayed of the UAE of an honourable retirement in Abu Dhabi.

Yemeni Ali-Abdullah Saleh repeatedly rejected GGC offers, until a rocket delivered him to a hospital bed in Jeddah.

Gaddafi's bubble was made of vanity and self deluding rhetoric, impregnable either by logic or advice from his few remaining friends—led by President Zuma—offering him a way out. South Africa was, at the time of going to print, still peddling 'an African solution to an African problem,' namely a negotiated settlement between Gaddafi and the rest of Libya.

The offer was laughed off by revolutionary Libyans.

Downing Street sources told *The Middle East* that British Prime Minister David Cameron was very much in support of the ICC and backs the NTC demand to put Colonel Gaddafi on trial.

The French put pressure on NATO not to target Gaddafi's family and regime convoys—some containing as many as 200 vehicles with armed escorts—as they headed south to Gaddafi's tribal stronghold of Sebha and from there across the porous Libyan/sub-Saharan borders to former French colony Niger, or to Algeria.

Human rights

Although the fleeing convoys carried large quantities of gold, cash and other valu-
ables, it was a more acceptable price to pay than that of further bloodletting, the
wisdom being that the more Gaddafi henchmen—and the hundreds of African
mercenaries—that leave Libya, the quicker the NTC can negotiate an honourable,
peaceful surrender for hundreds of hard-core Gaddafi loyalists that still hold out in
towns like Sirte and Sebha.

Evidence that has emerged of torture and massacres has further disturbed the
civilian population. To restore law and order, the NTC need to disarm civilians
turned gunmen. Not just the rebels—hardly any of them with army discipline—but
also Gaddafi's former loyalists. Even the members of the majority, who have no
intention of opposing the NTC, told *The Middle East* that, with police nonexistent,
they would be keeping their firearms for protection of their family and property.

Although most of the atrocities were the work of Gaddafi's henchmen and his
mercenaries, incidents of unruly behaviour by young, armed revolutionaries have increased since the fall of Tripoli. Several incidents of mob lynchings of African men
suspected of being mercenaries were reported. In reality, most of the victims were
illegal immigrants from sub-Saharan nations trying to make their way to southern
Europe and the hope of a better life.

During their meeting in London with British officials, a mere 10 days before
rebels took over Tripoli, British officials expressed concern about the ability of the
NTC to stabilise a post-Gaddafi Tripoli.

The first priority of the still-Benghazi-based NTC will be to start the task of nation building in earnest, with the big question—whether pertaining to the construction of basic infrastructure, or a workable political institution—by whom?

Military power?

Unlike Egypt where the army stepped in, first to stand guard when police vanished
from the streets, then to remove President Mubarak, there has been no army with a
recognisable structure in Libya. Seeing the army as a potential threat to his power,
Gaddafi preferred to franchise strong brigades led by his sons and to run Libya as a
Mafia-style family business.

The NTC were advised by London to rebuild the army in western-trained units,
devolved from political power and headed by officers who defected from Gaddafi's
regime early in the revolution.

The NTC are urged to recall the police—also marginalised by Gaddafi—and rebuild improved security services, not least to win the goodwill of the general population.

Colonel Gaddafi built little in the way of functioning infrastructure. Libya's oil
sector, including refineries, wells, pipes and oil terminals, employed only 43,000
nationals. Likewise, most services and construction projects were mainly manned
by migrant labour from North and sub-Saharan Africa and skilled staff from Eastern
Europe.

In addition to the challenge of law and order, which will mean disarming thousands of undisciplined young men, there will be the mammoth task of persuading

public sector workers to return to jobs running basic utilities such as water, energy and transport. Nearly three quarters of basic daily services including street cleaning were carried out by an army of thousands of migrant workers, most of whom fled Libya during the six months of the revolution.

The economy is another challenge. With guest and migrant workers gone, and massive infrastructure building required, large numbers of skilled and educated Libyans are expected to return from the diaspora. The next two years are expected to see record numbers of Libyans employed in their own country.

There were no political institutions in Libya. A draft constitution was circulated to different parties in August, NTC sources say, to introduce amendments and suggestions. A referendum is planned for within six to nine months, to provide a framework for the political system.

New rule

The NTC, whose members are banned in the draft constitution from standing for office, then gives way to an appointed transitional government. It plans to spend 12 months of debate among wider groups and parties for a final constitution drafting; this could be extended to 20 months, at the end of which parliamentary and presidential elections would be held.

All NTC members interviewed indicated their desire for reconciliation among all Libyans. However, "those with blood on their hands" will not be welcome for inclusion in the transition period, the NTC assured *The Middle East*.

The Berber pink flag was flying in many locations in Benghazi and Tripoli alongside the NTC tricolour (King Idriss's independence flag of 1951) with crescent and star. Under Gaddafi's Pan-Arab nationalism, Berbers were not allowed to speak their Amazigh language or fly their flag. The new draft constitution removed ideological adjectives from the official name of Libya, like 'Socialist,' 'Arabic' and especially the meaningless *Jamahyriah*. The new constitution simply refers to the Libyan Republic. A good sign of inclusivity and acceptance of a rainbow of tribal and ethnic diversity.

The constitution on face value seems positive in highlighting the need for free speech, rule of law and equality, but liberals and Libyans, especially women, find faults. They cite certain articles seen as being a threat to universal human rights, especially the rights of women. Articles declaring Islam as the official religion of the state and Sharia (Islamic law) as the principal source of legislation have been wrongly, though widely, utilised in the past to suppress free expression, demonise opposition, erode minority rights and even facilitate the banning of political parties, publications, books and works of art by the subjective branding 'contradictory to Sharia' law.

Human rights organisations and democratic Libyans became suspicious at the sudden disappearance of the draft constitution from the NTC website when criticism of some articles was aired. As yet, there is no judiciary system worth speaking of in Libya and rewriting the penal code, and training judges and lawyers, will prove far more challenging than it ever was in Iraq.

My Walk Through the Valley of Death

By Janine di Giovanni
Newsweek, October 24, 2011

When Janine di Giovanni arrived in Libya, she hoped to find a triumphant nation basking in newfound freedom. Instead she was confronted with a land haunted by the ghosts of Gaddafi's reign of terror.

When I first arrive in Tripoli, long past midnight on a hot September night, driving in from the Tunisian border, the smell of burning rubber permeates everything. Near Fashloom, the first neighborhood to rise up against Gaddafi, there are a row of littered, desecrated shops and a scarecrow of the dictator hanging from the electricity wires.

There is also the flag of the new Libya—modeled after the one from the days of King Idris—flying. The restaurants and shops are not yet open, but there are tea sellers with vast silver pots working street corners. Even at midnight, there is heavy traffic, mainly soldiers sitting in the back of trucks, and everyone seems to have a gun. The sound of AK-47s firing in the air—in celebration, not war—is unnerving. And it is constant.

And people are tentatively coming back. The borders are packed with some of the million expatriates now returning after nearly four decades in exile. They gape at their old neighborhoods. Some are here to find out their own secret histories, some to open up old wounds, some to discover exactly what happened to people they loved who died under Gaddafi's rule.

In one southern Tripoli neighborhood, Yarmuk, the stench of death lingers after 45 people were summarily executed.

Yarmuk was once a place full of Gaddafi pride, and the base for his 28-year-old son Khamis's political and military headquarters. His was the feared 32nd Brigade, an elite "protection military unit" of 10,000 men.

Khamis's HQ was behind 12-foot gray cement walls wrapped with barbed wire, with an enormous entrance topped by an imposing eagle. Local people say it was a son's pathetic attempt to model his base after his father's elaborate compound, Bab al-Aziziya. Khamis means "Thursday" in Arabic, and some Libyans joke that Gaddafi's son had an inferiority complex about his name and that there was constant infighting between all the male heirs about who would succeed their father as the next Libyan dictator.

A month on, Khamis is believed to be either killed in battle or in hiding with his father. His former compound is now filled with weeds growing in the fierce

Mediterranean heat. But the fear in Yarmuk remains because people still remember when they heard bullets in the night, and the sound of men screaming, in the last days of the fall of Tripoli.

There are places in the world, like Srebrenica in Bosnia, like Hama in Syria, where the ghosts of death linger long after the event. You smell them and you see them even before you arrive: these are haunted places. In a small field, part of the compound, belonging to the 32nd Brigade, a guard leads me to a corrugated-iron warehouse, terra-cotta colored, about 30 feet by 50 feet. I'm not so far away when I begin to feel a familiar sensation: something evil happened here.

The guard says it was used for farm supplies; someone else says auto supplies. There is an exploded pickup truck with the Khamis Brigade insignia, and the field is scattered with objects the prisoners left behind—a single sandal, perhaps lost while fleeing; a plastic bag of toiletries hanging on a nail in the wall—but otherwise the place is eerily silent.

It was here the Khamis Brigade killed the detainees—some of them innocent men—on Aug. 23. At one point, at least 150 were crammed into the warehouse, without water or sanitation, in the raging heat.

Instead of releasing the men, Khamis himself arrived, according to survivors. He gave orders. Then the killers tossed grenades into their crammed cell, then machine-gunned them, then tried to get rid of the remains by pouring gasoline around the cell and burning it. Two days later, witnesses who came across the warehouse told Human Rights Watch that they saw the smoldering remains and, outside the warehouse, two corpses.

A few weeks later, the stench of burned flesh encircles me; the charred, blue-gray bones can still be seen; felt under my feet are the remains of the men who died here. There are sprays of bullet holes in the door and, inside, a bloody mattress and burned clothes. In one corner is a cluster of singed hair. Outside is the killers' graffiti, scribbled before their act of vengeance: "GOD, KADAFFI AND LIBYA." And next to it, "DEATH TO THE RATS." "Rats" was Gaddafi's pet name for rebel fighters. But some of the men were not even fighters: they were simply in the wrong place at the wrong time.

> *There are places in the world, like Srebrenica in Bosnia, like Hama in Syria, where the ghosts of death linger long after the event.*

As Libya comes back to life, the stories of the last days of the atrocities are beginning to emerge. One of the dead from the Khamis massacre was a 46-year-old beekeeper named Abdulhakim Khaditha al-Kabir. He was the father of three children. He was seized on June 18. Abdulhakim's crime was that he was coming home from his farm past curfew when he was stopped by Khamis's men. He was in Souq-al-Jumaa, one of the first areas to rise up against the dictator. They accused him of being a rebel fighter. "His bee farm was near Bani Walid," explains his brother, Khaled, 41, describing a town that is one of the last pro-Gaddafi strongholds. "I don't think he knew why they put him in that warehouse. But inside, it was terrible. There were 150 men there, fed every three days, with one bottle of water a day for all of them."

Most were political prisoners, Khaled says, including a famous judge who was imprisoned, then released, simply for being close to Mustafa Abdel Jalil, the head of the National Transitional Council.

"But most, like my brother, they were there by mistake," Khaled says at his home in Tripoli on a scorching autumn day, as his brother's fatherless children play silently nearby.

Khaled says that when his brother was brought in for questioning by Khamis's men, he was tortured, and "they planted a Kalashnikov in his car and said it was his. But my brother did not own a gun. They lied. And then they killed him." But in the final days of Gaddafi, with all brutality unleashed, truth hardly seems to matter. And on the way out of Yarmuk I see scrawled across a concrete wall "The Devil Is Muammar Gaddafi."

One evening I have dinner with Huda Abuzeid. She has a cut-glass British accent, but she is thoroughly Libyan, and is now working as an adviser to the NTC. She is here to see the rebirth of her country, which she left when she was 4, but also, on some psychological level, to find closure for the murder of her father, Ali Abuzeid, a leading dissident.

Huda was 22 when her father, a trained accountant, was murdered in November 1995 by Gaddafi's men in London in the grocery shop he owned near the Edgware Road, an area populated by Arabs. It was Huda who found his body, knifed to death—"his face viciously marked, a final spiteful act by his killers"—and Huda who had to keep her 14-year-old brother from coming inside the shop after she called the police. "I was in shock," she says now, her voice emotional at the memory. "I just remember the phone ringing and ringing . . . and trying to keep my brother outside so he would not see the blood."

Ali Abuzeid was the founder of the National Front for the Salvation of Libya, an anti-Gaddafi group in exile. But he had left the group some time before, believing that regime change could not come from those abroad but rather had to be borne by those inside Libya.

Huda, still torn by the murder of her beloved father, says, "He was a man from the western mountains of Libya, a man who was respected for his word, a man well liked and strong-willed." Imprisoned in Libya for a year in 1976, he took his young family and left for the U.K. with a bounty of millions of dollars on his head. He must have known that Gaddafi's regime would one day get to him. "My childhood was spent worrying about him every time he traveled," she says, recounting that once, on a trip to Tunisia, she had to leave when they found out a hit squad had been sent to assassinate her father for a failed attempt to overthrow the regime. Gaddafi called her father a "stray dog" in one of his infamous speeches that followed.

The Libyan dictator's powers stretched way beyond his own country.

In the weeks before her father's death, Huda, who was working for the BBC, noticed that he seemed especially agitated. The fact was, he had been threatened for the past two months but decided to keep the news from his family.

The worst part of her father's death was that his murderers went unpunished. The case was not investigated thoroughly, even though Ali was a British citizen by then. Huda was told off the record by police officers that they were "not being allowed to do their job properly." Indeed, the police were unable to access the Libyans they felt might be responsible; and two weeks after her father was killed, a Libyan diplomat, Khalifa Bazelya, was expelled from Britain for spying on Libyan dissidents. Information that later came to light said that both MI5 and MI6 had long suspected Bazelya of acts of violence in the U.K.—yet they never had the chance to question him about Ali's death.

"No one has given an adequate description of why they deported him so quickly and why they did not question him about the murder," Huda later wrote. "I began to see there were higher agendas being served.

"My father's murder," she added, "is only one of a long list of crimes that have been committed by the Libyan regime and have gone unresolved."

But today, she is back in Tripoli trying to work with a country that has not known democracy or how to build institutions for 40 years. It's challenging, but it is also painful. "I was numb for 10 years after his death," she says quietly. "I had so much to do. Protect my mother and siblings. I worked and tried not to think of my father as dead. We left everything, all his clothes, still in the same place." Even his reading glasses, she says, stayed where he had placed them.

During the start of the Libyan revolution, she was in London editing a film she had made about Egypt. Even as she watched television with "my heart squeezed," she thought the Libyan revolution "would be over in a week." Yet she bought a camera, headed to Benghazi, the seat of the resistance, and offered her services. "Suddenly, I spoke the same Arabic I had spoken with my family my whole life," she says. "I was back in my own country. I felt free! When I saw the flag, I wanted to cry." She says she always thought she would never get to Libya until she was very old. "I saw my father live with the failed revolution, and now I am living what he could not see," she says. "I realized, finally, Libya was free."

In Benghazi and Tripoli, I meet a lot of young people like Huda Abuzeid: Libyans who had been forced to leave, were educated to high standards abroad, and are now back to build a new country.

But nation building, especially in a place that was ruled by fear for so long, is "not going to be easy," admits Mazin Ramadan, director and senior adviser to Ali Tahouni, the new finance and oil minister. Ramadan settled in Seattle in 1984 to be part of the high-tech boom and came rushing back when the revolution started. "Libyans don't imagine an Iraq-type scenario here," he says. "They imagine it will be like Europe, France, the U.K.—I have even heard they want it to be like Switzerland." He laughs and orders a macchiato—Libyans, due to their Italian colonization, probably drink more coffee than those from the Starbucks state. "People expect Coca-Cola to run from spigots in their kitchens!"

Change, Ramadan says, for the traumatized Libyans who were taught from Gaddafi's infamous "Green Book" and had to whisper anything remotely sensitive and who disappeared and were tortured and killed if they weren't careful, has to be visible. He reminds me that the war is actually still going on. Elections, most people predict, will take 18 months or more; this is a population that has never voted—let alone chosen between political parties. "Remember, for an entire generation under 40," he says, "there was only Gaddafi."

One evening as the heat drops, we go to Gaddafi's old compound, Bab al-Aziziya, a 2.3-square-mile area that now resembles a grotesque Disneyland. Once people get through the lines of traffic—especially on a Thursday night, the start of the Muslim weekend—they still wait for hours to see the home of their now demystified leader. It's disappointingly ordinary and suburban. People bring their children and snap photos of them on their mobile phones holding borrowed AK-47s. Across a patch of grass is the home of Saif al-Islam, Gaddafi's Western-educated son who once regaled London's jet set with his parties and his thoughtful demeanor. People try to loot whatever is left and throw trash in Gaddafi's old swimming pool. Children flash V signs and wave the new flag and wait to see the network of underground tunnels where Gaddafi showed off his cruise missiles. It makes me wonder about the next generation—children of this revolution, and how they will be educated in democracy.

Dr. Faisal Krekshi, 55, head of the recently renamed Tripoli University, says that during the Gaddafi regime, the school was a "center of propaganda. If you wanted to be promoted, you had to be loyal." Educated in the West as an ob-gyn, he decided to return and teach his people during the regime. Gaddafi trusted him and made him the family gynecologist to his daughters and wife, but as soon as Krekshi could, which was in February 2011, he defected to the rebels and worked from within a sleeper cell. Now he is back running the university, and some say this thoughtful, intelligent man is Libya's best chance to be an honest, solid politician.

During the NATO bombing, he says, "Gaddafi was taking dead bodies from my hospitals—the bodies of dead rebel soldiers—and planting them in places where NATO had struck, then bringing out the media and saying, 'Babies are dying,'" he remembers. "There was nothing that was beyond him."

So what lies ahead for Libyans? Krekshi is careful, because he is concerned. He says Tripoli University is the most important educational institution, but also the most dangerous.

"It is capable of immense brainwashing," he says. "One could easily get 120,000 students on the streets in a matter of hours. That's the power of propaganda. So we have to be careful where we go, how we do it." The lessons to be learned in Libya, he says, are about transparency.

"And there cannot be revenge," he says, referring to Iraq. For example, the former dean, a known player in the regime, was told specifically not to come back to campus after Gaddafi fled. But he did—and the angry students quickly arrested him.

"I said, don't touch him," Krekshi says. "They wanted me to take him to prison." He sighs. "Healing will take a long time. That is one thing that is for certain."

Black and White in Libya

What Will Happen When the Honeymoon Ends?

By Åsne Seierstad
Newsweek, October 23, 2011

"I see now, Gaddafi made mistakes." Mabruk, a young physics teacher, considers his words for a while before he continues. "But he gave our people everything. Modern houses, jobs, a new hospital, a nice school. I was fortunate enough to shake his hand when he visited Tawergha, just before the revolution."

Gaddafi's visit to Tawergha, a small town between the port city of Misrata and his hometown of Sirte, took place in February after the revolts in Tunisia and Egypt had started gaining traction. It would be the last time Gaddafi benevolently handed out money and privileges in exchange for support. And he did gain support from the black inhabitants of Tawergha, of whom several joined his security guard. "We had everything but freedom," Mabruk says to me and adds, "Now I, too, am a revolutionary. But what does it matter when it does not show?"

Because the color of the Libyan revolution is white. Or at least as fair as the skin of Arabs and Berbers along the Mediterranean coast. Despite Libya's having a significant black population, no blacks are represented in its current transitional government, and there are no blacks among the economic or cultural elite. Amnesty International and Human Rights Watch have both reported cases of arbitrary arrests, torture, and execution of blacks in detention, not least blacks from Mabruk's hometown. Tawergha had more than 30,000 inhabitants, but is now ethnically cleansed. The buildings stare vacantly out toward the deserted streets. Corpses of dogs and cats lie next to laundry hung out to dry on the day the inhabitants fled. The National Transitional Council seems to employ classic Gaddafi methods. If this tolerance for revenge remains as pervasive as it is today, Libya's new leaders have already lost the struggle to obtain a better image than their predecessor.

Muammar Gaddafi was a master at divide and conquer. By doling out privileges to some and withholding them from others, by the use of force and intervention, he nourished strife within his own country. He often set neighboring tribes, provinces, or cities against each other, leading to a number of conflicts, such as the one between Tawergha and neighboring Misrata. Misrata sided with the rebels; Tawergha's leaders remained loyal to Gaddafi.

He curried favor on the African continent more than in the Arab world, and today blacks are fair game. I've met black Libyan mothers who missed several sons, abducted from the streets, never to return.

> *If this tolerance for revenge remains as pervasive as it is today, Libya's new leaders have already lost the struggle to obtain a better image than their predecessor.*

A huge political void opened up during the meltdown of Gaddafi's regime. What to fill it with remains an unanswered question. The hundreds of armed brigades patrolling the country in Misrata, Benghazi, Tripoli, and the Nafusa Mountains are subject to neither civilian nor military control. The various militias have sufficient access to arms for a small conflict to escalate to full-blown warfare.

In Tripoli I met with Judge Ahmed Naass in the local council. Having worked for 40 years as a judge under Gaddafi, he had "nothing to be ashamed of," he said. "What do you mean?" I asked. "I was only an employee. I had no power. I did what I was told."

He has new bosses now, and will by all accounts once again do what he is told. Libya's elders have learned from Iraq, and have chosen not to do away with everybody who had anything to do with the previous regime. In Iraq, Paul Bremer had demanded the removal of all members of the Baath Party from their positions, creating a huge vacuum. Retaining Gaddafi's system on all levels, however, hardly bodes well for human rights and the rule of law, which have been the stated goals of the Libyan revolution.

And yet, while many Gaddafi minions remain in their positions, what Libyans call "filtering the system" has already commenced. Judges have been killed. One of Naass's colleagues was shot down in the street.

Libya is a country brimming with plundered firearms. In Naass's neighborhood alone, where he himself holds the keys to the arms depot, 6,000 weapons have been stolen and only 400 reclaimed. He shows us the slim results of having gone from door to door to collect the weapons. "If you want to start a revolution in your country," an obese bearded man says, giggling to me, "you can get your weapons here." He turns out to be the local baker, a devoted Salafi. "Don't talk like that," the judge hisses to him in Arabic. "Show some restraint."

Restraint might be exactly what Libya needs in the power struggle, in the reorganization of the armed forces, in the prison system, in the lust for revenge among people who suddenly can speak freely, act freely, and think freely. In a country where 150 newspapers have been established in a matter of months, many of them produced on a voluntary basis, rumors flow freely. Stories of brigades of black men specializing in rape abound, detailed with reports of how they tote packets of Viagra donated by Gaddafi.

Something else that made an impression during my visit to Libya was the pervasive religiosity. In a reeducation center for prisoners, the inmates, former Gaddafi loyalists—injured and wounded for the most part—were to be cleansed through the Quran. Their "reeducation" consisted of reading the Quran from dawn till dusk. The leader of the center, Imam Haitem Muhammed, a Quran teacher for children before the war, told me he wanted Libya to become a modern, Islamist state. "Sort of like Saudi Arabia," he explained.

Another encounter was with a medical student named Ehab, who was worried about "bad Islamism," as he called it.

"We have freedom now, but it's not a good freedom. There are weapons everywhere. If the rebels remain in Tripoli, this will turn into a new Somalia. They control the streets," he insisted, "not the government. There have been conflicts here of a kind we've never seen before."

But the brigades celebrating in Tripoli do not want to go home. Misrata has gone through hell and wants something in return. Benghazi started it all and has a proprietary feeling about the revolution. The Berbers from the Nafusa Mountains want recognition for having freed Tripoli. The emancipation of Tripoli is now, in the vernacular, called the "Chocolate Revolution," as the capital was barely touched by fighting and emerged from the revolution after others in Libya suffered enormous losses.

"We have lived for 42 years in a police state, and now no one is in charge. Who will take care of the streets, if not us?" says the local commander of the Zintan brigade, Yousef Ghabash. He stands with his legs wide apart, full of self-confidence. He had soldiers under his command; he had his Kalashnikov and more. In Zintan, located in the western mountains, he used to work as a bus driver. This is another aspect of the revolution: the intoxicating taste of power, the feeling of wind blowing in his beard, the comradeship under the moon at night. How can he go back and drive a bus in a small provincial town after this?

He might be shaving his beard now. He was supposed to wear it until Gaddafi fell. But although Gaddafi is dead and this beard might have gone, many battles remain. There will be struggles for control of the country, the armed forces, the streets. And when all that's over, a conquest still remains for Yousef. He wants to find a girl to marry. All he knows about that is "I want to go on a honeymoon to Europe."

But for Yousef, as for Libya, life will not be easy when the honeymoon is over.

❖

Åsne Seierstad is a journalist and author from Norway. She has covered wars in Afghanistan, Iraq, and the Balkans, and now covers the Arab world for Newsweek. *She is the author of* The Bookseller of Kabul *and* The Angel of Grozny. *She lives in Oslo, where she was born.*

False Ending

Muammar Gaddafi is dead but the women of Libya remain fearful

By Sophie McBain
New Statesman, October 31, 2011

"I was one of the few women who went out to the first protests in Tripoli on 22 February, and shortly after that I joined the 17 February Youth Coalition, a rebel group," Mounia al-Saghir says quietly. "We had a medical section, a communications section, and later, of course, a military cell." She is 22, veiled, soft-spoken and fearless—a student, an NGO worker, and now a revolutionary.

We speak on 20 October, on the evening of Muammar Gaddafi's death. Mounia says that she is "overwhelmed," but sounds calm as she recalls the worst of the past few months. Her group organised a failed assassination attempt on Saif al-Islam Gaddafi in July and one of the women behind the plot was arrested.

"They electrocuted her and beat her. She had 16 broken bones. She didn't drink, she didn't eat anything." Mounia, too, had a narrow escape after smuggling videos and instruction manuals abroad. When a police car pulled up outside her home, she was forced to spend a month in hiding while her father was repeatedly interrogated by the secret services. "I thought they would beat or torture him," she says.

Mounia is a close friend. We met in late 2008 when I first moved to Libya to work for the United Nations, and then often for coffee on sunny seaside terraces when Tripoli was still a sleepy Mediterranean town. Although she had vaguely mentioned her previous political work, I was unprepared for her stories. War changes everything, however—a point that takes on new meaning when you watch unhappily and guiltily from the sidelines, as I did, as your former home is ripped apart by conflict.

Gaddafi's gory, televised end marked more than the removal of a figurehead or even the dismantling of a political system. It tore through Libyan society. Now, Libyans will be renegotiating not only the relationship between citizens and the state, but also their relationships with each other. Women such as Mounia, who risked their lives for the anti-Gaddafi struggle, do not want to relinquish their new-found freedom, power and respect.

In denying any meaningful form of popular political expression, Gaddafi treated both sexes equally. Social conservatism generally proved a greater constraint on women than the legal system and it was even all right to care about women's rights—provided you adhered to the state-sponsored feminism. When Alaa Murabit co-founded a women's development NGO last year, a charity led by Gaddafi's daughter Aisha quickly forced her to shut it down.

Today, the reformed Voice of Libyan Women (VLW) has about 60 signed-up members and a network of 1,500 volunteers. It developed from Murabit's activities during the revolution when she began calling on the women of her home town, Zawiya, to help smuggle medical supplies for her makeshift field clinic. "To ask for rights, women have to do something," she explains. "During the revolution, women did that. They did everything that a man could do."

Murabit says that she is more interested in choice and education than in sexual liberation, more concerned with freedom than with imposing any particular lifestyle on women. "We are not telling anyone to go out and work if they don't want to. We're just saying, 'Know that you have a choice,'" she says. "I'm not saying, 'Let your daughter go partying all night.' I'm just saying, 'Let them have an education, give them the same opportunities as your sons.'"

For better or worse

A few female protesters have made it on to the National Transitional Council (NTC). Najla al-Mangoush, one of a handful of women who joined the first demonstrations in Benghazi in February, is now head of public engagement. She insists that she is not interested in power.

> In denying any meaningful form of popular political expression, Gaddafi treated both sexes equally.

"A political role is not my dream," she says. "My dream is to play a big role in my community, to give something to my country, to be in a position where I can make a difference. A lot of women are like me. Libyans don't dream of being something political, because we felt all these years that those involved in politics were bad men."

These women represent a small yet influential segment of the population: educated, politicised, from the relatively liberal coastal cities. The deeper you travel into the desert, the more conservative Libya becomes. What has become of the shy, cloistered women I met in the oasis town of Kufra, where I didn't see a single woman walking in the streets? Or the forgotten Bedouins who live in abject poverty—what say will they have in a free Libya?

Despite their hopes, none of the women I speak to feels confident for the future, and the liberation speech on 23 October by the NTC's Mustafa Abdel Jalil has not helped. The VLW issued an angry response. It wrote: "He had so many more important issues to address. However, he focused on polygamy. Not only that, [he] thanked women for their roles as 'mothers, sisters and wives.' Need we remind him of the countless women who got arrested, killed and raped during this revolution?"

Mounia sounds sad when I call her after Jalil's speech. "Sometimes, I worry that things could get worse for women, rather than better," she says. Yet she is also defiant. I know she means it when she promises: "I will keep on fighting for women's rights. They can throw me in prison. I'm not scared."

Libyan 'Crossfire'

By Charles Krauthammer
The Washington Post, October 27, 2011

You've got your Mexican standoff, your Russian roulette, your Chinese water torture. And now, your Libyan crossfire. That's when a pistol is applied to the head and a bullet crosses from one temple to the other.

That's apparently what happened to Moammar Gaddafi after he was captured by Libyan rebels—died in a "crossfire," explains Libya's new government. This has greatly agitated ACLU types, morally unemployed ever since a Democratic administration declared Guantanamo humane. The indignation has spread to human rights groups and Western governments, deeply concerned about the manner of Gaddafi's demise.

Let's begin at the beginning. Early in the revolution, Gaddafi could have had due process. Indeed, he could have had something better: asylum (in Nicaragua, for example) with a free pass for his crimes. If he stepped down, thereby avoiding the subsequent civil war that killed thousands of his countrymen, he could have enjoyed a nice, fat retirement, like that of Idi Amin in Saudi Arabia.

Like Amin, Gaddafi would not have deserved a single day of untroubled repose. Such an outcome would itself have been a gross violation of justice, as he'd have gone unpunished for his uncountable crimes. But it would have spared his country much bloodshed and suffering.

Such compromises are fully justified and rather common. They are, for example, the essence of the various truth and reconciliation commissions in countries transitioning from authoritarianism to democracy. In post-Pinochet Chile and post-apartheid South Africa, it was decided that full justice—punishing the guilty—would be sacrificed in order to preserve the fragile social peace of the new democracy.

The former oppressors having agreed to a peaceful relinquishing of power, full justice might have ignited renewed civil strife. Therefore, these infant democracies settled for mere truth: a meticulous accounting of the crimes of the previous regime. In return for truthful testimony, perpetrators were given amnesty.

Under the normal rule of law, truth is only a means for achieving justice, not an end in itself. The real end is determining guilt and assigning punishment. But in war and revolution one cannot have everything. Justice might threaten peace. Therefore peace trumps full justice.

Gaddafi could have had such a peace-over-justice compromise. He chose instead to fight to the death. He got what he chose.

That fateful decision to fight—and kill—is the prism through which to judge the cruel treatment Gaddafi received in his last hours. It is his refusal to forgo those final crimes, those final shellings of civilians, those final executions of prisoners that justifies his rotten death.

He could have taken a de facto amnesty for all his previous crimes, from Pan Am 103 to the 1996 massacre of 1,200 inmates at Tripoli's Abu Salim prison. To reject that option and proceed to create an entirely new catalogue of crimes—for that, there is no forgiveness. For that, you are sentenced to die by "crossfire."

So he was killed by his captors. Big deal. So was Mussolini. So were the Ceausescus. They deserved far worse. As did Gaddafi. In a world of perfect justice, this Caligula should have suffered far more, far longer. He inflicted unimaginable suffering upon thousands. What did *he* suffer? Perhaps an hour of torment and a shot through the head. By any standard of cosmic justice, that's mercy.

Moreover, Gaddafi's sorry end has one major virtue: deterrence. You are a murderous dictator with a rebellion on your hands. You have a choice. Relinquish power and spare your country further agony, and you can then live out your days like Amin—or like a more contemporary Saudi guest, Tunisia's Zine el-Abidine Ben Ali. Otherwise, you die like Gaddafi, dragged from a stinking sewer pipe, abused, taunted and shot.

> *That fateful decision to fight—and kill—is the prism through which to judge the cruel treatment Gaddafi received in his last hours.*

It's not pretty. But it's a precedent. And a salutary one. One that Syrian President Bashar al-Assad, for example, might contemplate. Continue to fight and kill, and expect thereafter no belated offers of asylum—not even the due process of a long, talky judicial proceeding in The Hague with a nice comfy cell, three meals a day and the consoling certainty that your captors practice none of your specialties: torture and summary execution.

Call it the Gaddafi Rule: Give it up and go, or one day find death by "Libyan crossfire." Followed by a Libyan state funeral. That's when you lie on public view for four days, half-naked in a meat locker.

5

Syria:
Twilight of the Assad Regime?

Pro-democracy protesters burn portraits of Syrian President Bashar al-Assad during a demonstration outside the Arab League headquarters in Cairo where an emergency ministerial meeting was held on November 12, 2011, to discuss the situation in Syria.

Deep Divisions:
Syrian Society and Politics

By Paul McCaffrey

In terms of geography, Syria has about the same area as the state of North Dakota. The country's population, at around 22 to 23 million, is comparable to that of Texas. Despite this relatively diminutive size, Syria has more than its share of political, ethnic, and religious fault lines. For decades, these fractures were concealed beneath the surface by political repression, but they came to light with the outbreak of antigovernment protests in 2011, as part of the Arab Spring revolutionary movement sweeping Arab nations beginning in 2010. Syria's ruling Assad regime responded to the demonstrations with a full-scale military onslaught that, according to December 2011 estimates, has left more than 5,000 people dead.

Given the spectrum of violence perpetrated by the Assads since the family's patriarch, Hafez, seized power by coup d'état in 1970, the recent death toll, though steep, is only a fraction of that incurred in earlier incidents. As of February 2012, the regime's bloodiest crime was the Hama massacre of February 1982, when the Syrian army killed between 10,000 and 40,000 people in response to unrest instigated by the Muslim Brotherhood.

The fractures in Syrian society are deep seated and longstanding. Some have troubled the region for centuries; others are of more recent vintage. During the colonial era between 1920 and 1946, when Syria was under French administration, a visiting British diplomat declared, "I haven't yet come across one spark of national feeling: it is all sects and hatreds and religions." Ethnically, Syria's population is only about 90 percent Arab; Kurds represent Syria's largest ethnic minority at around 9 percent of the population. The Kurds have an uncertain and unenviable status in the Syrian Arab Republic. Over the years, they have been subjected to widespread discrimination and, at times, even full-scale ethnic cleansing. There are also about 500,000 Palestinian refugees in Syria who are not entitled to Syrian citizenship and form something of a permanent underclass. Iraqi refugees are a presence as well; at the height of the insurgency against US and coalition forces in Iraq, an estimated one million Iraqis fled to Syria.

But it is along religious lines that the most troublesome divisions in Syrian society emerge. The nation is about 74 percent Sunni Muslim, nearly 13 percent Alawite, 10 percent Christian, and 3 percent Druze. The Sunni population is centered in and around the capital of Damascus and the cities of Homs and Hama. The Druze are settled mostly in the south, around the so-called Jabal al-Druze ("Mountain of the Druze"), also known as Jabal al-Arab ("Mountain of the Arabs"). The Kurds and Christians are found mostly in the northern part of the country, which is dominated by the city of Aleppo. The Alawites are settled in western Syria, along the Lebanese border.

Generally speaking, Shia and Sunni Islam are the two major denominations of the Islamic faith, their divergence resulting from a dispute over the Prophet Muhammad's rightful successors that developed larger theological implications over the centuries. In Syria, the Sunni-Shia bifurcation further complicates Syrians' attempts to maintain positive relations despite their religious diversity. The Druze evolved from the Ismaili subgroup of Shia Islam and adopted elements from other faiths and philosophies to such an extent that most Muslims no longer count them as members of the Islamic community, or *Ummah*. How the Druze see the issue is not entirely clear. Druze doctrine is shrouded in secrecy, with only the most pious and devout initiated into the greater mysteries of the faith. Further, while Druze are required to speak the truth to one another, they are permitted to deceive non-Druze to protect both the faith and the faithful. Consequently, outsiders know next to nothing about their religion.

Slightly less opaque is the Alawite population to which the Assad family belongs. Like the Druze, the Alawites are a secretive offshoot of the Ismaili branch of Shia Islam, and like the Druze, their status as Muslims is a matter of some dispute within the Islamic community. In general, Shia are more likely to recognize Alawites as fellow Muslims while Sunnis are more inclined to view them as heretics. In terms of self-perception, the Alawites consider themselves Shia and Muslim. Certain tenets of the Alawite faith suggest Christian influence: Alawites believe in incarnation, or God/Allah assuming human form, and they celebrate certain Christian holidays. Alawites also have their own Trinity, made up of Ali, a relative of Muhammad, as well as his first convert and the first Imam in Shia Islam; the Prophet Muhammad; and Salman the Persian, a companion of the Prophet Muhammad. Alawites are thought to embrace a more casual approach to the study of the Koran and believe in a process of reincarnation.

Much of Alawite doctrine is not precisely aligned with more orthodox interpretations of Islam, thus the heresy charge is a common one and has often influenced how the Alawites have been treated. When Syria was part of the Ottoman Empire, the Alawites were saddled with onerous tax burdens and, for much of recent history, occupied the lower rungs of the Syrian socioeconomic ladder. Under the French Mandate for Syria and Lebanon, which lasted from 1920 to 1943, though French troops remained until Syrian independence in 1946, Alawites and other Syrian minorities were patronized by the colonizers, and Alawites were recruited into the ranks of the colonial military. Following Syrian independence in 1946, thanks to their training by the French, Alawites such as Hafez al-Assad rose to positions of prominence in the new country's armed forces. When Assad took power in 1970, the Alawites achieved significant influence and held onto it into the twenty-first century, retaining their clout throughout the reigns of Hafez and his son Bashar, who assumed the presidential mantle upon his father's death in 2000.

It is hard to overstate what the Assads' ascent meant to Syria's sectarian hierarchy. As the Middle Eastern historian Daniel Pipes wrote in *Greater Syria* (1990),

"An Alawi ruling Syria is like an untouchable becoming maharajah in India or a Jew becoming tsar in Russia—an unprecedented development shocking to the majority population which had monopolized power for so many centuries."

At 10 percent of the population, Syria's Christian community is the country's second largest minority after the Alawites. Even in the face of the Arab Spring uprising and its subsequent repression, Christians have remained one of the Assad regime's most loyal constituencies. This is due in part to years of patronage. Like the French, the Assads have favored minorities, Christians among them, at the expense of the Sunni majority. In addition, according to press reports, Syrian Christians—and Alawites—have expressed trepidation about what the fall of the Assads could mean for their communities.

Since the end of the four-hundred-year Ottoman rule of Syria in 1918, Sunni Arabs have seen their influence in Syrian affairs diminish. To the French, they posed the biggest potential threat to colonial rule and were thus kept in a state of subjugation. In the postcolonial era after 1946, Sunni Arab political power in Syria has been directed into two distinct movements: political Islamism of the Muslim Brotherhood variety, and secular pan-Arab socialism. The latter ideology has been the most widely applied governing doctrine in Syria and the larger Arab world over the past sixty years, but it has largely failed to live up to its promises of seeking to unite Arab groups, promote women's emancipation, and free Arab nations from the constraints of colonialism.

Egyptian ruler Gamal Abdel Nasser was the face of pan-Arab socialism in Egypt's early postcolonial era. His initial achievements, while notable, did not bring about the Arab unity and prosperity he envisioned. A brief attempt to merge Syria and Egypt into one nation, the United Arab Republic (UAR), lasted a mere three years, from 1958 to 1961, and was ended by a coup in Syria. Nasser could not deliver in the Arab world's conflict with Israel either. His brinkmanship led instead to humiliation and defeat in the Six-Day War of 1967, during which Syria lost the Golan Heights to Israel.

The indigenous Syrian model of pan-Arabism—the Baath Party, in power from 1947 to 1966—has been discredited as well, especially among Sunni Arabs. Following independence in 1946, the nation tried its luck with a democratic system but failed to overcome its numerous ethnic and religious divisions. A series of military coups followed. By the late 1950s, fearing a communist takeover, Syria's leaders were begging Nasser to annex their country. Describing his countrymen to Nasser, the frustrated Syrian president Shukri al-Quwatli reportedly observed, "Half claim the vocation of leader, a quarter believe they are prophets, and at least ten percent take themselves for gods." In Syria's first twenty-four years of independence, the national government changed hands twenty-one times, based on various machinations and coups. Eventually the Baath Party came to power in 1963, the same year Baathists seized control in neighboring Iraq. Due to internal dissent among Syria's Baathist rulers, long-term political stability was not achieved until Alawite Baathist politician Hafez al-Assad staged his coup in 1970.

Under the Assads, the Baath Party retained its central place in Syrian affairs. According to the Syrian Constitution promulgated in 1973, the Baath Party is "the leading party in the society and state." Founded in the 1940s by two Syrians— an Arab Christian and a Sunni Arab—the Baath Party, which translates to "renaissance" in Arabic, sought to subsume the various sectarian divisions within the Arab world (and the arbitrary borders imposed on it by European colonizers) by promoting Arab socialism. Instead, in both Iraq and Syria, Baathist regimes have tended to pursue sectarian agendas while paying lip-service to pan-Arab unity. Under the rule of Saddam Hussein in Iraq, especially, Baathist ideology supported a thuggish, genocidal, and expansionist regime intent on ensuring Sunni Arab dominance in a nation composed largely of Arab Shia. In Syria, the Assads have empowered the Alawites and other minorities at the expense of the majority, like the French rule of Syria; and like the Hussein regime in Iraq, they have safeguarded their power by constructing a police state.

Given the failure of pan-Arab politics, major opposition to the Assads throughout their rule has come from the Sunni Muslim Brotherhood. The Brotherhood rejected the secular nature of the Baath Party and dismissed the Assads as heretics due to their Alawite faith. An armed Islamist insurrection broke out in 1976. Six years later, Islamist resistance was crushed in the Hama massacre, in which Syrian military forces responded to the Muslim Brotherhood uprising in Hama by killing thousands of civilians. The ruthlessness displayed at Hama not only quelled the challenge to the regime, but also served as a warning to other potential opponents. At Hama, the Assads had declared that they would stop at nothing to hold onto political power. The show of brutality had the desired effect: no viable resistance to the Assads arose for nearly three decades.

By virtue of its longevity, the Assad regime has to be counted as one of the most enduring dictatorships in recent memory, especially considering Syria's underlying sectarian tensions. Moreover, during their reign, the Assads extended their power beyond Syria's borders, sending troops to Lebanon in 1976 and ruling the neighboring nation in all but name for well over a generation. In a tumultuous region, they have maintained and expanded their influence without the help of massive oil wealth or foreign aid. Consequently, barring intervention by the North Atlantic Treaty Organization (NATO), it may be safe to assume that the Assads will continue to crack down on Arab Spring protesters and will not relinquish power except by force of arms.

Islamist calls for a "day of rage" against the Bashar al-Assad regime in February 2011 did not result in particularly effective protests, partly because the Syrian government took stringent measures to quell rebel opposition. Syria is not like Tunisia, Libya, or Egypt, countries whose insurgents successfully ousted their rulers. Syria's population is not ethnically or religiously homogeneous, and its demographic contours make it especially difficult to construct a unified opposition to the dictatorship. Thus the potential for a prolonged stalemate and a full-blown civil war is much more severe in Syria than other Arab Spring nations with a more unified oppositional front.

In November 2011, the Arab League voted to suspend Syria's membership after the Syrian government failed to reduce military attacks on activists. Although the

League launched an official investigation into Syrian affairs in December 2011, the mission was put on hold in January 2012 because of unabated violence. Syria has not responded to Arab League requests that Assad step down from his role as president, although Assad has several times promised to initiate discussion with oppositional forces in the interest of peaceful resolution.

As of February 2012, Syria once again became a focus of international attention when unrest in the country escalated. Numerous suicide bombings and organized attacks by the Free Syrian Army (made up of Syrian military defectors) were met with Syrian government bombardment of Sunni Muslim areas. United Nations (UN) attempts to condemn Syria had been vetoed by Russia and China. The United States and other countries including France, Spain, the UK, and Italy, as well as some Arab states along the Persian Gulf, withdrew their embassies from Syria in response to the country's increasing instability. News reports were limited in scope and many relied on social media for communication from within Syria. The UN announced its inability to confirm the death toll beyond 5,000 in December 2011, while some groups allege that more than 7,000 people have died in Syria since the beginning of antigovernment protests in 2011.

Syrian Stalemate?

The Middle East, November 2011

A special report on developments in Syria from our correspondent in Damascus.

Facing into the New Year with no let-up in the nationwide protests apparent, both the Syrian regime and the protest movement are hanging on.

The regime's efforts to quell the uprising had cost the state $2 billion to last August, a figure that may have doubled by now. Its political legitimacy has been shredded to pieces in the countryside and provinces.

Protests, though still numerous, have decreased in size over the past few months due to the state's heavy-handedness, and perhaps because of a growing climate of fear and street fatigue. The organised opposition have failed to draw significant elements inside Syria to their cause, chiefly, the city-based business classes. The country's minorities, 25% of the population, are utterly sceptical of the Syrian National Council (SNC) opposition.

A solution seems as far off as ever with the United Nations saying 3,000 people have been killed since the unrest began.

Syria's complexities are both numerous and intertwined. The country's business classes can be loosely split into those that precede the Ba'athist regime (broadly anti-Assad) and those who became rich through the patronage of the establishment (pro-regime). The former group, though they would prefer the regime to go, are fearful of civil war and the consequent loss of capital and business. The latter can be expected to back the regime to the end, providing it with funds for its crackdown on protesting elements.

Further, the country's religious minorities are mightily fearful of the Sunni majority. Governed by the Assads, they refer to the leadership of the regime as 'one of our own.' Alawites and Shia for different, if related reasons, and Christians are quick to believe that all women will have to wear a hijab and red shoes to indicate that they are not Muslims should the Assads be toppled.

The international response to the unrest in Syria has also been divided. Russia and China's veto of a UN Resolution last month condemning the violence used by the regime against Syrian civilians has heartened the authorities no end.

The UN Security Council failed to pass the resolution with South Africa, which abstained from casting a vote, saying: "We were concerned that this resolution should not be part of a hidden agenda to yet again institute regime change," referring to the case of Libya.

The US ambassador to the UN, Susan Rice, was furious at the time, saying "The United States is outraged that this council has utterly failed to address an urgent moral challenge . . . Today, the courageous people of Syria can now clearly see who on this council supports their yearning for liberty and universal rights—and who does not."

The proposed resolution, which did not even contain the word 'sanctions,' would have been reviewed in 30 days. It had also been 'watered down' three times.

Deep unrest

Those demonstrating and being shot in the streets across Syria were devastated. But since then both Russia and China have issued statements pointing to the fact that the Syrian government should act on its pledges of reform.

"We think that the Syrian government should move faster to implement the reforms to which it has committed and expedite an inclusive political process with the participation of all stakeholders," said a spokesperson for the Chinese foreign ministry on 11 October.

For the suffering demonstrators in Syria, Libya's NATO-assisted success may have killed the appetite for further military intervention. However, western powers are determined not to abandon the protest movement, and have vowed to continue pressing the Syrian government through sanctions and rhetoric.

Back in Syria, a series of events in early October saw tension across the country ratchet up.

Reports of the first woman killed in custody drew outrage from international human rights organisations. It later turned out the girl was alive, and was interviewed by Syrian state television saying she ran away because her brothers abused her.

The number of assassinations spiked in the early days of October with Syrians from various religious backgrounds shot in Homs and elsewhere. Academics and a nuclear scientist were gunned down separately in the city during a five-day period. In the northern province of Idlib, a policeman and other symbols of state authority were targeted. The 21-year-old son of Syria's Grand Mufti, Ahmad Badir Al Din Hassoun, was reportedly shot dead when driving on the highway between Idlib and Aleppo on 2 October.

The regime's media machine has been effective and has successfully portrayed the message that it remains both strong and right. It has achieved several coups over what it calls the 'lying and insidious international media.' It managed to show a former defected officer of the Syrian army denying previous claims he made that soldiers were ordered to shoot civilians. It claims *Al Jazeera* and others are doctoring news reports to show Syria in a bad light.

On 12 October, thousands of pro-regime supporters gathered in Damascus in support of the president. On Syrian television religious leaders spoke to the crowds of a united Syria. People waved Russian, Iranian and Chinese flags. However, the majority of those in attendance were army conscripts, state workers and school children, ordered from offices and schools. There was little spontaneous support from Damascenes on the street.

In Damascus the fear factor remains strong, despite an obvious lack of concern for those being killed in the dozens in the countryside. Posters and signs stating

'Thank you Russia' are ubiquitous throughout the capital. Syrian Christians post 'I am sanctioned' on their Facebook accounts.

The regime still believes itself to be strong, and on the streets of the capital a relative calm has returned. People are back in cafes and restaurants. Though wealthy Syrians are not spending as in the past, most are buying clothes and visiting restaurants to deal with what many call the 'boredom.' Most in Damascus have tired of not being able to visit the country's coastal region or to visit Turkey and Lebanon.

A solution seems as far off as ever with the United Nations saying 3,000 people have been killed since the unrest began.

But protests have returned to many urban centres that had been silenced by force in the past. In Qatana, a town of about 70,000 people located 30 kilometres southwest of Damascus, protesters have began to return to the streets following a military crackdown last July. Men dressed in green uniforms and holding batons walk uneasily among the local population in the evenings. After evening prayers, tension in the town rises fast.

Few offer predictions of what the final result of the revolution in Syria may be. Either the regime falls, through an internal coup, or the crackdown proves so successful protestors simply stop taking to the streets. The regime's promises of reform will satisfy few as long as killings and detentions continue to take place. Municipal elections have been called for 12 December—the first time such elections have taken place under Ba'ath rule—in what can only be regarded as an attempt to appease the 'silent majority,' those living in the country's two largest cities, Aleppo and Damascus.

Tales of the cities

It is in these two cities the effects of international sanctions are beginning to kick in.

On 22 September, state media reported that foreign goods taxed 5% or more were banned from entering Syria, save some foodstuffs and medical equipment. There would be no more cars, French perfume or Pepsi. There was uproar among the business classes and urban dwellers.

A Sunni Damascene, who imports generators and generator parts, was white with rage when meeting this correspondent for *The Middle East* at a cafe in the capital. He said he and other importers approached the ministry for the economy shortly after the ban was issued to plea their cases and were told the decision did not come from the ministry, but from 'above.'

"Listen, in any case, I will pay the Lebanese smugglers the same amount I have to bribe the Syrian officials to get access to my goods. So for me it's almost the same," he said. This businessman's rage will have lessened only slightly following the cancellation of the imports ban.

When the ban was announced, car prices rose 20% in a single day. Fruits and vegetables at or on the way to the border had to be thrown out. Moreover, even though the ban has been reversed, the price of food staples have shot up. Cigarettes and eggs, for example, have risen 30%. With winter fast approaching, the sound of the horn from the trucks selling the *mazout* heating oil to households is unusually absent. Today, queues outside gas stations often reach a quarter of a mile in length.

However, it appears the establishment is at least taking into consideration internal demands. After just 12 days the ban was revoked, though the return of foreign products to the Syrian market had yet to materialise by mid October. A salesman at a car dealership outside Damascus said: "You know how the system works, they need some time."

Whether the populations of the towns and villages under attack from state terrorism around the country see fit to give the regime 'time' remains to be seen. The Syrian youth will only become more restless as the months tick on because as Syrian officials stated in the past, Syria needs $10 billion in FDI per year to meet the demands of a rapidly increasing workforce. Predictions for FDI this year see it amounting to about $500 million—just 5% of expected requirements. The future for the economy, and by extension the 22 million Syrians and the regime, seems increasingly bleak.

Outside input

Economic factors are likely to be some of the most critical is deciding what happens next. The EU oil embargo is set to begin this month [November] while employees of the overburdened state sector await their annual bonuses in December. With the government almost broke, paying out these vital extras seems unlikely, which would in turn increase resistance to the regime's tactics inside the vital state sector, a sector populated by individuals earning just $270 per month.

A Christian hotel owner in the Old City of Damascus recently said he had not received a booking since last spring. "The bookings that were made for after last March were cancelled. The only enquiries I get are from friends and past guests asking if I am OK," he says, asking not to be named.

Alawite communities in parts of the capital have reportedly been armed by supporters of the government. In central Syria, the Free Syrian Army, a hotchpotch of defected soldiers led by a small number of Sunni officers, has vowed to take the fight to the regime. In Rastan, a town of about 40,000 inhabitants, locals fought back against the army on two occasions during the past few months. It took the army four days to quell the second uprising in the town in late September and early October. But numbering around 10,000 and located in often isolated pockets around the country, the militias are no match to the might of the Syrian army.

The spectre of civil war grows with each passing day, developing into a self-fulfilling prophecy as feared by Syria's minorities for years, and often such twisted logic and sectarian loyalty comes up in conversation, conquering plain reason.

"I don't blame the government," says the hotel owner. "I blame the international community and *Al Jazeera*. They are making a big conspiracy against us." Even faced with the ruin of his business, this man, like almost all other Christians, continue to side with the regime.

The regime still believes itself to be strong, and on the streets of the capital a relative calm has returned. People are back in cafes and restaurants.

Syria's Assad on the Ropes?

By Patrick Seale
The Nation, September 12, 2011

President Bashar al-Assad is fighting for his political life, perhaps even for life itself. His brutal repression of the protest movement in Syria has earned him international condemnation. Calls for him to step down have come from President Barack Obama and from the leaders of Britain, France and Germany. The Arab world's heavyweight, Saudi Arabia, has recalled its ambassador from Damascus, as have several of the smaller Gulf states. The UN's high commissioner for human rights, Navi Pillay, has presented a report to the Security Council describing, in gruesome detail, the killing and torture of civilian protesters. There are moves afoot to ban imports of Syrian oil to European markets, which provides about 30 percent of the state's income.

Yet Assad remains defiant. He seems determined to fight to the end. Undeterred by harsh repression, the Friday demonstrations have swollen week after week, and their tone has hardened. Increasingly, the strident call is for the fall of the regime. Angry protesters say that over 2,000 of their number have been killed and over 13,000 arrested, many of them savagely tortured, while the regime retorts that it is fighting a foreign-inspired "conspiracy" and that 120 security personnel have been killed by "armed gangs." A sectarian civil war on the Iraqi or Lebanese model is every Syrian's nightmare. No one really wants that—neither the regime nor the vast majority of the opposition. There is, however, a fringe element that believes any regime, however extreme, would be better than the present one.

The opposition faces a stark choice: either go all out to bring the regime down, as some would like, or cooperate with it in building a new and better Syria. The first course is hazardous: if the Baathist state is torn down, what will replace it? The second course requires an act of faith: it means accepting that Assad truly wants to implement radical reforms and effect a transition to democracy by means of a national dialogue. He has attempted to launch such a dialogue, but has so far failed to convince—largely because the killing has continued. In August, for example, he signed a bill introducing a multiparty system, but no such reform can be implemented while the violence persists.

The regime has not distinguished itself in the trial of strength. Slow to grasp the nature of the popular uprising, it has been incompetent in confronting it. The security services, like Assad himself, seem to have been taken by surprise. By resorting to live fire against protesters at the start, in the city of Dara'a in southern Syria, they displayed indiscipline and arrogant contempt for the lives of citizens—the very contempt that, in one country after another, has been a motor of the Arab Awakening.

The speeches Assad has given since the protests started have been public-relations disasters—far from the rousing, dramatic appeal to the nation that his supporters had expected and the occasion demanded. Above all, he has failed to rein in his brutal security services and put an end to the shootings, arbitrary arrests, beatings and torture that have aroused international condemnation. Meanwhile, the Baath Party—"leader of state and society," according to the notorious Article 8 of the Syrian Constitution—has been virtually silent, confirming the widespread belief that it has become a hollow shell, concerned only with protecting its political monopoly, its privileges and its corrupt patronage network.

If the regime has shown itself to be weak, the opposition, however, is weaker still. It wants to challenge the system, but evidently does not yet know how to go about it—apart, that is, from staging riots and publishing videos of brutal repression by government forces. It is split in a dozen ways between secularists, civil rights activists, democrats and Islamists of various sorts; between the opposition in Syria and exiles abroad, who are among the regime's most virulent opponents; between those who call for Western intervention and those who reject any form of foreign interference; between angry, unemployed youths in the street and venerable figures of the opposition, hallowed by years in prison, most of them in late middle age. In a gesture of conciliation, the regime lifted a travel ban on several of them, including veteran human rights campaigner Haitham al-Maleh, 81, who, to his great surprise, was allowed to leave Damascus to attend an opposition gathering in Istanbul in July. But no coherent leadership has yet emerged, some say because its members, at least those inside Syria, fear arrest.

The July Istanbul meeting was the second of its kind to be held in Turkey, and seems to have enjoyed some support from Prime Minister Recep Tayyip Erdogan's AKP, a ruling party of conservative Islamic coloring. But neither conference brought to the fore a united leadership or a clear program, let alone anything that might look like an alternative government. The opposition factions that have so far declared themselves—the National Democratic Grouping, the Damascus Declaration signatories, the National Salvation Council, the local coordination committees in Syria—are loose groupings of individuals with little real structure and few novel ideas, save for the goal of ending rule by the Assad family and its cronies once and for all.

The truth is that, as Tunisia and Egypt are discovering, it is exceedingly difficult to bring about a transition from an autocratic, highly centralized, one-party system to anything resembling democratic pluralism. It is not something that can be done in a weekend or even in a month. In Europe it took a couple of centuries. In Syria—and, for that matter, in most Arab countries—there is no experience of free elections, and there are no real political parties, no free trade unions, no state or civil society institutions, no separation of powers, no independent judiciary, little real political education. The Syrian Parliament is a farce.

Everything in Syria will have to be rebuilt from the ground up—including the ideology of the state. The old slogans of the post–World War II period—anticolonialism, revolutionary socialism, Baathism, radical Islamism, Arab unity and Arab national-ism, Arabism itself—will all need to be rethought, discarded or brought up to date.

As in Egypt and Tunisia, a key puzzle will be how to integrate Islamist movements into a democratic system. In Syria, the Muslim Brotherhood has been banned—membership is punishable by death—ever since it conducted an insurgency against the regime of former President Hafez al-Assad, Bashar's father, from 1976 to 1982, which ended in a massacre at Hama. According to Human Rights Watch, between 5,000 and 10,000 people were killed as the government fought to regain control of the town from Islamist insurgents. These events have been seared into the collec-tive memory of most Syrians. But they mean different things to different people. For the regime, Hama was a necessary action that saved the country from Islamist terrorism. For the opposition—and especially for Sunni Muslims—it was a criminal massacre that, some would say, must be avenged.

There is, therefore, understandable uneasiness among sections of the popula-tion, especially the Christians (10 percent of the population) and the Alawis (about 12 percent). The regime is dominated by the latter, a branch of Shiite Islam, who are heavily represented in the officer corps and security services. They would be an immediate target if an extreme Sunni regime were to come to power. As Syria is a mosaic of sects and ethnic groups, the need for tolerance, reflected in an es-sentially secular government, is deeply ingrained. Many worried secularists look to Turkey as a model because Erdogan's AKP has shown that Islam is compatible with democracy.

The Need for Neutral Intermediaries

Since the task of bringing democracy to Syria is so vast, and since any viable transi-tion must inevitably take time, some observers have come to the view that a dia-logue between regime and opposition would be the safest way forward. But how to start, when the two camps are separated by an abyss of hate? Clearly, the regime must first stop killing its citizens and the opposition must accept the notion of a gradual transition. A cooling-off period is urgently required.

A peacekeeping mission, staffed by neutral countries such as India, Brazil and Turkey, could do the job. Jimmy Carter could oversee it. His moral stature and his record of conciliation are widely admired. The task would be to create the condi-tions for a serious exchange of views and hold the regime to its promises of real democratic reforms. Free elections under international supervision should be the ultimate goal.

Assad's Syria claims legitimacy on two main counts: for standing up to Israel and its American backer, and for having given its citizens—at least until the present cri-sis—a long spell of security and stability even if the price paid was an absence of po-litical freedoms. Every Syrian knows the terrible fate suffered by two of its neighbors: Lebanon because of its savage civil war (1975–90), and Iraq because of the horren-dous bloodletting of the Sunni-Shiite conflict, unleashed by the US invasion of 2003.

So Assad may be on the ropes, but he is far from finished. Some hardline pro-testers reject any notion of dialogue with him. Other opposition figures are more flexible but insist that the killing must stop first. As repression has intensified, the hardliners are gaining ground.

There are three scenarios that could bring the regime down: a split in the army and security forces; a major dispute within the regime or within the Assad family; or a catastrophic economic collapse. All are possible, but none seem imminent.

Except for some defections, the army and security forces have stayed loyal to the regime. So long as this remains the case, it will be difficult for the opposition to topple it. The ruling family and the regime continue to present a united front. There have been rumors of disputes between the president and his hardline brother Maher, commander of the regime's Praetorian Guard. But little of this has emerged in public view.

The economy is, of course, a source of great concern. Syria's tourist trade has collapsed, domestic investment has dried up and the Syrian pound has taken a battering. After the Arab Spring's first moment of euphoria, most people now realize that the problem is not just one of forging a new political system, whether in Syria or indeed in Tunisia, Egypt or Yemen. It is also a question of tackling the huge social and economic problems Syria and other countries in the region are facing: exploding populations; rampant youth unemployment; an impoverished middle class and a semi-destitute working class; a soaring cost of living; a semi-bankrupt government; policies of economic liberalization that have benefited only a tiny and corrupt elite; and neglect of workers' rights, whether on the land or in shops and factories.

The rich monarchies of the Gulf can spend their way out of trouble, and are doing so. Saudi Arabia, for example, has announced plans to spend $70 billion on low-cost housing. Syria, with about the same size population, can only dream of such figures. Kuwait, Qatar and the United Arab Emirates, highly prosperous sheikdoms with vast sovereign wealth funds, have promised to help Tunisia surmount its current difficulties. Money has also gone to Egypt, Oman and Yemen, a country of special concern to Saudi Arabia. Syria, too, will need bailing out if the crisis continues. But on whom can it rely? If times get really hard, its Iranian ally might well help out with a billion or two. But Iran has its own problems.

The Syrian economy can probably stumble along for several more months without imperiling the regime. Syria has proved it can withstand sanctions, mainly because, unlike most Arab countries, it can largely feed itself—this year's wheat crop is estimated at 3.6 million tons. With an oil output of 380,000 barrels per day, and plenty of gas, it also has a measure of energy autonomy. Although Europe is moving closer to a ban on imports of Syrian oil, imposing a worldwide ban would be difficult. In short, for all its faults and weaknesses, the regime is no pushover.

Assad's Assets

Bashar al-Assad is in deep trouble, but it does not yet look terminal. After the NATO intervention in Libya—not to mention the conflicts in Iraq, Afghanistan and Pakistan—no external power, and surely no Western country, has an appetite for military intervention. Russia has started to express its alarm at what its Syrian friends are doing, but it will almost certainly block condemnation of Syria at the UN Security Council, as will China. And Syria is too central to the stability of the eastern Arab world for any of the neighboring Arab states to be in a hurry to destabilize it. While the Saudis and several other Gulf states have recalled their ambassadors, and the Arab League and Gulf Cooperation Council have urged Assad to stop the killing, they have not called for him to step down.

Compared with other Arab countries that have experienced this year's revolutionary wave, Syria is something of a special case. Tunisia, for example, is geographi-

> **As violence intensifies in Syria, the frightening specter looms of a bloody sectarian settling of accounts.**

cally largely immune from the boisterous currents of Arab politics (although it has had to take in refugees from Libya). Events in Libya, too, violent as they have been, have had little impact on the Arab world. Even Egypt's revolution has not so far radically changed the Arab political map. Egypt is still self-absorbed, trying to sort out its own immense problems. It will no doubt in the future have a major impact on the Arab world, and on Arab-Israeli relations, but not quite yet.

Syria, in contrast, lies at the heart of the politics of the eastern Arab world. It is on the fault line of the Sunni-Shiite divide. It is Iran's main Arab ally. It is Israel's most obdurate opponent. It was, until the present crisis, the linchpin of Turkey's Arab policy. As Turkey's relations with Israel cooled, a Turkish-Syrian alliance was formed that has been of great importance for the region's geopolitics. Strains have arisen because of the brutality of Syria's security forces, but Turkey has by no means abandoned Syria. It would like to play a key role in stabilizing the situation, and has urged Assad to discipline his forces and stop the killing.

Syria is still the dominant external influence in Lebanon, in alliance with Hezbollah, the strongest party and the most powerful armed force in that country. Israel and the United States continue to demonize Hezbollah as a terrorist organization, whereas it is, in fact, no more than a Shiite resistance movement, which managed to evict Israel from Southern Lebanon after a twenty-two-year occupation (1978–2000). Indeed, it was Israel's occupation that created Hezbollah. To Israel's fury, Hezbollah has acquired a minimal capability to deter further Israeli aggression; it demonstrated its strength when Israel last invaded Lebanon, in 2006. Israel would dearly like to disrupt the Tehran-Damascus-Hezbollah axis, which in the past three decades has been the main obstacle to its regional hegemony. But it would not be easy to do so without incurring grave risks.

Hezbollah has attracted some criticism, especially from Syria's opponents in Lebanon, for siding with Assad's repression. Its heroic image of confronting Israel has been somewhat dented. But it remains true that Syria, Iran and Hezbollah have together shouldered the confrontation with Israel and the United States ever since the 1979 Egypt-Israel peace treaty removed Egypt from the Arab equation and exposed the rest of the region to Israeli power. This was evident in 1982. In the same year that the Syrian army perpetrated the massacre at Hama, Israel invaded Lebanon, killing more than 17,000 people in an attempt to destroy the PLO and wrest Lebanon from Syria's sphere of influence, bringing it into Israel's orbit. Had Israel been successful, Syria's security would have been fatally undermined and Israel would have reigned supreme in the Levant. However, the late Hafez al-Assad managed to thwart the Israeli plan. He used to claim it was one of his greatest triumphs. It protected Syria and kept Lebanon in the Arab camp.

All these many relationships—with friends as well as enemies—would risk unraveling if the Assad regime were to fall. This is the great worry in the region and beyond, and is one reason Bashar al-Assad may yet survive.

If the protests in Syria become more threatening and the killing continues, no one should expect the regime to go down without a fight. Indeed, few regimes are ready to commit political suicide or willingly surrender to their enemies, especially when severe retribution is threatened. Under father and son, the Assad regime has lasted for more than four decades, survived many a crisis and seen off many an enemy. In this, its ruthlessness is no different from that of others.

China had its Tiananmen Square massacre and Russia its bitter war in Chechnya. Iran crushed the Green Movement, which tried to topple President Ahmadinejad. Secretary of State Hillary Clinton has cast aspersions on Assad's legitimacy and called on the international community to stop doing business with Syria, but Syrians know very well that America's record in hunting down and destroying its enemies is no better than their own, and perhaps a good deal worse. When it was attacked on 9/11, that great bastion of democracy invaded Afghanistan in 2001, then Iraq in 2003 on fraudulent, trumped-up charges. Hundreds of thousands died, and several million were internally displaced or forced to flee abroad. Syria still plays host to more than 1 million Iraqi refugees, victims of America's war.

As violence intensifies in Syria, the frightening specter looms of a bloody sectarian settling of accounts. It is already a case of kill or be killed. That is why all those who care about the Syrian people and about regional stability should work to ensure that a national dialogue take place as soon as possible, with the aim of bringing about a transition of power by democratic means rather than by civil war.

❖

Patrick Seale is a British writer and journalist specializing in the Middle East. His books include The Struggle for Syria; Asad of Syria: The Struggle for the Middle East; *and, most recently,* The Struggle for Arab Independence: Riad el-Solh and the Makers of the Modern Middle East.

Assad's Hope of Survival

By Ed Blanche
The Middle East, August 1, 2011

Tehran reportedly has sent seasoned covert operators to prop up the Damascus regime and prevent the collapse of a key ally in Iran's expansionist strategy.

President Bashar Al Assad of Syria is fighting for the survival of his iron-fisted regime, dominated by the Alawite minority to which his family belongs, amid the staggering political turmoil that has turned the Arab world upside down since the start of the year.

But he has few friends in the Arab world. His only true ally is Iran, and, by all accounts, it is doing all it can to preserve the Damascus regime, a vital element in Tehran's drive to expand its influence across the Middle East.

Tehran has a lot at stake here and its apparent engagement in Syria's increasingly brutal crackdown against dissent reflects the anxiety in Tehran about the possibility of Assad's regime collapsing.

If Tehran loses its air-and-land bridge into Lebanon, through which it funnels missiles and other weapons, Islamic Revolutionary Guard Corps (IRGC) advisers and combat teams to support Hizbullah in its war against Israel, Iran's expansionist objectives in the Levant and westwards into Egypt and North Africa will be seriously curtailed.

"There's a deeply integrated relationship here that involves not only support for terrorism but a whole gamut of activities to ensure Assad's survival," said Michael Singh, a former senior director for Middle East affairs for the US National Security Council during President George W. Bush's administration.

Enduring alliance

The Americans and their allies have been striving for years to woo Syria away from Iran to isolate the Islamic Republic and break what has been one of the most enduring alliances in the fractious Middle East, where strategic regional partnerships have a habit of collapsing.

Splitting Syria from Iran would end an alliance forged in 1980 by President Assad's father, Hafez, who died in June 2000. Back then, Iran was fighting Iraq's Saddam Hussein, Assad's big rival.

But the alliance did not go down well in the Sunni-dominated Arab world, which saw no good coming from a fundamentalist Shi'ite regime in Tehran.

Nothing much has changed, except perhaps the level of alarm among the Sunni regimes, as US power in the region wanes and Iran's is on the rise.

The Iran-Syria bond has not been broken. It is difficult to determine with any exactitude the extent of the Iranian support Assad's regime is getting. But it should be viewed through the prism of how disastrous the fall of that regime would be for Tehran's strategic ambitions in the region, in particular being able to challenge Israel on its own doorstep.

It stands to reason, then, that Tehran's support is largely covert.

Damascus strenuously denies it is getting Iranian help, although western military analysts say regime forces lack the training, equipment and numbers to deal effectively with the uprising.

Tehran denies it is providing such support. But if the Americans and Israelis are to be believed, Iran has stiffened Damascus' massive security establishment with some heavy hitters in Iran's covert operations apparatus, already active in the Gulf and the Levant in expanding Iran's influence.

> *Syria is Iran's gateway to the Levant, and Tehran's most valuable proxy, Lebanon's Hizbullah movement.*

Syria is Iran's gateway to the Levant, and Tehran's most valuable proxy, Lebanon's Hizbullah movement. Hizbullah challenges Israel from the north and provides support for the Palestinian militants of Hamas, who rule the Gaza Strip and create a southern front against the Jewish state.

US and Israeli sources say that the IRGC and its covert strike arm, the Al Quds Force, are now operating throughout Syria, reportedly with some Hizbullah operatives from Lebanon, to back up elite Syrian army units dominated by the Alawites.

But these forces, the most loyal to the regime, are limited to the 4th Division and the Republican Guard, which essentially form the private army of Assad's hotheaded younger brother Maher, backed up by armed paramilitaries known as shahiba.

As the uprising has spread, these forces have become overstretched, and the regime has been reluctant to call in other divisions, consisting largely of Sunni troops whose loyalty is questionable.

The question is: If the crisis deteriorates, would Tehran send in troops to aid Assad, just as Saudi Arabia sent Gulf Cooperation Council forces into Bahrain in March to bolster the tiny kingdom's beleaguered Al Khalifa dynasty?

An Iranian move like that would be seen as provocative in the extreme in the Sunni-dominated Arab world, and beyond.

In retaliation for Iran's alleged support for Assad, the United States and the European Union have imposed sanctions on top IRGC commanders, including Maj. Gen. Qassem Soleimani, commander of the Al Quds Force, and Brig. Gen. Mohammed Ali Jafari of the IRGC and his deputy commander, Gen. Hossein Taeb.

The Tehran regime is deeply concerned that the Damascus regime may fall. In a recent online broadcast, Syrian protestors chanted "freedom" as they burned an Iranian flag, a sight that must have shaken Iranian leaders.

"The majority of the Syrian populace . . . see Iran as part and parcel of the problem," said Jubin Goodarzi, author of *Syria and Iran: Diplomatic Alliance and Power Politics in the Middle East.* "So Tehran is worried that if the regime does collapse, any new regime would, at the very least, be very cool—or outright hostile—to Iran."

Of all the uprisings taking place across the Arab world after decades of repressive rule, the upheaval in Syria is the most worrying for Tehran.

If Bashar Al Assad is forced from power and replaced by a more representative regime from the Sunni majority, "it will be a major blow to Iran's foreign policy, in terms of ideological aspirations, projecting its power in the eastern Mediterranean and trying to participate—whether substantially or symbolically—in the Arab-Israeli conflict," says Goodarzi, a Middle Eastern specialist at Webster University in Geneva.

Surveillance support

The Iranian regime's experience in putting down a widespread protest movement of its own two years ago is clearly aiding Assad's forces in Syria, particularly when it comes to countering internet-linked uprisings such as that sweeping Syria.

IRGC and Hizbullah cadres are reported to be closely involved in the Damascus regime's efforts to contain the spreading uprising.

Special sniper teams have been reported in action against street protests, picking off ringleaders. Other teams advise Syrian military units on the ground how to contain and splinter street demonstrations.

These techniques were used to great effect by the Tehran regime against Iran's "Green Movement" following the hotly disputed 2009 presidential elections.

Iran is also reported to have supplied sophisticated surveillance equipment that is helping Syrian security authorities track down opponents through Facebook and Twitter accounts on the internet. These operations have resulted in the arrest of hundreds of Syrians in their homes in recent weeks.

"Having weathered a social networking revolution of its own, the Iranians have developed techniques and insights into combating Facebook-assisted uprisings," observed Joshua Landis, director of Middle East Studies at the University of Oklahoma, who lived in Syria for many years.

"The clearest sign of Iranian assistance is Syria's development of cadres of pro-regime youth who can spread regime-friendly voices on the internet, websites and blogs."

The key figure in the Iranian operation is Gen. Mohsen Chizari, a senior officer in the Al Quds Force, whose personnel have played a key role in the Syrian crackdown since at least mid-April, US intelligence sources say.

Chizari, Gen. Qassem Soleimani, the Al Quds Force commander, and the organisation itself were the subject of US economic sanctions in May for what Washington said was their complicity in the Assad regime's "human rights abuses and repression of the Syrian people."

Chizari is a seasoned clandestine operator who played a major and highly effective role in destabilising Iraq after the US invasion of March 2003 and establishing an overarching Iranian presence in its traditional enemy.

He was captured with another Al Quds Force commander by US troops in Baghdad in December 2006 at the compound of Abdel Aziz Al Hakim, a leader of the Iranian-backed Islamic Supreme Council of Iraq.

The Iranian commander reportedly had detailed reports about Iranian weapons shipments into Iraq to foment trouble against the Americans and their allies and data on explosive projectiles that caused scores of US casualties.

Chizari and his companion were later returned to Iran under an exchange for British marines captured by the Iranians in the northern Gulf.

The shadowy general's reported presence in Syria would seem to underline Tehran's determination to support Assad's regime to the fullest extent with clandestine operations by the Al Quds Force, and to coordinate Hizbullah involvement in backing up the embattled regime in Damascus.

"Syria's alignment with Iran and its backing of local paramilitary and terrorist clients are not flimsy marriages of convenience," observed Israeli analyst Jonathan Spyer.

"They were, and are, the core of a successful regional policy. Through it, Damascus has magnified its local and regional influence, and obtained an insurance policy against paying any price for its activities. This insurance policy is now paying dividends," he added.

"Syria's alignment with the regional axis led by Tehran represents Assad's best hope of survival. Indeed, Western fear of Iran is the crucial factor making possible the crackdown in Syria and hence the survival of the regime.

"The fall or weakening of the Assad regime in Syria would constitute a serious body blow to Iranian regional ambitions.

"Its resurgence under the protective tutelage of Tehran, by contrast, would prove that membership of the Iranian alliance provides a handy guarantee for autocratic rulers hoping to avoid the judgment of their peoples."

Out of the Shadow of Fear

A rare inside look at Syria, a land where the regime rules with a murderous impunity.

By Åsne Seierstad
Newsweek, June 5, 2011

He walks barefoot through the streets. The air is fresh with night, the sky at its darkest. He stretches his legs and inhales the scent of spring.

Some cars drive by, lighting up the sidewalk as they pass. Sand and gravel cover the soles of his swollen feet. His stomach pains are intense. His neck hurts. "This was just a holiday," they told him. "Next time, it's business."

He arrives at a metal door in Yarmouk, on the outskirts of Damascus, and presses the doorbell. A confused face appears in the door hatch, then bursts out: "So, they got you a new haircut!"

Abid is jostled into the apartment. The ones who were asleep come shuffling. The laughter, it seems, won't stop. Abid is out of jail.

The engineering student is one of thousands who have been detained and imprisoned since the revolt in Syria started in March. People have been plucked away from schools and mosques, from public squares and streets. The authorities are quick to arrive on the sites of the protests. Men in civilian clothes, called the "ghosts," are watching.

Surveillance dominates every aspect of life. The secret police—the Mukhabarat—is divided into an intricate system of departments and subdepartments; no part of society is left unexamined. A network of agents spans Syria. Some have tenure; others work part time. Who could be a better observer than the greengrocer by the mosque or the hospital night watchman? Who can better keep tabs on a family than the schoolteacher who asks what Daddy says about the man on the posters?

The man on the posters has pale, close-set eyes, is well groomed, and has a curiously long neck. On one variant he wears sunglasses and a uniform. On others, he looks like a banker. An ophthalmologist, he was reeled in at his father's death to replace him as Syria's dictator. His name is Bashar al-Assad. His deposition is the goal of the nascent upheaval.

One Friday Abid found the resolve to join a demonstration after prayers. He hardly saw they were surrounded before he felt a stinging pain on his neck. The electric shocks chased through his body. He fell, lost consciousness. When he awoke, several others were lying around him.

The Mukhabarat had appeared, in plain clothes, from nowhere. Now they dragged him, and a hundred others, to waiting white vans. The demonstrators were taken to the outskirts of Damascus.

"We sat in rows in a *riad*, a courtyard, surrounded by high walls. Our hands were tied behind our backs, and we were forced to kneel. I counted the prayer calls from the mosque to keep track of time. Our legs became numb. When told to stand up after the last call from the mosque, none of us could. I buckled over, was beaten, forced to stand, and fell again. At night, we were stuffed into a cell. We stood upright, 12 men, on a few square meters. Next morning we were taken out to the *riad* again. After three days we were tender, and the interrogations could start."

Some were tortured for hours and came back bloodied. The one who suffered the most was an Alawite, a man belonging to the same Shia minority as the Assads, and considered a turncoat. Abid was more fortunate. "I am a member of the Baath Party. The beatings I received were not as harsh."

Abid became a party member while growing up in Daraa, the city where the revolt began. Holding a membership is sometimes required to get into college, to get a job, or to rise in the power structures.

But Abid had had enough. With only one year left of his engineering studies, he risked it all in order to take part in the Syrian Spring. "It's now or never. The train of freedom is leaving. We can jump on it, or we can let it go by." A voice sounds from the far end of the sofa: "Listen to him. Two weeks in jail and he's already Mandela!"

The authorities' aim is obvious: to strangle the protests at birth. Not to do as in Cairo and wait until the squares get crowded. Whereas the gatherings in Tunisia and Egypt rapidly grew to number in the thousands, Syrian authorities mercilessly beat down on groups of 25, 50, or 100.

"Getting a thousand people out on the streets here is like getting a million people out in Cairo," says Abid's host.

His living room is about twice the size of Abid's cell. Air is scarce. Everybody smokes, and cigarettes are lit with finished butts. It's midnight. Outdoors, children are still in the streets. Some are traipsing around on their own, trash crackling beneath their feet. Others are half asleep on Daddy's arm, on their way to bed. A couple of greengrocers are still open. A kebab skewer keeps rotating. Life goes on.

Syrian political life revolves around Bashar al-Assad. The real power figures are Bashar and his younger brother, Maher, commander in chief of the Republican Guard, an Alawite-dominated elite force, the only army allowed inside Damascus. Their father, Hafez al-Assad, the Air Force pilot who took power in 1970, is remembered as a shrewd politician. Belonging to the Alawite minority—merely 12 percent of the population—he built a power base of mainly his own clan. His son has lacked the experience to navigate in the national and regional political terrain and has lost some support.

Evening falls again. Alia hums as she concentrates on her penmanship. "When danger approaches," a Syrian proverb goes, "sing to it." Some girls gather around a desk in a high-rise apartment building. There are a pair of scissors, sheets of black paper, pencils, and a box of chalk on it. Alia makes an outline in pencil and fills it in with chalk. The Venetian blinds are drawn. You can never be too safe, even on the seventh floor with an open view.

The words gradually take shape beneath Alia's purple-polished nails. "Stop the Killing." On another poster, written from right to left: "Stop the Violence." Discussion ensues on the spacing of the words on the third poster, but their message is clear. "Stop the Siege of the Children in Daraa."

Daraa, a sleepy town in the desert on the Jordanian border, was where it all started. One afternoon in March, some boys wrote antigovernment graffiti on a wall. They were detained by the security forces and taken to the local police station. And then silence.

> *Terrorists, Al Qaeda, and Israel are behind the revolt, according to Syrian media. A handful of men have confessed on state TV.*

Their parents searched for them, asked around. Nobody knew. They went to the authorities and were sent packing. The local sheik joined the fathers at the office of the head of security in town.

"Give us our children back," said the religious leader. He removed his headband—called an *ogal*—and placed it on the table, a symbolic gesture to indicate the importance of the request. If you ask for something, be prepared to give something in return, says the Quran.

"Forget your children. Go get new ones," the head of security allegedly replied.

The sheik asked him to show mercy, for God's sake.

"If you can't make more children yourselves, send your wives and we will fix it," the security boss is known to have said.

The disappeared children. The staggering insults. More and more people gathered around the building. They were turned away, but they came back.

A week passed before the children were released. They had been severely maltreated. Skin and flesh had been beaten off the knuckles of their hands. Some were said to have had their fingernails pulled out. YouTube videos of the kids were distributed on the Net. The protests spread to other cities.

Damascus remained an island of calm until the end of March, when spontaneous protests started occurring even there. There was no coordination, no defined leadership. The time and place for the demonstrations had to be transmitted from mouth to mouth, from friend to friend. And they had better be real friends.

The girlfriends on the seventh floor are planning the first women-only demonstration in central Damascus. The following Monday they will meet on one of the better streets in a Damascene shopping district. They will stay in stores until the strike of 3, when they will gather and roll out their banners. They will run when the police arrive. And they plan to vanish, like shadows, into the side streets.

Terrorists, Al Qaeda, and Israel are behind the revolt, according to Syrian media. A handful of men have confessed on state TV. "My mission was to make untruthful videos," said one. "The money came from Saudi Arabia," said another. "People are forced to go out and protest," said a third.

The girls shake their heads at this. "I just want a good life," says Alia. She works in a production company specializing in soap operas for the Palestinian market, and has a lot to lose. Her job. A boyfriend. Parties on the terraced roof. "You feel very small under this regime," she says in halting French.

"Everything is from the government down. Until now, I've asked my friends to stay away from the protests. I've said, let's wait a little. But the killings have changed people. Too much blood. We can't just let them keep on." Elias, the apartment's only male inhabitant, shows remorse. "I'm full of fear," he says. "I've never participated in any protest. I am not a brave man."

Elias and Alia belong to religious minorities. He is Christian, she is Druze. "I'm afraid of what may come," says Elias. "The regime has a good policy when it comes to minorities, keeps the country in balance. I'm afraid of Islam, afraid Syria will become a new Iraq." The regime preys on this fear. It tries to convince Christian leaders, representing a 10th of the population, that Islamists may take over. Across the border, in Iraq, half the Christian population has fled persecution.

The chalk on the banners smudges; the writing becomes blurry. White writing is innocence; the black background, power. The idea was so nice. Alia blows off the excessive dust and adds more chalk.

One of the girls finds the solution. "Hair spray! We'll fix it with hair spray!" The spray spreads out all over the room. Hair spray has never smelled more of revolution.

"I apply not my sword, where my lash suffices, nor my lash, where my tongue is enough" are the words of Muawiya, the first caliph of the Umayyad dynasty in Damascus. He was a master of *hilm*—grace and forbearance—and used force only when absolutely necessary. When he proclaimed himself caliph in 661 in opposition to Ali, Muhammad's son-in-law, the split that divided Islam into Sunnis and Shias was a reality.

This Friday the Umayyad Mosque is stage to a modern drama. The mosque is the only legal gathering place, and still strictly monitored by the security forces. Every word from the imam's mouth is noted.

The bazaar is empty. The stalls are closed. Iron shutters protect glass jars and baskets. A whiff of cardamom rests over the spice market. The leather craftsman has left behind a faint tang of hide, the soapmaker a trace of lavender. The tourists have gone; only the locals are left, small boys on bicycles, grandfathers on their chairs. Police units on motorcycles have closed off several streets. Some plan a protest after prayers.

The silence is oppressive. The area teems with Mukhabarat. Everyone knows who they are, even though they act like normal men. They squat on curbsides, lean against walls, sit on benches or together by doorways. They're dressed in shirts and trousers, like other men. Though they might be more broad-shouldered than the average Syrian, and certainly have a stronger proclivity for leather jackets, the clothes aren't what set them apart. It's their glance.

They possess a way of looking that is inquisitive but not curious. It's one-way; they want to take, not meet. Their conversation, or lack thereof, is the other giveaway. Between most people there is at least a little chitchat. These men hardly talk, and when they do, they do it without facial expressions, without a jab in the side, a poke on the shoulder. They don't talk like people really talk. They are on assignment.

As prayers are about to end, a cold wind trembles. The sky above the mosque darkens, splits, and rain starts hammering down. Water splashes on canopies that give way under the weight. A man tries to keep the water out of his entrance with a broom. Suddenly white frozen pearls drum on roofs and tarps, make the jasmine fall off the trees and drown in puddles. "God is great," says a man who follows the hailstorm from his doorway. "I've never seen this in Damascus before. It is protection from God. People will stay calm. So they won't get killed today," he says with a sigh.

It's as if the deserted street, shuttered stores, and everything that drowns in the storm emboldens the man. He talks about his brother, who narrowly avoided a government sniper last Friday. "It brushed by him here," Tarek says, pointing to the side of his throat. The bullet peeled off the outermost layer of skin during a demonstration in Zamalka. Several people were killed.

The snipers shoot to kill. Not many, just enough to frighten. The orders are said to be no more than 20 a day, but many Fridays the numbers have been higher.

Like other Syrians, he talks about The Fear.

"It's injected into us at birth," he says softly, demonstrating an imaginary needle. "It makes us bow our heads, turn away, distrust each other. Everyone can be reported. If you happen to be rude to a policeman or he doesn't like your face, you can disappear for years. Do you know when I've been most frightened? When I've seen the Assads on TV. I ordered my sons to sit and listen in reverence. You had to be careful around the children. But everything changed in March. I told my boys what is happening in our country. The oldest one came with me to the protest last week. But my 5-year-old daughter cried when I said Bashar had to go. 'I love Bashar,' she cried. The way we've taught her. 'No, you should hate him,' I explained. 'But I love him,' she sobbed."

Tarek points to the poster above the door. "They came with him 10 days ago. 'Paste him up,' they ordered. I was afraid not to. This is my living, after all. Others pasted him up too. No wonder my daughter is confused."

In the fashionable shopping district of Damascus the atmosphere is somber. Elegant, minimally clad mannequins view passersby with an arrogant mien. The cashiers stand listlessly with resigned expressions. There are no pictures of the president. The regime does not paste over the clean windows of the upper class. The poorer the district, the more posters.

Shirin paces the floor of her fashion store in tight jeans and flat suede Uggs. She had planned for a spring sale, but then came the bloodbath in Daraa. "Advertising while people are being killed felt wrong," she says.

But the successful businesswoman has little sympathy for the protesters—"Some young rebels running around making trouble"—and supports Bashar al-Assad. "We have an excellent foreign policy. We are independent, and produce all we need, except for some spare parts for airplanes. The sanctions have taught us self-reliance. We don't need foreign intervention, as in Libya. And what's so wrong about Gaddafi? I always thought he made a lot of sense."

But as a matriarch with three sons, she is upset about the arrests of the youngsters in Daraa. "The president should have ordered the hanging of the local chief of security," she opines. "The way he treated the parents was a declaration of war. They're Bedouins down there, divided into clans. I worry extremists will exploit the situation and wind people up."

She sighs. "I really love this country. This is where I want to live. Live now."

In a café downtown, Mouna takes a sip of her Barada beer. She has the burning eyes of a sleepless activist, staying every night in a different place. The Mukhabarat could have arrested her for her eyes only.

It all started with her leftist father, who barely avoided the purges of the 1970s. Mouna remembers his comrades' white skin, having survived the jails of Hafez al-Assad.

After the demonstrations in Egypt, Mouna went home to her parents. "My father and I sat with our mint tea and talked for hours. He said: 'It's coming here! It's spreading. It's your turn now.'" She draws her breath and looks around. "I used the Internet, email and Facebook, like the Egyptians. Soon I began receiving threats. 'We're coming to get you,' they say. When I ask who they are, they answer, 'You know who's talking.'"

Mouna gets annoyed at the next question. "We've grown up to believe there's nothing to do about this society, and you already ask me who we want as a new leader. No candidate has materialized between March and April. What I want is to participate in society," she says firmly.

She disconnects her cell phone from its charger when it starts chiming. It's a dying phone and needs charging three times a day. Mouna's slight body begins to shake. She holds her phone in one hand and clasps her hair with the other.

"When? Where?"

She stares into the air. "I have to go," she says. "My friend has been arrested. The secret police came to his home."

The next day, there are more girls than usual on a specific Damascene shopping street. They walk in pairs. To those in the know, discerning who is there on an assignment is not difficult. They look around nervously. They keep tossing their heads. They have flat-soled shoes. Like the men outside the mosque, they talk without facial expressions. One pair here, another one there. Three. Four. A small gathering. A larger one.

Suddenly, they open their purses and hold up their banners. Some written on cloth, some on paper. Each woman has her slogan.

Stop the Killing. Stop the Violence.

They start walking silently to the square with the looming bronze statue of Hafez al-Assad. None of the bystanders says a word. They pay attention, in disbelief. The girls cross the roundabout to get to the statue. A minute passes. Two. Maybe three. They are surrounded. White vans and scores of men in plain clothes pop up from nowhere. They tear posters out of the girls' hands, throw the women to the ground. "Whores," the men shout. "Cows!" Some lie on the ground. One refuses to release her poster and screams as her finger is broken.

But most have fled. They disappeared over the square, into the side alleys. Every girl for herself. As they had planned. It's all over in a matter of minutes. A white van drives away with four of the girls. The other vehicles depart from the scene.

The square appears as if nothing has happened. But something has happened. Something has begun.

❖

Seierstad is the author of The Bookseller of Kabul *and, most recently,* The Angel of Grozny: Life Inside Chechnya.

Inside the City of Fear

By James Harkin
Newsweek, November 28, 2011

James Harkin is one of the few non-Syrian journalists to get into Homs. There, in the midst of murderous civil strife, he befriends a brave 18-year-old who dreams of a free Syria.

It's an abrupt twist to a conversation as I settle into my seat on the bus from Damascus to Homs: an 18-year-old boy tells me in no uncertain terms to get off, to leave the bus. We've known each other just five minutes, Mohammed and I, after he introduced himself while we were loading our luggage into the hold of the bus. I'd invited him to sit beside me at the back. With his shock of curly black hair zipped up in the hood of a stripy cardigan, he looked like the lead singer of a retro boy band. "But why? Why do you want to go to Homs?" he asks again and again. Oh, I don't know, I say: I'm touring around. This spooks Mohammed, as well it should: Homs, in recent weeks, has become a place of immense peril, the epicenter of an increasingly violent uprising against the regime of Bashar al-Assad.

I don't want to tell Mohammed I'm a journalist. Journalists are, as a general rule, barred from entering Syria, and definitely not allowed to wander around unsupervised. They are most certainly not allowed to get on a bus to Homs. I don't want to get the boy into trouble. "Tourists in Homs? There are none," he says. He looks at me quizzically for a few moments, as if he's trying to get the measure of me: what kind of Western tourist would be so idiotic as to park himself on the bus to Homs? And then, just as the bus revs its engines, his tone becomes more urgent. "I fear for you, I want you to get off the bus. Get off." It's as if he's only just realized that I must be mad—or a journalist. People are beginning to stare. Almost everyone else on the bus is an old man; maybe young men know better than to take the bus to Homs. The bus pulls away and I shrug my shoulders, but Mohammed is deadly serious. "You can still get off. Get off now."

For the next two hours we talk. Perhaps it's because I'm a foreigner, Mohammed is mighty voluble. He's an engineering student from Homs, but since the antigovernment demonstrations began, he hasn't been able to attend college in the city. Homs, where he lives, is home to just over a million people, right in the heartland of Syria. It's where Syrians go to flee the bustle of Damascus and relax in its cafes and restaurants and to watch soccer (Homs boasts two popular soccer teams, Al-Karamah and Al-Wathba). Not anymore; since March, when its people rose up to complain against economic injustice and demand more political freedom, and its armed forces replied with guns and repression, the city has been under a fierce siege. Most of the city is under total military lock-down, Mohammed tells me. No one can go out; everyone stays at home. "There are tanks in the streets where I live. You can't really walk around; it's dangerous." His father is a headmaster in a local school, but even he hasn't been able to go out to work. Everyone knows someone who's been killed or injured in his area. "Yesterday my sister saw a body in the street, and she's been crying ever since." Does he mean districts like Baba Amr, I ask, places from where gruesome but unverified clips of bombed buildings and dead bodies have been turning up on YouTube? Mohammed becomes insistent, frustrated with his inability to get the message across: "No, not just there. It's everywhere. You will see."

I did see—and hear. Later that day, in Homs, I'd chat with the manager of a pastry shop who, when he was sure he was out of the earshot of others, told me he believed as many as 5,000 people had been killed in the city in the last six months. The day after, the same man walked me to the now-infamous clock tower in the city's main square where a demonstration of 70,000 people in April was met with adamant violence by the authorities. There, chillingly, he played out the act of firing a machine gun into imaginary crowds. Rat-tat-tat-tat-tat. Since the demonstrators were ejected from the main square, the battles between them, the Army, and unknown armed groups have fanned out into different areas within the city limits. Some residents of Homs have taken up arms, either to defend themselves and their communities against the Army and the police or to go on the attack. Amid reports of growing sectarian tension between Sunnis and Alawites, the conflict has grown more shadowy and difficult to fathom; the only thing people know for sure is that more bodies are found on the streets every day.

The living stay at home. Everyone sits tight and waits. Many homes in the city are doing without gas, electricity, or hot water; even in the city center, where I stay, there is no hot water to be found. In the morning, people walk around the city center, as if stretching their legs after their hours of being cooped up indoors. But the claustrophobia, the feeling of everyone watching and being watched, is intense. When I venture outside—everyone cautions me against it—I feel like every Syrian is staring at me. There's shooting, I'm told, in an area just a few hundred yards away from the hotel where I'm staying. Demonstrations still take place in areas of the city, often after a funeral or Friday prayers. In a cafe I see two waiters racing to a window and leaning out of it excitedly; one of them thought he could hear chanting going on in a different part of the city. I follow them to the window but strain to hear anything. In the early afternoon, even the center of the city begins to shut down. By early evening an informal curfew is in place and an unnatural quiet descends on the entire, empty city. Staring out at the main square from an otherwise vacant hotel, the place looks haunted, as if all its residents have been stolen away.

Mohammed has been luckier than most. For the last few weeks he's been shuttling back and forth between Homs and Damascus for a part-time work placement, and now he's returning home. The roles between the two cities have been reversed; now it's the hectic pace of Damascus that is a breath of fresh air from the eerie watchfulness of Homs. All the same, Mohammed misses his family; he has nine brothers and sisters, all of them living in and around Homs. Occasionally his mobile phone goes off, and he speaks to one of them to hear their news and tell them he's safe and on his way back home. Like most people in Homs and a great majority of the Syrian population, his family is Sunni. Many of the current protesters are Sunnis who believe they've been discriminated against under the Alawite regime—that President Assad has doled out jobs and influence to Alawites like himself, followers of an unorthodox branch of Shiite Islam. In return the government is claiming that the protests are being masterminded by Sunni extremists, stoked by Syria's foreign ill wishers in Saudi Arabia and even inspired by Al Qaeda. Mohammed doesn't want to discuss religious divisions within his country, which he seems to think have been greatly exaggerated. He's keener to know about the West. "Is it true that you hate us Muslims? We just want to live in peace." For the most part, however, the tone is playful, curious. I show him my swanky new iPhone, thinking that this is how to impress a Syrian 18-year-old. But

> *Amid reports of growing sectarian tension between Sunnis and Alawites, the conflict has grown more shadowy and difficult to fathom; the only thing people know for sure is that more bodies are found on the streets every day.*

it doesn't even register; he thinks I'm asking him to type in his telephone number. "Are you married?" he wants to know, asking a question that no Arab male fails to ask of a Westerner, man or woman. No, I say. "Why not?" he wants to know. I ask him the same question, and he says with a giggle that he doesn't even have a girlfriend. That's something for the future, he says—something else, besides a better country, for a young Syrian to hope for.

Rewind to the bus ride, Damascus to Homs. Our conversation is becoming animated, and an old man in a headdress sitting beside us opens an eye from his half-sleep, wondering what we could be talking about in my English and his, half-garbled but still intelligible. These are Mohammed's fellow townspeople, and he seems relaxed around them. He's never been outside Syria, never really been anywhere apart from Damascus and Homs, but he's relentlessly interested in the rest of the world. I tell him I live in London. He's fascinated: "Is it beautiful? How do people live there? What are the buildings like?" He hopes to go see it one day when he's finished his studies.

Have I been to Iran, he wants to know. He'd really like to go to Qatar, to see the architecture there and to work. He wants to travel and to see the world, he says, but it's often difficult for Syrians to get visas even to other Arab countries. (It's a complaint I hear again in Homs from another young man, that the Arab League nations that are so concerned about the human rights of Syrians—this is four days after the country has been suspended from the League for its repression—are less generous when it comes to granting visas to its citizens to live and work. Does he think the situation might improve? In a year or two, yes. He doesn't want to leave for good; he wants a job and a better life, but most of all he loves Syria. "I am very sad for my country," he keeps saying. He says it over and over again, as if talking in code.)

As we talk, we pass a succession of military vehicles traveling in the same direction: trailers, long green buses, munitions vehicles, but mostly trucks with soldiers sitting in the back, smoking and sleeping. Truck after truck in a great, rumbling convoy; I count at least 50 of them. Then there's the occasional huge gun mounted on a lorry, the tank beached at the side of the road. Mohammed keeps nudging me to look at it all. Neither of us says anything, but he frequently fixes me a stare as if to say, "I was right, wasn't I? You should have left the bus." In return I raise my eyebrows, as if to get across the seriousness of the situation I've gotten myself into.

My companion has become my lookout, counting down at regular intervals how many kilometers it is until our arrival at the bus station just outside Homs. It is just after midday. The only safe place, he tells me as we near Homs, is now the city center itself. Together we devise a plan. He's going to write down the name of a hotel there and then I'm going to show it to the taxi driver, go there directly, and not go out again until I leave.

As I get off the bus I tell him to give me a few minutes, that I have a pressing need to use the facilities. "No, no, no," he says. "Wait. You can do that at the hotel. Just wait five minutes." Carrying sports bags, looking firmly at the ground, we march past prying eyes and toward the first available taxi—like bank robbers walking away from a job. As I get into the taxi he embraces me goodbye, and then changes his mind. No, he says, I'm going to come with you, then jumps in the back of the car. For most of the journey Mohammed and the taxi driver talk to each other in Arabic. From what I can understand they seem to be discussing the worsening violence. They're discussing me, too—how could they not?—but I trust Mohammed's judgment. On arrival we spend 15 minutes walking around searching for the entrance to the hotel, looking, all the while, utterly conspicuous. We find what used to be the entrance, but it is shut, as if permanently. Together we find a side entrance down an alley, and what looks like a private, disused elevator that will take us up to the hotel.

On the way up to the sixth floor we exchange telephone numbers, and he tells me to call him if I need anything while I'm in Homs. I thank him profusely and implore him to stay in touch, that he must let me know if there's anything I can do to help when I'm back in London. The following day, as my fears of arrest grow, I'll delete his name and number from my phone, just in case the police want to know how I got in and who I've been talking to. In any case, he doesn't seem very interested in polite offers of assistance from random foreigners. It's only later that I realize just what a help he's been. The anonymous business hotel he's brought me to makes perfect cover for a visiting journalist. Never get a taxi on your own, someone in the city advises me; if the driver is friendly with the authorities there's a good chance he'll take you straight to the police station and you'll be deported, possibly after being roughed up. Two days after I leave, a Syrian news cameraman was discovered dead on the main street in Homs, according to the New York–based Committee to Protect Journalists. He was found with his eyes gouged out.

In the hotel lobby I offer Mohammed some money for his journey home, but he won't accept it. I've taken you out of your way, I say. I want to give you some money; you need to get home. I take out a large Syrian bank note and try to force it into his hand, but he is not having any of it. In any case he's changed his mind about going home; one of the telephone calls he took was from home, he says, and they've told him it's too dangerous to go back there. He's going to stay with his sister instead, who lives in a safer part of town. One final embrace and Mohammed is gone, back into his world of grim menace, leaving me in the hands of a hotel manager who turns out to be just as gently solicitous as Mohammed was.

6

Elsewhere on the Arabian Peninsula: Bahrain and Yemen

(AFP/Getty Images)

Bahraini Shiites hold an antigovernment rally in the village of Qadam, West Manama, as tensions remain high in the kingdom on November 25, 2011.

A Country Divided: Yemen's Plight

By Paul McCaffrey

Of all the nations to experience political upheaval during the Arab Spring, Yemen presents one of the more difficult cases. Situated on the southwestern shore of the Arabian Peninsula, Yemen faces a number of challenges that pose serious threats to its future. While the population of the Arab world is rapidly expanding, in Yemen it is exploding; currently numbered at nearly twenty-five million, it is increasing at a rate of around 3 percent per year. Even the most advanced and dynamic economy would be hard-pressed to accommodate such growth, and Yemen's economy is neither. Unlike its neighbors, Yemen is not blessed with vast oil reserves, and what it does have is expected to be depleted in the next decade.

More alarming still is the state of the nation's water resources. Some expect Yemen's capital city, Sanaa, to run out of water in the next generation. Much of this strain is blamed on khat, a mildly narcotic plant. Nearly nine out of ten Yemeni men and a significant percentage of Yemeni women chew khat, and according to official reports, Yemeni families spend more on khat than on food. Despite the country's high rates of malnutrition, much of the arable land is devoted to khat cultivation. A durable plant, khat is easy to grow—if there is enough water. Khat fields are generally inundated twice per month. Yemen's arid climate yields little in the way of rainfall, so its water is harvested mostly from fast-depleting underground aquifers.

Prior to the Arab Spring uprisings, many analysts, both Yemeni and foreign, attributed the long tenure of the ruling Ali Abdullah Saleh dictatorship in part to the country's khat habit. Chewing the substance, they contended, had lulled Yemenis into a haze of complacency. The Yemeni journalist Ali Saeed al-Mulaiki joked to Dexter Filkins for the *New Yorker*, "If the Yemeni people didn't chew khat, they would think about their future and about their lives, and there would be a revolution."

Even without its population and resource issues, Yemen would still face a difficult path. The country suffers from deep internal divisions. Historically, Yemen has been two countries: North Yemen and South Yemen. Unification only occurred in 1990, and the period since has seen its share of upheaval. Yemen's population is about 53 percent Sunni and 45 percent Shia, with the latter adhering mostly to the Zaidi branch of the faith. Sunnis are predominant in the southern lowlands of Yemen, while the Shia inhabit the mountainous north. Further thwarting national unity are strong and enduring tribal loyalties. Such allegiances are especially strong in the countryside, where the national government's influence is weak. Many tribes have their own heavily armed militias. The combustible atmosphere led Saleh to declare that governing Yemen was like "dancing on the heads of snakes."

The partition of Yemen into North and South Yemen occurred in 1839, when the British seized the southern port of Aden and the surrounding area from the Zaidi imamate that then ruled most of the country. In the centuries prior, Yemen had en-joyed periods of independence interspersed with stretches of colonization, whether by the Ottoman Empire or the Egyptian Mamluks. The Ottomans returned in 1849 to take control of North Yemen.

North Yemen achieved its independence from the Ottomans in 1918 and was ruled at first by a series of hereditary imams, beginning with Imam Yahya Muham-mad Hamid al-Din. Imam Yahya died during a failed coup d'état in 1948 and was succeeded by his son, Ahmad, who led the nation until his death in 1962. Before Ahmad's son, Muhammad, could secure his reign, a group of Yemeni army officers seized power, declaring a Yemen Arab Republic (YAR). A civil war ensued, each side receiving foreign support. Gamal Abdel Nasser, the president of Egypt, backed the republicans and sent troops to assist them. At its peak, the Egyptian military pres-ence in North Yemen comprised an estimated seventy thousand troops. To thwart Egyptian influence, Saudi Arabia financed the royalists. The two sides battled on and off for the next five years, with neither faction achieving a decisive victory. Sapped by the effort and facing threats closer to home, Nasser withdrew Egyptian troops in 1967. The royalist and republican forces reached a truce in 1970, and a democratic constitution was adopted. Despite the reconciliation, the imamate was not restored and the YAR endured under the leadership of President Abdul Rahman al-Iryani.

Al-Iryani was deposed by a coup d'état in 1974 and went into exile in Syria. The coup plotters, led by Colonel Ibrahim al-Hamdi, suspended the constitution and installed a military council to rule the country. Al-Hamdi was assassinated in October 1977. His former chief of staff, Ahmed Hussein al-Ghashmi, succeeded him. In June 1978, a South Yemeni agent killed al-Ghashmi with a bomb planted in a briefcase. Saleh, a charismatic army officer stationed in Taiz, traveled to Sanaa, North Yemen's capital, and convinced military leaders to back his candidacy and the Yemeni parliament to elect him president.

Following the colonization of Aden, the British extended their reach through-out South Yemen, incorporating the country into British India. As the years pro-gressed, Aden became a largely Indian city as the British imported laborers from the subcontinent. In 1937, the British separated South Yemen from India. The British established the Federation of South Arabia in 1962, incorporating its colonial ter-ritories in and around Aden with the surrounding tribal lands. The Federation did not last long. Following World War II, sustained opposition to British rule developed in South Yemen. By 1965, this opposition became violent. The two principal inde-pendence groups, the Front for the Liberation of Occupied South Yemen (FLOSY) and the National Liberation Front (NLF), initiated attacks on British forces. Two years later, the British withdrew, as did much of the colony's foreign labor force. As the struggle for independence neared its end, the NLF eclipsed the FLOSY and on November 30, 1967, declared South Yemen's independence. The Federation of South Arabia became the People's Republic of South Yemen. The NLF instituted a one-party state under Qahtan Muhammad al-Shaabi. In 1969, al-Shaabi was de-posed by a Marxist faction of the NLF led by Salem Ali Rubayi. Rubayi took over the leadership and the next year changed the country's name again, this time to the People's Democratic Republic of Yemen (PDRY).

As the fighting between royalist and republican factions raged on in North Yemen, South Yemen went in an entirely different direction. Instead of looking to Egypt or Saudi Arabia, Rubayi aligned the PDRY with the Soviet Union and other communist countries. Internal crackdowns, meanwhile, persuaded thousands of South Yemenis to flee north. In 1972, border clashes between North and South Yemen nearly led to full-scale war. The dispute ended peacefully, with a ceasefire arranged by the Arab League, and the leaders of the YAR and PDRY declared their intention to unify. Despite this pledge, unity was still eighteen years away.

In 1978, Rubayi was overthrown and executed. Abdul Fattah Ismail emerged to lead South Yemen and replaced the NLF with the Yemeni Socialist Party (YSP). Renewed border clashes between the PDRY and the YAR led to another Arab League–sponsored truce and a new unity pledge. Nevertheless, the PDRY supported a leftist insurgency in North Yemen. In 1980, Ismail went into exile, and Ali Nasir Muhammad took leadership of the PDRY. Once installed, Muhammad took a less confrontational approach with North Yemen, withdrawing the PDRY's backing of the insurgency.

In 1986, civil war broke out in South Yemen as Ismail returned from overseas and with his supporters sought to reclaim control of the country from Muhammad. Though Ismail was killed in the month-long conflict, Muhammad was deposed and fled to North Yemen with about sixty thousand loyalists. Among the few in the leadership ranks of the YSP to survive the violence, Ali Salim al-Bidh, a member of the Ismail faction, became South Yemen's new head of state.

Faced with diminishing aid from the Soviets and the prospects of oil reserves along the shared border, al-Bidh pursued unification with Saleh's North Yemen. After negotiations, a framework for unity was established in 1988 and a proposed constitution approved in 1989. Finally, on May 22, 1990, with Saleh as president and al-Bidh as vice president, the Republic of Yemen was officially declared. The following year, the people approved the constitution in a national referendum and in 1993 voted for a national parliament.

Despite these hopeful developments, the Republic of Yemen, like its forbears, showed a marked lack of stability. Al-Bidh, claiming the south was being marginalized, withdrew to Aden in 1994. On May 21, he declared the Democratic Republic of Yemen in an attempt to restore South Yemen's sovereignty. The military forces of the YAR and PDRY had never been integrated and soon massed on their former borders. Clashes erupted, and over the next two months, aided by Muhammad's supporters, Saleh's northern forces drove south, capturing Aden on July 7.

With his power secure, Saleh won the presidency by vote of parliament on October 1, 1994. He claimed a second five-year term through a national election in April 1999. That term was extended to seven years by constitutional amendment in 2000, and in 2006 he was reelected.

Though he has managed to hold onto power for more than thirty years, Saleh has had few achievements other than his longevity. In a fractious country, he has maintained an uneasy peace by essentially buying it, instituting a complicated system of bribery and providing regular payoffs to tribal leaders in exchange for votes and acquiescence. Official corruption is rampant, with those closest to Saleh using their positions to enrich themselves. Meanwhile, South Yemen has yet to be fully pacified. Though Saleh is a Zaidi himself, his rule has been challenged in the north by supporters of the Zaidi cleric Hussein al-Houthi. The conflicts between Houthis and Yemeni security forces have resulted in thousands of casualties. The disorder in the country has made it a useful base for al-Qaeda terrorists, who have launched numerous attacks from Yemen since 1992, including the suicide bombing of the U.S.S. *Cole* in October 2000.

Arab Spring protests in Yemen first occurred in January 2011 as demonstrators, inspired by events in Tunisia, called for Saleh to resign. The regime responded with violence and repression, and Saleh instituted a state of emergency. In the face of this brutality, high-level operatives in the government and military began to defect to the opposition, and more and more people joined the protests. By March 2011, his situation becoming untenable, Saleh opened talks with the opposition only to break them off soon afterward. In June, a rocket attack on the presidential compound severely wounded Saleh and before long, forced him to leave the country for medical treatment in Saudi Arabia.

Saleh returned to Yemen in September, but his grip on power was slipping. On November 23, 2011, he signed a pledge to cede authority to his vice president, Abdrabbuh Mansour Hadi, and a national unity government in exchange for immunity from prosecution. Despite the pledge, many doubted Saleh's sincerity and expected he would find some way to sabotage the deal and cling to power. In January 2012, Saleh left Yemen to seek medical care in the United States but vowed to return in time to lead his party in the new presidential elections scheduled for February 2012.

Whether Yemen has truly entered the post-Saleh era is unclear as of this writing. Equally unclear is what a post-Saleh era will look like and whether it will yield better outcomes than the dictatorship. Saleh has not left many enduring institutions. Poverty, illiteracy, and malnutrition are rampant. Filkins, writing in the *New Yorker*, observed, "Yemen is not Egypt: it has virtually no middle class, a weak civil society, a marginal intelligentsia, and no public institutions that operate independently of Saleh."

The divisions and instability in Yemen—a separatist movement in the south and a fundamentalist insurgency in the north, combined with well-armed and loosely governed tribal groups—have led many observers to worry that the country could descend into chaos. Some have even suggested that Yemen is in danger of becoming a failed state, another Afghanistan or Somalia. The human toll of such a potentiality would be enormous. With its lack of resources, comparative isolation, and large but impoverished population, Yemen is uniquely ill-equipped to weather increased and sustained deprivation. Given such concerns, Yemen stands as one of the Arab Spring's more worrisome iterations.

Chill Winds Follow Dawn of the Arab Spring

By Brian Dooley, Nick Redmayne, and a special correspondent in
Damascus
The Middle East, July 2011

While Tunisians and Egyptians are adjusting to a new era of democracy, others in the region continue to petition for social and political reforms. In this issue, three TME contributors send their on-the-spot reports from Bahrain, Benghazi and Damascus.

From Brian Dooley in Manama, Bahrain

You wonder if the men who come to arrest people in the middle of the night wear black ski masks because Bahrain is so small they might be recognised when out shopping with their families. No one seems to know exactly how many people have been seized like this in the last few months—the government told me it didn't really know, what with new people being arrested virtually every day.

Since 14 February, around 1,000 people have been detained in a government crackdown against reformers.

The protestors were overwhelmingly Shi'ite Muslims, as are the majority of Bahrainis, calling for a democratically elected government and an end to discrimination in employment and other areas of Bahraini life.

The government broke up the reform protests—centred around Manama's Pearl Roundabout—in a crackdown marked by excessive force: at least seven people were killed. Certain elements started to call for more radical reforms, including an end to the monarchical rule of the Sunni Al Khalifa dynasty. Some protests turned violent, and there are reports a number of anti-government protesters entered the university and attacked students and Asian migrant workers. More injuries and three deaths were reported.

The country's security forces, backed by 1,000 troops from neighbouring Saudi Arabia, stormed protestors at the Pearl Roundabout area and cleared pro-reform demonstrators in a show of force, causing further injuries and deaths.

Since then, the country has seen a wave of arbitrary arrests, widespread and credible reports of torture, attacks on Shi'ite religious sites, large numbers of people suspended or fired from their jobs, at least four deaths in custody, and a number of other deaths of civilians on the street under suspicious circumstances.

Risky situations

The Bahraini government has put dozens of people on trial in military courts, and two Shi'ite men have been sentenced to death. Bahrain's King Hamad bin 'Isa Al Khalifa lifted the State of National Safety, announced on 15 March, on 1 June, two days before a decision was taken by the Grand Prix authorities to allow the Bahrain event [postponed from March because of the conflict] to go ahead towards the end of 2011 if political conditions allow.

Doctors and other health professionals have been particularly targeted. Medicine is a common career for Bahraini Shias, who are prevented from employment opportunities in many areas of the government and other professions.

One medical professional, a woman, took substantial risks in telling me what happened to her.

Her treatment in custody is typical of the many reports emerging from those who have been released:

> *"Four masked men came and took me for an interrogation from the hospital where I was working. They blindfolded me and took me to the Investigation Office. They were verbally abusing me, saying the doctors at the hospital were sectarian, only treating Shi'ite patients—I was blindfolded the whole time.*

> *They wanted me to say that doctors took injured people for operations unnecessarily, claiming those with very minor injuries were made worse on purpose, resulting in death in two cases.*

> *They said we wanted to hurt Bahrain's international reputation. I said no, patients were really bleeding badly, some from live ammunition wounds, and we didn't make their wounds worse.*

> *The policewoman started to beat me. They took me to another office—I was standing the whole time, about three hours. It was terrifying; I was hoping I'd die. You don't know how long it will continue, what they will do next. They repeat the same questions over and over and if they don't get the answer they want they beat you.*

> *They accused me of taking drugs from the hospital to the medical tent at Pearl Roundabout [where there was a makeshift medical centre]. I said I had not, but still I was badly beaten and told I was a whore and my mother was a whore. The interrogation went on all night except when they made me sing the national anthem and other songs.*

> *In the early hours of the morning they let me lift my blindfold just enough to sign something, though I wasn't allowed to read what it said. The next day I was taken by the military police for further interrogation and then I to sign something else I couldn't read. I was finally moved to jail where the other detainees were. They didn't allow me to call my family for a week. I was begging them to call my children, who were alone, but they refused.*

> *After some weeks in jail I was taken—with a group of other detainees—back to the Investigation Office. We were terrified. They took more than a dozen of us. We were called in to a room one by one. I had to sign a document to say I hadn't been beaten. Then, about midnight, I was released."*

Legal proceedings

The US government has been notably muted in its criticism of the crackdown.

To many pro-democracy activists in Bahrain there has been a frustrating double standard used by the Obama Administration, which for many weeks had been vague and unspecific in its tepid condemnation of the Bahraini government's abuses while outspoken on violations in Libya, Syria, Tunisia and eventually Egypt.

> **The Bahraini government has put dozens of people on trial in military courts, and two Shi'ite men have been sentenced to death.**

The President did finally get specific in mid-May, criticising the attacks on Shia mosques and other Shia places of worship, more than two dozen of which were demolished between the start of April and the middle of May.

The lifting of the State of Safety in June might make little real difference. Bahrain's military courts will still be sitting, processing hundreds of cases, including a prominent show trial of 21 leading government opponents. An assortment of human rights defenders, bloggers and political opposition leaders are being tried under heavy security for charges including 'insulting the military.' Some of them claim they have been severely tortured and threatened with death.

According to the law, the King must sign the final death warrants before anyone faces a firing squad.

Some are relying on a magnanimous gesture from him, commuting the sentences, as a signal that the line has been drawn under the protests and that it is time for Bahrain to move on; others remain sceptical.

Nick Redmayne reports from Benghazi

Walking towards the heart of revolutionary Libya on Benghazi's corniche, I'm accosted by Bashir, a former flight officer with Libyan Arab Airlines. Bashir picks up a plastic bottle from a pile of rubbish, "It makes me ashamed. Still it's 42 years, 42 years can you believe it? To think we'll be in good shape after three months, it's too much."

Save for localised attempts at acrid incineration, refuse has been piling up in parts of the city. With government tanks poised to crush the uprising, the Keep Benghazi Tidy campaign has understandably taken a back seat.

However, change may be afoot. A few hundred metres from the Mediterranean, Ibrahim is overseeing a group of boys wearing fluorescent jackets. Some sweep walkways, others paint kerbstones alternately black and white. "Because of the problems, the schools are closed right now. We give them something useful to do. Our association is organising to make the city better. Do you want to see our office?"

Five minutes' drive later, in a middle-class Benghazi suburb, a small office is proudly emblazoned 'Ras Abaydah Charitable Association.' Inside, 21-year-old Mohammed speaks English clearly and deliberately. "We have a mixture of people helping, doctors, accountants like Ibrahim—all kinds of people. Younger people help us with the cleaning, painting, things like that." I follow Mohammed across the street, where he opens the doors to the local headquarters of the former Revolutionary Committee—the insidious eyes and ears of the ruling regime in Ras Abaydah. "We're taking this over. Can you believe this place? I've lived here all my life and it's only now that I get to see inside." In one room an older man sits filling plastic bags with sugar from a sack. In another, piles of basic foodstuffs await distribution. Mohammed points to a black bin liner and says, "Since the revolution, prices have increased so much. We give out about 150 of these to underprivileged families each month." Another helper opens the bag and displays the contents—tea, pasta, tinned fish and rice. "We buy this food with donations, or sometimes food arrives at the port and we get a telephone call to collect it." On the next floor, Mohammed shows me a corridor of smaller rooms. "Here we plan a clinic, 13 consulting rooms—there's plenty of space. Of course we can't do all this at once, but slowly. Maybe after three or four months, giving food to the people, there will not be such a thing, but the other work will continue for a long time."

Outside, another young man, Abdul Salam, is taking the breeze in front of his home. I ask how life has been in this part of Benghazi. "It's hard. I have three friends missing—alive or dead? But I don't know anyone who is affected mentally in a bad way. They all share the same idea. They are sad about the injuries, they are sad about the young people dying, but in general it's worth it, there is a price to pay and it's worth it, and everybody understands it."

Walking back to the car, we pass a Bedouin tent somewhat incongruously erected on wasteland. A middle aged man, Abu Faris, sits at the entrance and motions to me to sit down, proffering coffee. "What are you doing here?" I ask. "Right now we take it in shifts to check who is coming, who is going—we look after each other." "How long will you be here?" I ask. Abu Faris takes a contemplative sip of his coffee. "You know, we as Libyans are a great tree, that for so, so, so long has not been watered. Now, maybe by Allah, maybe by what has been going on around us, maybe because we arrive at a moment and we're just fed up, but it's started. We have been watered. And in our roots there's still life. When Gaddafi goes, then we'll take this tent down and return to our homes."

From a special correspondent in Damascus

Day by day, the Assad regime comes under increased pressure as revolution sweeps across the country and the regime intensifies its crackdown on the demonstrations. Since the start of protests, the Assad regime had been utilising security personnel detached from the majority of Syria's population to do their dirty work. But their numbers cannot any longer keep up with the increasing multitudes of demonstrators, who are spread across large and distanced geographical locations.

In the beginning, the Assad regime used only Maher Al Assad's Fourth Division, and the Republican Guards, handpicked and trained specifically to follow the Assad family's orders. Later, it began using Iranian Revolutionary Guards and Hizbullah militia, Ba'ath party members, and Al Shabbiha, the Assad-sponsored thugs, to quell the national uprising.

Taking sides

The Assad regime was forced to turn to such 'foot soldiers' after numerous incidents where the Syrian Army refused to shoot unarmed civilians. There are reports of soldiers executed by security agents accompanying army divisions for not shooting at protesters, and others of soldiers joining the protesters and shooting security agents. In one incident, it is rumoured, a soldier shot Jameel Assad, one of the President's cousins and head of one of the regime's 15 security agencies, for ordering brutal attacks against unarmed civilians.

Thus, with its inability to trust the regular army, the regime had been shuffling the same units between Dera, Latakia, Banias and Homs, killing hundreds and arresting thousands more, while trying to cause discord between the army and the people.

The number of protesters killed by the ruling regime is escalating by the day, despite official denials. Mass graves had to be dug in Dera: meanwhile, in Latakia, fire trucks were employed to clean the blood off the streets. The number of 'missing' is now so large that the detained are housed in private warehouses rented by the regime in Homs, and grain silos in Dera.

However, although thousands are dead and missing, there are millions more who continue to fight against their oppressors. Most low-ranking soldiers are against the Assad regime and are only in uniform because of Syria's mandatory army recruitment system.

When all else fails and the Assad regime has to utilise them to suppress protests in 'critical' areas such as Deir Ez-Zor, Hama, Hasakeh, Ar-Raqqa, and Idlib, defections and dissentions—already at an all-time high—will soar.

The regime knows morale is nonexistent and desperate to throw a cloak of secrecy over events such as the Fifth Division commander and a handful of his soldiers who managed to wreak major damage on the ranks of the Fourth Division in Dera before being wiped out for their refusal to slaughter innocent civilians.

If the regime wishes to avoid other such scenarios, it might only use its Fourth Division, Republican Guard, Shabbiha, Ba'athis, and hired thugs, but these will eventually dwindle and collapse.

Inclusion of Bashar Al Assad in the newly imposed sanctions by the US and the EU is a new development but more international support is needed at this crucial point. Support for the Assad regime needs to be dismantled piece by piece if further 'official' murder and mayhem is to be avoided.

Bahrain Commission Issues Brutal Critique of Arab Spring Crackdown

By Elizabeth Dickinson
The Christian Science Monitor, November 23, 2011

An independent commission presented its findings to Bahrain's king, offering the tiny Gulf country a road map for moving beyond the violence of recent months and repairing relations with the US.

An independent commission in Bahrain today documented abuses by the country's security forces during Arab Spring uprisings and offered a set of recommendations that could help the oil-rich kingdom restore its image with Western allies.

Before an audience that included the king, dignitaries, activists, and foreign media, the head of the Bahrain Independent Commission of Inquiry (BICI)—respected Egyptian lawyer M. Cherif Bassiouni—also decried a culture of impunity among the country's leaders. Mr. Bassiouni called for another independent body to ensure that changes are made to prevent a repeat of the violence.

How the report is implemented will affect not just the 1.2 million inhabitants of this tiny Gulf peninsula, but the country's geopolitical future as well. The United States, which houses its Fifth Fleet in Bahrain, suspended a $53 million arms sale pending the report's findings. Acting on the recommendations may be Bahrain's last hope to put the violence behind it.

"In every crisis, there do come forks in the road," says Salman Shaikh, head of the Brookings Institution in Doha. "On one path you get to an intensification, and then the other path does offer an opportunity for compromise and to make progress. This report does offer that [opportunity] because we all know that we needed something that would help a new political agreement, and that is first and foremost what is needed.

"If [these] recommendations are taken seriously, then you may well find that you're able to turn the corner."

Systemic abuses

The BICI, established June 29 with a budget of $1.3 million, was part of the government's response to protests that rocked Bahrain since majority Shiite protesters first took to the streets to demand a more representative government in February.

Drawing on 9,000 testimonies, the 500-page report offers an extensive chronology of events, documenting 46 deaths, 559 allegations of torture, and more than 4,000 cases of employees in both the public and private sector being dismissed for participating in protests. It also criticized the security forces for many instances when "force and firearms were used in an excessive manner that was, on many occasions, unnecessary, disproportionate, and indiscriminate."

For example, hooded men systematically broke into suspects' houses between 1 a.m. and 3 a.m., "terrorizing" the inhabitants, the report says.

Torture is also documented explicitly. Cases of electrocution, stress positions, hanging, beating detainees on the soles of their feet, and verbal abuse were among the violations cited.

> *Torture is also documented explicitly. Cases of electrocution, stress positions, hanging, beating detainees on the soles of their feet, and verbal abuse were among the violations cited.*

Notably, it found that certain abuses, such as destruction of property, "could not have happened without the knowledge of higher echelons of the command structure"—an indication that abuses were systemic.

Bassiouni blamed the Sunni government's crackdown—which has included such tactics as night raids and the dismantling of religious structures—for exacerbating sectarian tensions in the Shiite-majority country. The report also discredited the government's arguments that the unrest had been stirred by Shiite Iran.

Speaking immediately after Bassiouni, King Hamad bin Isa Al Khalifa promised to examine the report and use it as a template for reform: " . . . we are determined, God willing, to insure that the painful events are not to be repeated, but that we learn from them and use our new insights as a catalyst for positive change," he told the audience. He vowed to set up a committee to examine the report and propose recommendations "urgently."

Last-ditch effort?

The report was seen as a last-ditch attempt to bring Bahrain's increasingly polarized sides together. Past concessions from the regime and attempts at dialogue have all fallen flat—in large part because the crackdown has continued.

To this end, the commission's findings included recommendations for establishing an independent body to implement reforms, training for security forces in upholding international human rights standards, compensation for victims, and the separation of the judiciary from the interior ministry.

Responding to these suggestions, the king promised to "waste no time in benefiting from [the commission's] work . . . your report provides a historical opportunity for Bahrain to deal with issues that are both serious and urgent."

Activists skeptical

Yet opposition activists remained skeptical that promises would come to fruition given that past promises remain unfulfilled, says Said Yousif, a member of the Bahrain Center for Human Rights.

"The king promised back in February to make an investigation and all that, but it seems to be that there was no change," says Mr. Yousif. "We hope that this time Bassiouni's recommendations will be implemented . . . Our [past] experience is different, but let's be optimistic."

Indeed, while the report was released to great fanfare at the king's Safriya Palace, on the streets of Manama, the mood was tense. By mid-morning, several small protests had erupted and security forces responded with tear gas.

Human rights activists say that the continued suppression of protests is just one example of how the same violations the commission is intended to report on continue unabated. "There are still violations ongoing," said Nabeel Rajab, president of the Bahrain Center for Human Rights. "This shows that [the government] doesn't yet have the political willingness to change things."

Political opposition cautiously optimistic

The main political opposition, Al-Wefaq, expressed cautious hope. Jassim Hussain, a former Wefaq member of parliament who resigned after the violent crackdown, says that his party was still interested in negotiating with the government to find a way out of the current political deadlock.

"I think [we have] made it very clear that dialogue is the only way forward," he says. "But for now, the ball is in the government's court."

The opposition's demands are relatively modest: Hussein says that Wefaq would like to see a more representative and responsive government, for example with a stronger parliament. Wefaq is also demanding an independent judiciary and a halt to what they see as the gerrymandering of voting districts.

Some analysts worry, however, that Bahrain has become too polarized for dialogue to even be an option. "It's not just regime and the protesters anymore," says Joost Hiltermann of the International Crisis Group. "Within those camps, you have the hard-liners and the doves." The intervening months of violence and mistrust, he argues, have empowered the hard-liners on both sides.

Within the regime, Hiltermann says that those who favor a harsh crackdown are "solidly on the saddle." And on the streets, he says, "A lot of people are not going to support Wefaq because they don't believe that they represent them. If Wefaq tries to represent 'the opposition,' they might well face street protests against them. They have to be very, very careful."

Divided They Stand

Yemen's fractured protest movement

By Haley Sweetland Edwards
The New Republic, April 28, 2011

On a recent rainy afternoon at the anti-government protest in Yemen's capital, an old tribesman, dressed in a long white robe belted at the waist with a foot-long dagger, danced hand-to-hand with a young man wearing tight jeans and a khaki jacket, more Williamsburg than Arabian Peninsula. The two men hopped and whirled in tight circles, their shoulders draped in Yemen's tricolor flag, their bare feet scuffing in unison on the dusty asphalt. In time with the music, the old tribesman brandished his dagger, slicing circles in the wet air, while the young man, daggerless, shook a red index card above his head like a referee, a potent symbol to anyone familiar with the universal language of soccer. "Red card!" he yelled in English. "Ali Abdullah Saleh, you're out!"

Walking the length of the mile-long intersection in front of Sana'a University—the epicenter of the anti-government protests and a place that resembles something between a music festival, a campaign headquarters, and a battleground—I'd gotten used to seeing such incongruous scenes. Just a few days before, I'd stumbled into a beige, wedding-style tent, where about three dozen protesters were sharing plates of chicken and rice. Upon discovering that I was a journalist, they erupted in a cacophony of opinions, thrusting their laminated ID cards at me, hoping to get their names in the paper. This group included a member of the Yemeni Socialist Party, an imam, an English teacher, and a member of Al Islah, Yemen's Islamist party. One young man, Yahya Mekhlafi, a political science student who quoted Montesquieu by heart, sat shoulder-to-shoulder with Thabit Hassan Al Sakkaf, a former tank driver who hadn't made it past elementary school. "We are all one now," says Mekhlafi in English. "Brothers," confirms Al Sakkaf in Arabic.

For 33 years, Ali Abdullah Saleh has ruled this fractious place by playing Yemen's factions off one another, arming rival tribes and encouraging local conflicts—a Machiavellian two-step that he once famously dubbed "dancing on the heads of snakes." In the past two months, however, a startling array of Yemeni citizens have gathered in huge protests to oust him—tribesmen and hipsters, socialists and radical Islamists, feminists and separatists, and rebels and former military officers. "We have figured out Saleh's game," a young protester named Anwar Al Kabodi tells me. "He is our only enemy now." But, while this newfound solidarity

---

has made Yemen's revolution possible, it may also, in the long run,
prove to be its greatest weakness.

I was deported from Yemen in
March, along with other Western
reporters. During my time there—
nearly a year altogether—I sometimes found it hard to think of this
nation of 24 million people as a
single country. Driving south from
the Saudi Arabian border, through
Sana'a and the eastern desert,

> *For 33 years, Ali Abdullah Saleh
> has ruled this fractious place by
> playing Yemen's factions off one
> another, arming rival tribes and
> encouraging local conflicts—a
> Machiavellian two-step that he
> once famously dubbed "dancing
> on the heads of snakes."*

through the painted canyons of the Hadramaut, and down to the rugged coastline
along the Arabian Sea, I have seen people's relationships to the central government,
to Islam, and to traditional tribal law change dramatically within the space of a few
hours. A post-Saleh Yemen would somehow have to be constructed out of these conflicting cultures and political forces.

The protests, as in Egypt and Tunisia, were jump-started by small groups of
disaffected young people, mostly from the western cities of Taiz, Aden, and Sana'a,
who felt alienated by the corruption and economic stagnation fostered by Saleh's
government. While these groups haven't formed a single organization, they share a
common goal: turning their homeland into a transparent and representative democracy. Last month, at the protests, a human rights lawyer described to me his vision
of a pluralistic, tolerant Yemen. After a while, though, I could barely hear him over
the sound of an Islamist preacher, his voice amplified by a crackling megaphone,
giving a sermon about how Yemen should be governed by sharia law.

Many of the young protesters I spoke to feared that their movement would be
co-opted by ultra-conservative Islamists—that is, the popular Al Islah Party, ubiquitous Salafi organizations, and sympathetic politicians, tribal leaders, and military
officers. One day, I watched Sheik Abd Majid Al Zindani, a radical cleric who has
been named a terrorist by the U.S. Treasury Department, climb onto the protesters'
central stage and give a bombastic speech envisioning Yemen as an Islamist caliph-
ate. Over the years, Zindani has advocated for morality patrols, rallied against legislation that would have banned child marriage, and threatened "global jihad" against
the United States. His words elicited both cheering and visible discomfort. "They're
going to think we're all terrorists," whispers Yahya Ali Ali, a student at Sana'a University. "Not all of us have this opinion."

Another major force is Yemen's powerful tribes, who have for decades sustained
themselves on a well-greased patronage system. In his heyday, Saleh provided important sheikhs with cash, cars, weapons, and an occasional school or paved road in
their region in exchange for their loyalty. This system worked rather well until this
past decade, when Saleh all but ran out of money. In late February, I met Hamid Al
Ahmar, a wealthy businessman in his palatial, Mediterranean villa-style mansion in
Sana'a. Hamid is the brother of Sadiq Al Ahmar, who heads Yemen's most powerful

tribal coalition, the Hashid Confederation. "We believe in a constitution in Yemen and institutions," Hamid told me. "It should be a good democracy." Yet sheikhs like Hamid Al Ahmar only stand to lose from such a system. They would, however, profit from having a new, wealthier strongman with whom to do business. "It's still in the tribes' interest to have a leader who is dependent on their demands," says Abdul Ghani Al Eryani, a Yemeni political analyst. "It's clear they do not foresee a democracy where they will be equal to every other person in the country."

Then there are the local tribal sheikhs, like 27-year-old Nasser Saber from Marib—a gas-rich region of impoverished villages, most of which lack electricity. Justice is dispensed by a council of local men according to a mix of ultraconservative tribal traditions and sharia law. I met Saber outside a hole-in-the-wall tea shop a block away from the protest. He came to Sana'a in the name of democracy, but his true priority is to provide his people with the services they need. He shares common ground with the youth movement and with powerful Islamist factions in the opposition.

There are regional divisions, too. The most obvious is in the south, where the tribes are less dominant: The region was an independent socialist republic until 1990, when it unified with Saleh's north Yemen. In 1994, the south tried to secede from the new union, but Saleh and his long-time ally Major General Ali Muhsin Al Ahmar recruited tribes and Islamists as mercenaries to brutally crush the socialists. For the last few years, much of the south has been outside of Saleh's control; it's here that Anwar Al Awlaki is believed to be hiding. For southern leaders, forming a government alongside tribal sheikhs and Islamists will be tough. Making matters more difficult, the southerners' nemesis, Al Ahmar, publicly joined the opposition in March.

Perhaps the most unpredictable player in this already volatile scene is an emboldened Al Qaeda of the Arabian Peninsula, one of the terrorist organization's strongest regional arms. The group has planned several attacks in Saudi Arabia and the United States, including, most recently, a thwarted plot last October to send bombs in UPS and FedEx packages to Chicago synagogues. Any new government in Yemen would have to contend with the group's growing influence.

In Sana'a, some of the young activists like to hang out at a posh coffee shop with a walled garden overflowing with bougainvillea. I spent an afternoon there with Sarah, a 23-year-old in a blue hijab. She asked that I not use her last name to protect her and her family. Sarah has a degree in sociology and cited Winston Churchill in her defense of a free society. Like many other young people, she is wary of the Islamist clerics and tribesmen who have rallied behind the youth's cause. "The tribes are motivated by blood, revenge, and power, that's all," she explains. "We are fighting for democracy beside people who don't have any interest in democracy."

❖

Haley Sweetland Edwards is a journalist living in Tbilisi, Georgia. She recently lived in Yemen on a grant from the Pulitzer Center for Crisis Reporting.

Yemeni President Hands over Power, but Little Changes

By Sudarsan Raghavan
The Washington Post, December 3, 2011

More than a week after President Ali Abdullah Saleh handed over authority to his vice president, the autocrat still exerts enormous presidential power, issuing decrees and engaging with world leaders. His family still controls the security forces, which activists say have continued to arrest and kill protesters. His portrait still hangs ubiquitously around the capital.

"Nothing has changed," declared Walid al-Ammari, 30, a Web designer and a leader of the protest movement demanding an end to Saleh's 33-year rule. "He's still the one giving the orders."

Even as the Obama administration and its allies applaud the power-transfer deal they pushed for as a major step toward a peaceful political transition, violence and mistrust continue to grip Yemen. The activists who spearheaded Yemen's 10-month-old populist revolt view the agreement as the latest attempt by Saleh to extend his rule over this Persian Gulf nation, which is plagued by poverty, a determined al-Qaeda franchise and an emerging humanitarian crisis.

"When we look at his history as president, he always maneuvers," Ammari said. "What he's doing now is rearranging his cards to play another game."

If Saleh remains influential, in whatever capacity, it could further divide Yemeni society and plunge the nation deeper into chaos. The United States fears that al-Qaeda might take advantage of the turmoil to create a haven from which to target the West.

On Saturday, violence again erupted in the south-central city of Taiz, a cradle of the rebellion, as government forces killed two civilians in a third straight day of shelling, which threatens to derail the agreement. In recent days, street battles between anti-government tribesmen and government soldiers have forced dozens of families to flee and left more than 15 people dead, medical workers and local officials said.

Mohammed Basindwa, an opposition politician who was appointed prime minister and tasked with forming a unity government, warned that "the continuous criminal shelling on the people of Taiz is an intentional act to foil the agreement." Basindwa called on Vice President Abed Rabbo Mansour Hadi, to whom Saleh has transferred his powers, to order an immediate end to the killings or else, he said, "we will reconsider our stances."

'Guarantor of security'

Saleh's loyalists insist he is sincere about ceding presidential authority, but they say he will be influential in Yemen in the months and years ahead. Even if the agreement holds, Saleh will remain head of the ruling party, with Hadi as his lieutenant.

"Ali Abdullah Saleh is a guarantor of security, and he brings balance in the Yemeni society," said Aref Al-Zouka, a senior ruling party official. "He has a right to play an influential role."

Al-Zouka blamed the opposition for the violence in Taiz and accused it of trying to sabotage the agreement, which was brokered by Yemen's gulf neighbors.

Even as the Obama administration and its allies applaud the power-transfer deal they pushed for as a major step toward a peaceful political transition, violence and mistrust continue to grip Yemen.

Three times, Saleh backed out of signing the deal. But after being threatened with sanctions and a freezing of his and his family's assets, he signed on Nov. 23 in the Saudi Arabian capital, Riyadh, in a ceremony witnessed by Saudi King Abdullah and Western and Arab ambassadors.

The deal allows Saleh to retain his title until elections, which are scheduled for February. But it also called for Hadi to immediately take over as interim leader. For the moment, the opposition and ruling party have agreed that Hadi will be the only candidate and would run the country for two years as a transitional figure until the next elections.

The agreement, though, was signed without input from Yemen's street activists or powerful regional groups. Both have rejected the deal, because it gives Saleh and his family immunity from prosecution and does not require a complete government overhaul.

"We will remain in the streets until we eliminate the whole regime," said Ali Saif al-Duba'i, 52, a merchant turned activist.

If the agreement holds, Saleh would become the fourth Arab autocrat to be ousted this year.

But since giving up formal authority, Saleh has sent telegrams to world leaders and ordered a governmental probe into an attack on protesters. He has also declared a general amnesty for those who committed "stupidities" during the revolt, with one exception: those behind the June bombing inside his presidential compound that seriously wounded him.

Even if he retires after the vote, many Yemenis are convinced Saleh will wield power behind the scenes. And many question whether Hadi has the strength to break away from Saleh and his family.

"Saleh will not let anybody make decisions freely," predicted Abdulla Almutareb, a businessman. "He will interfere with everything. For 33 years he's been involved in everything. It will not be easy for him to step down and keep quiet."

So far, the unity government has amounted to a reshuffling of political elites.

On Thursday, officials announced the composition of the unity government. The ruling party would remain in charge of key ministries such as defense, foreign affairs and oil, while opposition figures—many of whom have held posts in Saleh's government—would get the interior, finance and education ministries.

Protesters say the leaders of Yemen's traditional opposition have hijacked the uprising. "It disappointed a lot of hopes," said Ammari, referring to the agreement. "They have divided the power. Now, the opposition is sharing power with the gangsters and the militias."

Senior opposition figures say they want significant changes in a post-Saleh Yemen but are deeply concerned that Saleh will seek to retain control. A smooth transition, they say, is possible only if the United States, Europe and Saudi Arabia apply constant pressure.

"They need to send two clear messages. The first is to Hadi: 'Go ahead. Do not hesitate. The international community is behind you,'" said Sakhr Al-Wajeeh, a senior opposition leader. "The second message is to Saleh and his family: 'If you play from behind the scenes, there will be consequences for you.'"

Clampdown in Bahrain

When protesters called for a republic, the US position changed, allowing a Saudi invasion.

By Scheherezade Faramarzi
The Nation, September 12, 2011

The trial was like a scene from a bad play: for seven hours in June, third-rate actors played the roles of unscrupulous prosecutors and a military judge fabricating evidence to convict twenty doctors and medical staff of trying to overthrow the Bahrain monarchy. The judge scolded defense attorneys when they cross-examined state witnesses, who testified under oath that Shiite Muslim medics had occupied Bahrain's main hospital and denied treatment to Sunni patients. He either objected to the questions or responded to them himself.

Of course, the court session in the capital of Manama was no act. Bahrain's justice system was using flimsy evidence to punish and humiliate not only health workers who'd treated injured antigovernment protesters during last winter's pro-democracy rally but also anyone who stood against the monarchy. At least thirty-three people have been killed in the unrest since the uprising erupted on February 14 in the capital's Pearl Square, with many protesters demanding a republic. Hundreds more have been wounded, many severely beaten by security forces while in the hospital, according to human rights groups.

"Who are these people prosecuting us, judging us?" Dr. B., one of the accused, remembers thinking as she and other defendants watched the surreal proceedings. "It's scary what they're capable of doing. The security forces shoot people, put bullets in their heads and then accuse doctors of breaking and smashing their brains and causing their death." Dr. B., who asked not to be identified to avoid government retaliation, had to sign a paper pledging not to speak to the media when she was released on bail after nearly two months in jail. "It looks like I'm with the worst actors in the world, like when you go to theater. It's so boring. But I have to watch it." If convicted on various national security charges, she and other defendants could be sentenced to as many as 130 years. At a minimum, they could be jailed 15–20 years.

After police killed at least five people three days after the protests began, demonstrators wanted nothing less than to tear down the whole system. They made dialogue with the government conditional on the ouster of King Hamad bin Isa al-Khalifa. The radical shift in their demands played into the hands of Saudi Arabia, which from the outset had opposed any reform. With a green light from the United

> *After police killed at least five people three days after the protest began, demonstrators wanted nothing less than to tear down the whole system.*

States, the Saudi-led invasion by the Gulf Cooperation Council (GCC) on March 14 killed any hope of reform and democracy. The troops arrived right after a visit to Bahrain by former US Defense Secretary Robert Gates. As host to the US Navy's Fifth Fleet, Bahrain is a key US logistical and command center not only for the Gulf but for operations in Iraq, Afghanistan and the Indian Ocean.

The crackdown did not end in Pearl Square. The government has since been carrying out a systematic campaign of violent repression against its citizens, which was not eased by the lifting of the state of emergency on June 1. Security forces are still deployed in the streets, protests are violently attacked, military trials continue, people are still arrested and tortured (several have died in custody), and Bahrain state television continues to sow sectarian hatred against Shiites.

The crackdown hasn't spared Shiite mosques: scores have been destroyed or seriously damaged, allegedly for not having building permits, giving credence to the common view that the government is trying to bring Shiites to their knees. With most activist leaders languishing in jail, Bahrain's opposition is all but crippled. Wefaq, the country's main Shiite opposition party, pulled out of the national dialogue in July and has said it will boycott a special parliamentary election scheduled for September.

Despite government attempts to polish its image, protests continue in villages outside Manama, which "send a message—especially to reporters and policy-makers—that Bahrain will never be stable if grievances are not addressed," says Husain Abdulla, director of the Washington-based Americans for Democracy and Human Rights in Bahrain. He says the underground resistance, mostly by youth, relies on Facebook, Twitter and websites like bahrainonline.org to organize gatherings. Videos posted on the web show small groups shouting, "Down with Hamad!" and clashing with riot police.

Meanwhile, the Saudis seem entrenched on the island, despite the withdrawal of some troops. "It's their opportunity to extend their hegemony in the Persian Gulf," says Ali Al-Ahmed, director of the Washington-based Institute for Gulf Affairs. "Bahrain has a rope around its neck; they've lost any legitimacy and ability to project power locally. The Saudis are going to dig in."

During the protests Bahrain's crown prince, Sheik Salman bin Hamad al-Khalifa, who was assigned the daunting task of arranging a dialogue, confided to a group of Shiite businessmen that the Saudis had given him a short deadline to wrap up talks or else they would take action. They wanted "this mess in Bahrain to be cleared up as soon as possible, before it spread to their country," says one businessman who was at the meeting.

According to Saudi and Arab observers, Saudi Arabia's powerful interior minister, Prince Nayef, wanted to invade at the end of February, less than two weeks after the protests began, but was discouraged by the Americans. So the Saudis started lobbying in Washington—with the help of the Bahraini ambassador there—to incite fear of Iranian involvement. "While in Bahrain, they were talking about dialogue and reconciliation; in Washington the message was that Iran was behind it," says Abdulla. Iran claimed the protests were inspired by its revolutionary Islamic ideology, something most protesters strongly deny. Indeed, there's no evidence of any Iranian role in the uprising.

Soon after the February 18 shooting of demonstrators, President Obama spoke to King Hamad on the phone, asking that he not militarily suppress the peaceful protests. The king obliged and withdrew his army from the streets, allowing the demonstrators to camp out in Pearl Square. According to Bahrain insiders, it was at the suggestion of Jeffrey Feltman, assistant secretary of state for Near Eastern affairs, that the crown prince appeared on state TV after the shooting and appealed for calm. He said that what had happened was unacceptable and invited the opposition to dialogue. As the protesters became more intransigent—and several opposition groups called for a republic—the American position changed, allowing a Saudi invasion. For the United States, the royal family was a red line. Secretary of State Hillary Clinton suggested that Bahrain, one of Washington's most subservient allies, had the sovereign right to invite GCC troops anytime it chose—something no US official said when the Communist government of Afghanistan invited Soviet troops in 1979.

Shiites and Sunnis alike say that since the arrival of the Saudis, the influence of Wahhabi doctrine—the ultra-conservative ideology that Saudi leaders and Al Qaeda espouse and that considers Shiites infidels—has permeated Bahraini society. Religious police now operate under the name of the Committee to Protect Koranic Values, a branch of Saudi Arabia's Islamic Affairs Ministry. "That is very scary. They might leave Bahrain one day, but they will continue to have influence not only from the outside but from within," says Abdulla. "The fear is, you bring more sectarian people or ideas into the country to create a political society that is nothing but Sunni."

No official census has been conducted to determine the Shiite-Sunni balance in Bahrain. Most international media estimate a 60–70 percent Shiite majority, out of a population of about 600,000 citizens. More broadly, Western media coverage has not given an accurate account of the country's demography, ethnicity and social makeup, instead oversimplifying to depict a Sunni minority ruling over a discriminated Shiite majority. The ruling al-Khalifa is indeed Sunni, but there's no evidence that it favors the ordinary Sunni population. Long before other Gulf states modernized, Bahrain boasted a relatively educated and politicized population, with dissent common among an opposition mostly made up of leftist Sunnis. In 1975, however, Parliament was dissolved, and the following year the Constitution was suspended. Many oppositionists were arrested, with leaders forced into exile.

Two years after the 1979 Iranian revolution, the Islamic Front for the Liberation of Bahrain, a group of Bahraini Shiites who had forged close ties with Iran, staged a failed coup. The organizers had planned to install a theocratic Shiite regime, an event that left a deep scar on Bahrain's Sunnis. Around the same time, Saudi Arabia began spreading its Wahhabi teachings to counter Iran's drive to export its Shiite ideology. The Bahrain government has also encouraged the spread of Salafi preaching.

Bahraini Sunnis insist—and Shiites agree—that their community is not aligned with the royal family just because they share the same faith. They dismiss claims that al-Khalifa represents them. The family, they say, rules as a tribe, and the army and police are there only to protect the tribe. It recruits only those who are loyal to it, including thousands of Sunnis imported from Jordan, Syria, Yemen, Iraq, Sudan and Pakistan, ostensibly to increase the Sunni percentage—and perhaps also because they would have no allegiances to ordinary Bahrainis, whether Sunni or Shiite. There are nearly as many senior government positions occupied by trusted and loyal Shiites as ordinary Sunnis. However, Shiites are almost never allowed employment in sectors like defense, police, state TV and radio, or the information ministry, though there's no law barring them. There are almost as many—if not more—wealthy Shiite businessmen as Sunni. "The political problem in Bahrain is not sectarian," says Abdulla.

Many Sunnis initially sympathized with protesters' demands for a constitutional monarchy, but they were at the same time worried that religious leaders would hijack the cause and set up a theocratic state if they came to power. The ruling family was seen as a barrier to such a threat. What ultimately turned many Sunnis against the protesters was their call for regime change. "Sunnis are boiling inside," said Mohammed al-Sayed a few days before the attack on Pearl Square. Al-Sayed is from the Al Eslah Society, which espouses the Muslim Brotherhood ideology. "Sunnis resent the way [Shiites] present these grievances as only their own, as though they are the only community that aspires to change." Sunnis also suffer from unemployment, the housing crisis, government corruption and lack of political freedom.

This year's events are bound to have a deep impact on the way the two communities perceive each other. Bahrain was a symbol of peaceful coexistence in the Gulf, with widespread intermarriage between Sunnis and Shiites. It's difficult to see how such coexistence will return to the island so long as the state media insult Shiites with impunity. By the time Saudi tanks arrived, even some of the more liberal Sunnis expressed relief that a feared civil war had been averted and that the streets had, in their eyes, become safe again. Their relief may come at the cost of fulfilling the promise of the Arab Spring.

7

The Poltical Economy of Revolution

(AFP/Getty Images)

Tunisian students hold placards as they demonstrate outside the Constituent Assembly in Tunis on December 1, 2011. Thousands of people, academics, students, and miners, protested to express their concerns about unemployment, religious fundamentalism, and corruption. The placards read: (right) "Guess who am I. The problem of the Niqab to mask other underlying problems"; (left) "Stop! Do not touch my faculty!"

The Economics of the Arab World

By Paul McCaffrey

Each of the twenty-two nations that compose the Arab world has its own unique economy. The petroleum-rich Persian Gulf nation of Qatar has an annual per-capita income of roughly $138,000 and enjoys economic growth rates exceeding 15 percent. Meanwhile, the poverty-stricken country of Sudan has an estimated per capita income of $2,830 and its economy has grown at one-third the rate of Qatar. A measure of caution is required before drawing broad conclusions about such a diverse set of economies. However, there are certain economic trends and factors that exert influence in most, if not all, Arab countries. Five in particular stand out: the high rate of population growth and the accompanying increase in the number of young people throughout the region, an increase in educational achievements among young Arabs, the ubiquitous influence of the state and public sector on economic development, the reliance on food imports to feed populations, and the primacy of oil reserves and other energy resources in driving the region's economy. These phenomena do not always weave seamlessly with one another. Indeed, two of the primary motivating forces behind the Arab Spring are the inability of rigid, state-driven economic structures to accommodate the vast numbers of young people entering the job market and to ensure that populations have access to affordable food.

The Arab world's population has doubled in the past thirty years. On average, the rate of population increase in Arab countries is around 2 percent a year. In Yemen and Sudan it is as high as 3 percent. While fertility rates have declined since the 1970s, falling from six children per Arab woman on average down to three, life expectancy has increased. Approximately 60 percent of the population is under thirty years of age. In some countries, three out of four people are younger than thirty.

The Arab world's youthful population has the potential to inject a degree of dynamism into its economy. But it has also been a source of instability. Most economies in the region have struggled to meet the challenge of integrating so many young people in such a short period of time, and mass unemployment remains a problem. On a larger sociological level, youth bulges are associated with societal unrest and tumultuous political change. Unrest among the region's young people has been a major motivating force behind the Arab Spring.

Only rapid and sustained economic growth will create the number of jobs needed to employ the influx of young people in the Arab world. The economies of Egypt and Tunisia grew at a respectable pace in the past decade. In Tunisia, economic growth averaged 5 percent a year, while Egypt's economy expanded at a rate of 7 percent per year between 2005 and 2008. In most countries such statistics would be enough to achieve prosperity. Yet both Egypt and Tunisia will require rates substantially higher than this to keep up with the number of new workers entering the economy. Despite enviable economic growth over the last ten years, the unemployment rate in Tunisia was over 18 percent and stood at around 30 percent among young workers in December 2010, when widespread political demonstrations led to the overthrow of the government.

A corollary of the youth bulge in the Arab world is an increase in literacy and educational achievement levels. Throughout the latter half of the twentieth century, Arab governments invested heavily in education, building schools, and expanding educational access. As a consequence, the Arab population is not only young; it is increasingly educated. Tunisia has led the way in improving education standards for young women. But even with advanced degrees, many young Tunisians still cannot find work. They are not alone. In Morocco and Algeria, for example, the unemployment rate is higher for college graduates than it is for those with only a primary or secondary education. The Arab world is struggling with the paradox of a well-educated but underemployed youth demographic.

Most Arab economies rely on the state and the public sector as the primary means of economic development. Unlike market economies, where the private sector is the economy's principal engine, in the Arab world, the state largely plans and implements development projects. States arrange the funding of economic initiatives and distribute the proceeds when income is generated. The Arab Spring has illustrated many of the shortcomings of the state-centered model. Lacking the oil wealth of the Persian Gulf states, the Tunisian and Egyptian governments could not create the conditions to keep young people off the streets. Whether a market approach would have resulted in less unrest is a matter of debate. Still, the cases of Tunisia and Egypt illustrate that the state-centered model, whatever its actual results, can fuel resentment and alienation among young people.

When the government is the principal source of economic development, those closest to the ruling regime tend to benefit the most. In Tunisia, Zine el-Abidine Ben Ali and his extended family were renowned for their extravagance and were widely suspected of corruption. Ben Ali relatives owned Tunisian properties as varied as banks, supermarkets, car dealerships, and radio stations, as well as tuna exports and natural gas rights. According to some estimates, the Ben Ali family controlled between 30 and 40 percent of the Tunisian economy. Some analysts compared the family to an organized crime syndicate, ruling the country through a combination of connections and intimidation.

In Egypt, similar resentments flared up around the regime of Hosni Mubarak, who maintained the country's presidency for thirty years. Mubarak's family was suspected of accepting kickbacks in exchange for facilitating real estate deals and otherwise using the nation's resources to enrich themselves. When the regime fell in February 2011, Mubarak and his sons were arrested and charged for their alleged crimes.

Across the Arab world, oil wealth has served as a stabilizing influence in many regimes. With the vast reserves of capital raised by energy exports, heads of state have instituted public works projects and raised wages at will, releasing vast sums of money into the economy and counteracting internal political unrest at the first sign of trouble. Nonetheless, in Muammar Qaddafi's Libya, state-control of the lucrative energy sector was not enough to quell public criticism of the government. Like Mubarak and Ben Ali, Qaddafi and his associates exercised de facto control over the economy, operating the nation as though it was a family business—and creating acrimony among the country's citizenry. Though Qaddafi had leveraged oil wealth and state repression, bribery, and brute force to dominate his nation since the late 1960s, these tools proved ineffective in the face of Arab Spring unrest, and with UN military assistance, his regime was toppled.

Qaddafi, Mubarak, and Ben Ali were, for the most part, nonsectarian in their distribution of the nation's resources. Instead of favoring a particular ethnic or religious demographic, they rewarded their family and friends. In other nations, the pattern of distribution may favor, or be perceived to favor, individual ethnic groups. In Syria and Bahrain, Arab Spring uprisings have been motivated by such perceptions. In Syria, many in the country's Sunni Arab majority feel the Baathist regime of Bashar al-Assad gives preferential treatment to its Alawite colleagues. In Bahrain, many in the country's Shiite Muslim majority have expressed misgivings about the Sunni Al-Khalifa monarchy, which they allege steers the nation's economic benefits to fellow Sunnis. Governments in the Arab world that maintain significant control over economic activity, whatever their accomplishments and excesses, often lack credibility among their people. As the Arab Spring has shown, this lack of legitimacy can lead to overthrow.

Another challenge facing the Arab world is its lack of water resources and a widespread shortage of fertile land. Resource issues, combined with a rapidly expanding population, have made the region one of the world's leading importers of food. Saudi Arabia and other Gulf oil nations import around 85 percent of their food staples. As Javier Blas of the *Financial Times* has stated, "[f]or decades, the agricultural policy of the Middle East and North Africa has been extremely simple: hydrocarbon exports pay for carbohydrate imports."

A dependence on foreign food supplies has left the Arab world especially vulnerable to fluctuations in commodities prices. For example, droughts in Russia can send food prices soaring throughout the region. Compounding the problem, the United Nations (UN) has estimated that global food prices have risen over 80 percent in the past ten years and are not expected to come down significantly anytime soon.

Though manufacturing and tourism, among other industries, play important roles in many Arab economies, the region's energy sector is by far the most important. Algeria, Libya, Kuwait, Iraq, Saudi Arabia, Oman, Bahrain, Qatar, and the United Arab Emirates (UAE), in particular, possess enormous natural gas and oil reserves. These resources have created vast wealth for individual nations, but they have also led to economic distortions. Energy wealth does not translate into a diversified economy. Moreover, though the energy sector is a mostly stabilizing presence, it can, at times, have the opposite effect. A sudden drop in petroleum prices, for example, can lead to immediate declines in living standards in oil-dominated states. While reliance on the energy sector can yield considerable benefits when prices are high, when prices tumble, the effects are painful. The result is a boom-and-bust atmosphere, the peaks and valleys of which are felt throughout the Arab world.

One outgrowth of the oil sector in the petroleum-producing states of the Arabian Peninsula, in particular, is the presence of guest workers. Foreign nationals from across the Arab world, as well as India, Pakistan, Bangladesh, and beyond, make up much of the region's labor force. The opportunity to work in the Gulf oil states has historically relieved some of the youth-bulge-induced pressure on non-oil-producing Arab nations, as excess laborers from more resource-poor nations, including Egypt and Jordan, journey to Kuwait or Saudi Arabia for employment. In some nations, the population of guest workers exceeds that of the native inhabitants. In Kuwait, for example, there are more than two foreign laborers and their dependents for every one Kuwaiti citizen. In Qatar, at least three quarters of the population of 1.7 million is composed of temporary workers and their families. In the United Arab Emirates (UAE), there are 8.9 million people, of whom fewer than 15 percent are UAE nationals. The presence of foreign workers creates a complicated population dynamic. Living conditions among the guest workers are often less than optimal. As noncitizens, migrant laborers likewise lack legal protections and often suffer from exploitation and abuse.

Within the oil-producing nations, wealth distribution patterns similar to those of non-oil-producing countries have emerged. The state is the central actor in the economy and determines to a large extent how the wealth is dispersed. As in Egypt and Tunisia, those closest to the regime tend to benefit the most, creating similar resentment about how equitably the country's bounty is shared.

Taken together, the five aspects of Arab economics discussed above will pose serious challenges in the years ahead. How to find work for the large and growing number of young people entering the job market will test government and economic structures over generations to come. But the employment issue is not the region's only challenge. Commodities prices are expected to continue their upward trajectory, and food insecurity in the region is likely to grow more severe over the coming decades, creating the potential for further social and political unrest. If hydrocarbon prices remain high, the Gulf oil economies may have an easier time negotiating difficulties. Egypt, Tunisia, and other countries that are not blessed with petroleum reserves may not be so lucky. The question of whether the state-dominated development model is capable of implementing solutions to these problems will be important in determining whether the years ahead will be stable or tumultuous for countries in the Arab world.

The Economics of the Arab Spring

By Adeel Malik
The Financial Times, April 24, 2011

The plight of Mohamed Bouazizi, a Tunisian fruit vendor who found that official harassment made his job impossible, may seem a mundane trigger for the historic Arab awakening. In fact, Mr. Bouazizi's self-immolation and the protests it unleashed prove that Arabs' political and economic grievances are two sides of the same coin, and that democratisation in the Arab world must be both economic and political for either to succeed.

The Arab countries vary greatly in their politics—their degree of authoritarianism and prospects for change—and in their economic structure. But they all need reform and, with few exceptions, they all suffer a similar economic ailment.

The fundamental dysfunction of Arab countries is that of the rentier state. In oil- and gas-rich countries, natural resources return far more than it costs to extract them. Capturing and controlling this surplus—economic rent—is the chief source of enrichment, hence both the means and the end of power. Meanwhile the tragedy of resource-poor Arab countries is that they create rent artificially when nature has given them none. Monopolies, regulation and bullying all serve to limit access to productive activity, which generates fantastic rewards for a favoured few at the cost of holding back whole nations.

Whatever the source of the rent, the rentier economy is a vicious cycle in which the concentration of economic opportunity and that of political power fuel one another. This is why dignity and livelihood are inseparable in the demands of the excluded Arab majorities that have finally raised their voice. It is also why the political revolutions across the region will succeed only if matched by economic transformations. Even as Egypt and Tunisia grope for political transitions, the economic challenge is urgent.

The immediate priority where the regimes are in flux is to get the economy working again while preventing the flight of national wealth. For the region as a whole, the long-run goal must be to dismantle the rentier state where it is possible, and loosen its grip on the rest of the economy in the resource-rich lands where it is not.

However welcome, the opening up of Egyptian and Tunisian politics brings uncertainty that poses a threat to the economy. A clouded future keeps foreign investment and remittances away; owners of wealth may try to move it abroad. Caution is needed. It is essential to crack down on corruption, but sectors controlled by cronies must be kept operating while ill-gotten gains are retrieved. Attempts to stop capital flight can easily trigger it, so foreign swap lines are better than capital controls.

Such policies require respected technocrats to be found to hold the economic levers—for now. Where constitutional reforms succeed, economic statesmanship will be needed to chart long-term reforms, including more competition. The redistribution of opportunities this entails will be resisted by those who enjoy the easy fruits of exclusive access.

Not all reform needs to be hard. Simply removing rules and practices that restrict entry into economic activities or access to credit will be popular and good for the economy. Dispersing control of the corporate sector is trickier. A protracted tug-of-war with past regime favourites can destroy the values being fought over.

Broader ownership and competition are necessary for a more market-based allocation of resources. But full liberalisation overnight could kill the patient. Such welfare policies as food subsidies and public job schemes are inefficient, but must be kept until they can be replaced by direct support of purchasing power for the poor (which itself would boost their freedom).

> *Whatever the source of the rent, the rentier economy is a vicious cycle in which the concentration of economic opportunity and that of political power fuel one another. This is why dignity and livelihood are inseparable in the demands of the excluded Arab majorities that have finally raised their voice.*

The region's corporate successes are those that escaped political meddling. Arab people power risks more populism. For democracy to be secured, however, the economy itself must be depoliticised.

Restructuring U.S. Foreign Assistance in the Wake of the Arab Spring

By Mathew O'Sullivan
The Washington Report on Middle East Affairs, September 2011

Foreign aid is the U.S. government's most significant and wide-reaching channel of involvement in the Middle East. Through financial assistance, Washington seeks to influence markets, militaries, societies and governments abroad. But just as recent popular uprisings demonstrate the Arab world's disapproval of long-standing regimes, so too do they indicate objection to the external powers that have backed and funded the region's status quo.

A recent poll by Zogby International reveals that favorable attitudes toward the United States in the Middle East are lower now than they were in 2008, during the last year of George W. Bush's presidency. This represents a marked shift from the relatively positive perceptions of the American government following President Barack Obama's Cairo speech in 2009. Polling conducted by the Abu Dhabi Gallup Center between March and April 2011 shows 52 percent of Egyptians opposing any sort of U.S. economic aid to their country at all.

Although these stances may be in part a product of the vocal political climate currently pervading the Middle East, they unquestionably reveal the need for a drastic transformation of America's financial engagement in the region. A new approach should stabilize Middle Eastern economies in order to bolster the progress of the Arab Spring, empower individuals to become involved in public affairs, and demonstrate that Washington is interested in supporting the people of the Middle East, and not just the governments that march in step with U.S. policy.

In the months since the Arab Spring blossomed, both President Obama and U.S. policymakers have sought to communicate a change in aid strategy—away from top-down statebuilding and toward increased civil society assistance, investments in small- and medium-sized enterprises, and public-private partnerships. Ideally, such efforts would bypass corruption-ridden state bureaucracies and allow communities to achieve prosperity and democracy through decentralized and locally tailored means. Obama's May 19 pledge of $2 billion to the Overseas Private Investment Corporation (OPIC) for new ventures in Egypt and Tunisia supports the government's recent and growing focus on producing bottom-up development by providing much-needed capital to entrepreneurs in the Middle East and by building bridges between U.S. and Arab businesses.

At a July 21 event hosted by the Modernizing Foreign Assistance Network (MFAN), Tamara Cofman Wittes, formerly with the Brookings Institution's Saban Center for Middle East Policy and now deputy assistant secretary of state for Near Eastern affairs, further conveyed the U.S. government's intent to transform its aid strategy, stating that "the citizens of the region have made their own priorities clear" and that Washington will redirect foreign assistance programs according to the demands and democratic framework put forth by the Arab public. Wittes cited the State Department's Middle East Partnership Initiative as an example: it distributes grants of $25,000 to $100,000 to civil society groups that are locally run and benefit their own communities. Such initiatives are extremely important—especially since historically, as noted by James Zogby of the Arab American Institute, eighty-two cents on the dollar of foreign assistance have remained in American hands through donations and payments to major development organizations and U.S. contractors.

> *A recent poll by Zogby International reveals that favorable attitudes toward the United States in the Middle East are lower now than they were in 2008, during the last year of George W. Bush's presidency.*

Despite these efforts, Washington's rhetoric on restructuring its foreign assistance still fails to overcome many of the weaknesses that have defined its Middle East aid policies and provided support to autocratic regimes for decades. In a review of the federal budget and appropriations for fiscal year 2012, Stephen McInerny of the Project on Middle East Democracy (POMED) describes burdens on U.S. foreign assistance, including "dysfunction in the congressional appropriations process," unsatisfactory levels of funding for democracy programs and civilian assistance throughout the region, and an enduring "imbalance between military and nonmilitary aid."

Funding cuts implemented by Congress have a particularly strong impact on nonmilitary programs, which are deemed less important to national security. These budget reductions are affecting civilian assistance projects in Iraq and risk worsening the situation in the country as the U.S. military withdraws. In addition, Congress tends to overlook certain countries (such as Morocco) where civil society is thriving but in need of cash, while pouring unmanageable sums of U.S. dollars into others where there is insufficient institutional capacity to effectively use the assistance (as is the case in Egypt).

Congress also complicates the effectiveness of U.S. aid by attaching conditions to aid funding. When debating the Foreign Relations Authorization Act for FY2012, some members of Congress—such as House Foreign Affairs Committee chair Ileana Ros-Lehtinen (R-FL) and Rep. Jeff Duncan (R-SC)—proposed amendments that would prohibit bilateral economic assistance based on the country's voting record in the United Nations and on the representation of certain non-secular government groups. The latter stipulation has routinely affected financing to the Lebanese government and the Palestinian Authority due to the political activity of Hezbollah and Hamas, respectively, and it is likely that Congress will impose similar restraints on Egypt based on the Muslim Brotherhood's involvement in the country's emerging democracy.

The greatest mishandling of U.S. foreign assistance continues to result from the inflated allocation of funding to defense and security over development. MFAN listed the need to "budget for civil-military balance" as one of the key elements of foreign aid the government needs to fix "in the days and weeks ahead." Yet in a July 19 POMED panel discussion on Capitol Hill, analysts voiced their doubt as to whether, due to legislative barriers, a shift of military assistance to development assistance could even be achieved in the short-run. It would be extremely difficult and almost impossible to initiate a massive direct transfer of funding from military to economic aid, explained Michael Ryan, senior research associate at The Jamestown Foundation.

Nonetheless, given the overwhelming burden of military financing on the U.S. foreign aid purse, a solution is essential. For the eight Middle East recipients of U.S. assistance analyzed by McInerny in his report on the FY '12 budget and appropriations—Egypt, Iraq, Jordan, Lebanon, Morocco, Tunisia, Yemen and the Palestinian Authority—more than 55 percent of resources, or nearly $2 billion of a total of $3.5 billion, are assigned specifically for military and security assistance. The largest recipient by far on the list was Egypt, whose government received $1.3 billion exclusively for military support out of a total aid package of $1.55 billion. This strategy is worrying given the position the military currently holds in post-Mubarak Egypt and the possible negative impact that strengthening the armed forces may have on the democratic process there.

McInerny's analysis did not include other major recipients of U.S. military aid, including Israel and Bahrain. Israel's $3 billion foreign aid package—all of it devoted to the military—will remain unchanged for the coming fiscal year. As evidenced by recent demonstrations in the country, however, Israel has a growing need for social programs as well.

Is there any hope for an improved system of U.S. aid to the Middle East, or will strategic interests and institutional hurdles continue to hamper the potential for American-guided economic development in the region? Ideally, budget constraints, research on the security benefits of civil society projects, and the questionable role played by domestic armed forces in the Middle East in response to the Arab Spring will deter U.S. lawmakers from distributing the majority of foreign assistance to militaries in the future.

On the development side of foreign assistance, the executive branch and State Department fortunately are well aware of the need to invest less through large, centralized agencies and more through local groups and firms focused on human rights, political engagement and job creation. As the Arab Spring shows, central governments and politicians cannot always be trusted with the responsibility of guiding widespread economic and democratic advances. Nor is the United States ordained to draw the roadmap for growth and governance in the region. In the Arab world today, progress toward prosperity and representative government is being driven chiefly at the sub-national level, and it will behoove the U.S. to provide support accordingly and trust that communities and local, private organizations are best suited to work toward their own development.

Populations throughout the Middle East may not want the U.S. to be a leader or architect in the region, but would welcome it as a partner in the pursuit of economic and political empowerment.

❖

Mathew O'Sullivan is a senior at Washington and Lee University and a former intern at the Washington Report.

Working-Class Revolutions?

The success of the insurgent movements correlates well with the strength of organized labor.

By Joel Beinin
The Nation, September 12, 2011

During the demonstrations in January and February that led to the ouster of Egyptian President Hosni Mubarak, Sabr Barakat, a retired steelworker and veteran labor organizer, witnessed groups of workers spontaneously marching from industrial areas outside Cairo toward Tahrir Square. Through his work with the Egyptian Center for Economic and Social Rights, established in 2010, Barakat maintains close ties to labor activists throughout Egypt. He believes workers' presence in Egypt's January 25 Revolution, as it is known, was expressed in its most popular slogans: "Dignity, Democracy, Social Justice"; "Bread, Freedom, Social Justice"; and, most direct, "We Want to Live! We Want to Eat!"

Similar demands for bread and social justice were frequently raised during the 4,000 strikes, sit-ins and other collective actions involving millions of workers since 1998, after the Egyptian government seriously began implementing the privatization program it agreed to in 1991. The program reduced public sector employment and promoted early retirement to make enterprises more attractive to private investors. Buyers sometimes carried out mass dismissals, although this was nominally illegal. "There is continuity between those strikes and the 2011 revolution," said Khaled al-Khamissi, author of the bestselling novel *Taxi*.

Kamal Abbas, general coordinator of the Center for Trade Union and Workers Services, agrees: "It was a revolution against poverty and tyranny and for freedom and social justice." Abbas and others established the CTUWS in 1990, after he was fired for leading a strike at the Egyptian Iron and Steel Company.

In contrast, Ahmad Maher, a 30-year-old engineer and a leader of the April 6 Youth Movement, a key player in the Tahrir Square uprising, claimed, "The workers did not play a role in the revolution. They were far removed from it." Maher's inability to perceive the role of workers is only partly attributable to class prejudice. After 2000 there were two largely parallel movements, of workers and the urban middle class. Only a handful of journalists and committed leftists maintained regular contact between them. The workers' movement was far larger and more sustained, but workers had no national leadership or unified program. They rarely made direct demands for democracy or regime change, as middle-class activists did after the

Kifaya (Enough!) movement burst on the scene in late 2004. Only in late June of this year did the April 6 Youth Movement begin to embrace key economic demands of the workers.

The conflicting assessments of Khamissi and Abbas, on the one hand, and Maher, on the other, reflect a continuing battle over the narrative and political import not only of the revolution in Egypt but of the insurgent movements throughout the Arab world. Are they simply rebellions demanding dignity and democracy? Or are they also movements for social justice?

The global neoliberal capitalist model was test-driven in Chile after the 1973 coup against democratically elected socialist President Salvador Allende. Subsequently the International Monetary Fund and the World Bank began installing the model throughout the global South. Just as elsewhere, there was popular resistance in the Middle East and North Africa.

Egypt led the way. Nationwide riots against IMF-inspired cuts in subsidies on basic consumer goods in 1977 compelled the government to restore the subsidies, but they were reduced stealthily over the next thirty years. In response, workers launched strike waves in the mid-1980s and early '90s. Labor protests have proliferated since 1998. In Tunisia the General Federation of Labor called a general strike in 1978, and there was widespread anti-IMF rioting in Tunisia in 1984. There were strikes by Moroccan workers and students in 1981, riots in poor areas of Casablanca in 1990 and protests over increases in the price of bread in 2008 that forced the Moroccan government to back down. There were food riots in Jordan in 1989. Algerians erupted in rage when the government voluntarily adopted an IMF-style economic program in 1988.

Job insecurity due to privatization of public enterprises, high rates of unemployment concentrated among youth, poverty and inflation have fueled mass dissatisfaction with authoritarian Arab regimes. Vegetable prices in Egypt increased 51 percent in September 2010 over the previous month, while meat and poultry prices increased 29 percent. Abu Mohamed, a garlic seller, told the liberal daily *al-Masry al-Youm*, "A family can't afford to buy tomatoes . . . can you imagine? The government has to do something about the economic problems of the people because this is how revolutions start."

The upper middle classes have expanded because of neoliberal growth in "success stories" (by IMF standards) like Egypt, Tunisia, Morocco and Jordan, but their conspicuous consumption is a slap in the face to the majority. The capacity of non–oil producing states—and even oil-producing countries like Algeria and Egypt—to deliver basic social services and a secure existence to their people has been undermined by budget cuts and privatization schemes demanded by international financial institutions.

The Egyptian Federation of Independent Trade Unions (EFITU) was established on January 30 as an integral part of the revolutionary process. Before the outcome of the uprising was certain, these unionists boldly challenged the legal monopoly of the Egyptian Trade Union Federation (ETUF), a key institution of the Mubarak regime. EFITU emerged from two decades of work by the CTUWS and the inspiring example of the Real Estate Tax Authority workers. In 2008 Kamal Abu Aita led 35,000 RETA workers in establishing the first trade union independent of the Egyptian state since 1957, repudiating the labor-control apparatus of three successive regimes.

Khaled Ali, a labor lawyer and director of the Egyptian Center for Economic and Social Rights, carefully noted, "The workers did not start the January 25 movement, because they have no organizing structure." But, he adds, "one of the important steps of this revolution was taken when they began to protest, giving the revolution an economic and social slant besides the political demands." He was referring to some sixty strikes in the last days before Mubarak's departure on February 11 and the first few days afterward. Workers have continued to strike and protest ever since.

Some ninety unions, most of them newly established, have affiliated with EFITU. Among them are eleven unions and a citywide labor council in Sadat City, where 50,000 workers are employed in 200 enterprises, mainly textiles, iron and steel, and ceramics and porcelain. There were only two unions in Sadat City before this year.

The lack of a national organization, leadership and detailed economic program has allowed personal rivalries and minor differences to weaken Egypt's independent labor movement. In the past, despite principled calls for the rule of law, local networks of trust were the primary weapon in defending workers and sympathetic NGOs from constant threats and close supervision by the Mubarak regime. The legacy of this "small picture" outlook shapes the conditions in which the various labor alliances are scrambling to assert their influence. Even ETUF has established new unions—an apparent effort to demonstrate that it can meet criteria the International Labor Organization has established for legitimate trade unionism.

In Tunisia, as in Egypt, mobilizations of workers and their families and neighbors years before the mass uprising were a vital element in the social pressures that culminated in President Zine el-Abidine Ben Ali's January ouster. Tunisia's national unemployment rate was 13–16 percent in the 2000s but as high as 40 percent in the southwestern phosphate mining basin of Gafsa. More than 70 percent of Tunisia's unemployed are under 30; indeed, youth unemployment is a key factor in popular revolts across the Arab region.

The Tunisian General Federation of Labor (UGTT), established in 1946, participated actively in the struggle for independence from France, achieved in 1956. These historic credentials allowed the federation to resist total subservience to founding president Habib Bourguiba. In 1989, two years after he pushed aside Bourguiba and seized power, Ben Ali imposed a collaborationist leadership on the UGTT. While continuing to defend collective-bargaining rights in the workplace, the federation abandoned its decade-long resistance to the neoliberal agenda and supported Ben Ali in successive fraudulent elections. However, pockets of radicalism persisted among teachers, postal workers and civil servants.

In January 2008, nearly three years before Mohamed Bouazizi's self-immolation ignited the firestorm of protests in Tunisia and across the Arab region, street demonstrations erupted in Gafsa and nearby Redeyef. Workers accused the state-owned

Gafsa Phosphate Company of nepotistic recruitment practices in collaboration with local UGTT leaders. The protests spread throughout the Gafsa governorate, with teachers, women, street youth and some local union branches joining in, demanding not only fair recruitment practices in the mines but a comprehensive jobs program. The oppositional press, radical students in the more prosperous coastal cities, and diaspora Tunisians in France and Montreal expressed support. The protests were brutally suppressed, but support for the people of Gafsa spread nonetheless. Clashes continued for months, culminating in the killing of two demonstrators by militarized police. Internet activists publicized the events in the mining towns. In desperation, the regime shut down access to Facebook in August of that year.

The 2008 Gafsa revolt was the most important social movement in Tunisia since the bread revolt of 1984. The difference was that in 1984 the UGTT supported the protest, while the 2008 movement was initiated by rank-and-file workers, the unemployed and their families, with both the UGTT and the regime targets of protest.

The next great wave of protests in Tunisia came in December 2010, after the suicide of Bouazizi. That month the UGTT leadership began issuing statements opposing repression of demonstrators, but it came out in full support of the movement only days before Ben Ali's demise. In a January 10 speech Ben Ali dismissed his opposition as "hostile elements in the pay of foreigners, who have sold their souls to extremism and terrorism." That day thirty workers stormed into the Gafsa regional UGTT office, demanding that the local leadership support the protests. Ben Ali's insensitivity impelled the national federation to authorize regional general strikes in Sfax, Kairouan and Tozeur on January 11, followed by a general strike in Tunis on January 14, the day of Ben Ali's departure. Working-class neighborhoods of Tunis rioted in celebration that night.

After trailing behind their constituency for more than a decade, the UGTT leaders have played catch-up in the new era. Three representatives were ministers in the first transitional government. Their resignation after only one day, on the grounds that members of the former ruling party, the Constitutional Democratic Rally, retained too much influence, led to the formation of a new government and the party's dissolution on March 9. In the run-up to Constituent Assembly elections scheduled for October, many trade union activists are aligned with the "modern democratic alliance" of leftist parties.

In the monarchies of Bahrain and Morocco, workers and trade unions, though less successful than in Egypt and Tunisia, have been an integral part of the democratic movements.

Since its establishment in 2004 the General Federation of Bahrain Trade Unions has been a thorn in the side of King Hamad, who presents himself as a business-friendly reformer while maintaining the absolute rule of his Sunni dynasty over the country's Shiite majority. GFBTU's sixty company-based unions represent 22,000 of Bahrain's 140,000 local workers in construction, textiles, insurance, petroleum, aluminum, airport services and other sectors. The federation has an exemplary record of opposing sectarianism and defending the rights of contract migrant workers, a large portion of the workforce. It advocates the unionization of domestic workers, mainly South and Southeast Asian migrants, who are inadequately protected by labor laws in all Arab countries. Thirteen of its union committee members are women.

On February 14, the tenth anniversary of a referendum on the National Action Charter of Bahrain, which has not delivered on its promise of democracy, young activists oc-

> *Of all the movements of the Arab Awakening, Tunisia's has the best chance of achieving a viable democracy with a strong voice for working people.*

cupied Pearl Square in the capital of Manama. Security forces violently attacked them at dawn on February 17. The GFBTU supported the protesters by calling a general strike for February 20. The strike was suspended on February 21, after security forces withdrew from the roundabout. When the king requested military assistance from neighboring countries, the federation again called for a general strike. Thousands of workers struck on March 13–22, as Saudi and mercenary troops using US-supplied weapons occupied Bahrain and brutally suppressed the democracy movement. More than 2,500 workers have been fired for joining demonstrations or participating in strikes (seventy have since been reinstated, but without their seniority). GFBTU leaders have been especially targeted—fifteen members of the executive board and more than forty union leaders, including the heads of the teachers federation, the nurses association and the Bahrain Petroleum Company union, have been sacked.

The GFBTU challenged the dismissals but cautiously agreed to participate in the "national dialogue," convened by the king on July 1, after three months of martial law. But after royal allies blocked even consideration of reinstating fired workers, the federation withdrew, following the lead of the Shiite-oriented Wefaq Party, the largest in Bahrain.

On April 21 the AFL-CIO filed a complaint with the US Labor Department. "The egregious attacks on workers must end, and the Bahraini government's systematic discrimination against and dismantling of unions must be reversed. These actions directly violate the letter and the spirit of the trade agreement," said AFL-CIO president Richard Trumka when the complaint was filed. "Workers must be reinstated to their jobs and the elected union leadership must be allowed to function without fear of reprisals. Failure by the United States to intervene to support workers and their democratic institutions would make a mockery of the labor protections included in the free trade agreement." The Labor Department is conducting a fact-finding investigation.

On August 4 the AFL-CIO executive council reaffirmed its support for the popular uprisings in Bahrain and across the Arab world and called on the Obama administration "to make a clean break with past practice and strongly support freedom of association, human and workers' rights in all its policies in the region as a matter of urgent priority . . . It is incumbent on the international community and the United

States in particular to follow the will of the people who are risking everything for better futures."

Morocco's February 20 Movement for Democracy, which was launched with the participation of some 200,000 people who demonstrated throughout the country, was supported by several trade unions affiliated with the largest federation, the Moroccan Union of Labor, and the entire Democratic Labor Federation (CDT). The latter also joined the February 20 Movement and others in advocating a boycott of the tightly controlled July 1 constitutional referendum. Members of both federations supported a Casablanca sit-in on May 1, International Labor Day, though the CDT presence was more substantial.

Meanwhile, a strong counterrevolutionary wind is blowing in Egypt. On March 24 the ruling Supreme Council of the Armed Forces (SCAF) issued Decree 34, establishing harsh penalties for engaging in strikes and demonstrations. It was implemented on June 29, when a military court sentenced five workers at Petrojet, an oil and gas services company operated by the ministry of petroleum, to one-year suspended prison sentences. Their offense: sitting in for two weeks in front of the ministry to demand that 200 workers employed for many years on a temporary basis be granted permanent status.

Well over 100,000 people defied scorching heat to demonstrate throughout Egypt on July 8, the largest protests since Mubarak's ouster. In Tahrir Square protesters raised the slogan "The Poor First" and endorsed the key demands of the independent labor movement: revoke Decree 34, dissolve ETUF and enact the new draft trade union law. The main squares of Cairo, Alexandria and Suez remained occupied throughout July, as millions of Egyptians rebelled against the SCAF's vast repressive apparatus and demanded more thoroughgoing democratic change linked to social justice. But on July 29 this liberal-left-social Islamist current was overwhelmed by a massive display of hyper-conservative Islamist political strength, when the Salafi movement bused several hundred thousand supporters from all corners of Egypt to Tahrir Square, routing all other forces by raising provocative and divisive slogans ("Sharia Law Now!"). Some observers have remarked that many observant Muslims were turned off by the excess; if that reflects widespread sentiment, the rally may be the high-water mark of post-Mubarak radical Islamist influence.

As if to confirm this, three days after the Islamist rally, workers scored a major victory: the cabinet nullified the fraudulent 2006 ETUF elections. Minister for Manpower and Immigration Ahmad al-Burai, who was nominated for his post by the CTUWS and EFITU, initiated this action. The ETUF executive committee has been disbanded, but it is unclear whether this will result in the well-deserved institutional demise of ETUF or simply its reorganization after new elections.

Of all the movements of the Arab Awakening, Tunisia's has the best chance of achieving a viable democracy with a strong voice for working people. That country's UGTT represents about 14 percent of the labor force of 3.8 million. It is the largest civil organization in the country, and its membership has increased 35 percent since January. Its members were a decisive force in the democracy movement. Their leadership, despite its history of collaboration with the old regime, is now on a progressive trajectory.

The importance of workers to the regional uprisings can be judged by their absence in Yemen, Libya and Syria, where fragile, state-controlled union federations have not joined the resistance. In Yemen and Syria, unions are politically weak because of the small number of urban workers, high rates of unemployment and labor migration. In Libya and Syria, state repression and the ever-present threat of violence, even before the 2011 opposition movements emerged, prevented workers and unions from developing independent social power.

The success of the Arab Awakening movements correlates well with the strength of their labor contingents: the more workers involved, the more likely a democratic outcome. (There is a lesson here for American democracy as well.) But workers have rarely demanded democracy in the abstract. As a February 19 declaration of Egypt's emerging EFITU proclaimed, "If this revolution does not lead to the fair distribution of wealth it is not worth anything. Freedoms are not complete without social freedoms. The right to vote is naturally dependent on the right to a loaf of bread."

Punishing Doctors in Bahrain

By Ala'a Shehabi
The Nation, October 31, 2011

Between September 25 and October 6, Bahrain's military courts handed out sentences that add up to nearly 2,500 years in prison. The 200-plus defendants, arrested during protests against the government in March, included medical personnel, teachers and political activists. There was one death sentence, for the killing of a police officer.

Among the most prominent defendants are twenty medical workers accused of attempting a coup, along with possession of weapons and occupying a public building (Salmaniya Medical Center, where a number of them worked). The prosecution of the medics—who received between five and fifteen years in prison for providing medical treatment to protesters—has sparked an international outcry. Among the less-known cases are thirty-two men sentenced to fifteen years each for an arson attack on a farm belonging to a member of the royal family, as well as a ten-year sentence handed down to the president of Bahrain's teachers union.

The sentences were criticized by United Nations Secretary General Ban Ki-Moon, and European Union High Representative Catherine Ashton urged the Bahraini government to accept a requested visit by the UN high commissioner for human rights. Meanwhile, the Obama administration has come under fire for striking a deal in September to sell $53 million worth of military supplies to Bahrain.

> **The prosecution of the medics—who received between five and fifteen years in prison for providing medical treatment to protesters—has sparked an international outcry.**

Hundreds of people remain imprisoned. According to Sayed Mohsin Alalawi, a prominent lawyer defending many of the accused, most of the cases rely on forced confessions. The convicted doctors and others have described beatings, sleep deprivation and threats of sexual abuse during the months of awaiting trial. On October 7, a 16-year-old boy was killed during protests near Bahrain's capital, Manama.

A week after the doctors were sentenced, Bahrain's attorney general, Ali Alboainain, suddenly announced that they would be retried in civilian courts, a development lawyers have interpreted as an appeal rather than a new trial. "No doctors or other medical personnel may be punished by reason of the fulfillment of their humanitarian duties or their political views," he said.

Yemenis Hopeless About Economy as Revolt Continues

More than 4 in 10 struggled to afford food for their families in the past year

By Richard Burkholder
Gallup Poll Briefing, November 8, 2011

Yemenis see their economy at a near standstill after months of violence and political instability. Fewer than 1 in 10 Yemenis described local economic conditions as good in late July and 3% saw the situation getting better. In addition, 5% said it was a good time to find a job locally.

Asked of Yemeni adults: Right now, do you think that economic conditions in the city or area where you live, as a whole, are getting better or getting worse?

Getting better	Staying the same	Getting worse	Don't know/Refused
3%	10%	84%	3%

July 23–29, 2011

This hopelessness largely reflects the extensive changes Yemenis are witnessing in the country's political environment that are making food and goods shortages and poor employment conditions worse. Already facing calls for his resignation, President Ali Abdullah Saleh was injured in an attack in June that required extended medical treatment in Saudi Arabia. Popular unrest has accelerated since his return to Yemen, spreading from the country's capital Sanaa in the north to Aden in the south.

Although many countries in the Middle East face serious economic, social, and political challenges, Yemen is particularly fragile. More than 4 in 10 Yemenis (42%) say there were times in the past year when they did not have enough money to buy food for themselves or families. Nearly 3 in 10 (29%) were unable to afford adequate shelter or housing for themselves or their families.

Asked of Yemeni adults: Have there been times in the past 12 months when you did not have enough money to . . .

	Buy food that you or your family needed	Provide adequate shelter or housing for you and your family
Yes	42%	29%
No	57%	71%

July 23–29, 2011

Not surprisingly, 7% of Yemenis say they are living comfortably, while fewer than one in three (31%) say they are getting by on their present household income. Similar proportions are finding it difficult (30%) or very difficult (32%) to get by. In short, nearly two-thirds of Yemenis find their personal financial situations challenging or untenable.

> *More than 4 in 10 Yemenis (42%) say there were times in the past year when they did not have enough money to buy food for themselves or families.*

Yemenis Face Other Challenges

Along with the economic limitations Yemenis are facing, Yemen faces additional challenges. For example, official figures indicate that the majority of Yemenis have not completed primary education.

Widespread corruption exacerbates all of these issues and is one of the main catalysts of the unrest. While Gallup did not measure perceptions about corruption in the July poll, Gallup asked about the subject in a separate poll conducted this past March. At that time, about one-third of Yemenis (34%) said they thought the government was doing enough to fight corruption.

Implications

Yemen is facing an economic crisis that is a cause *and* a result of the country's current unrest. The country "is on the verge of a true humanitarian disaster" on par with that of Somalia, a U.N. Children's Fund's representative for Yemen said at a press briefing in late October. Gallup's recent polling—on food, housing, employment opportunities, and living standards—demonstrates how dire the situation has become.

Survey Methods

Results are based on face-to-face interviews with 1,000 adults, aged 15 and older, conducted July 23–29, 2011, in Yemen. For results based on the total sample of national adults, one can say with 95% confidence that the maximum margin of sampling error is ±3.8 percentage points. The margin of error reflects the influence of data weighting.

The Island at the Center of the World: The Silencing of Bahrain's Crisis

By Derek Henry Flood
Terrorism Monitor, May 12, 2011

Bahrain's state television recently announced that the Kingdom's "State of National Safety" emergency law, which allowed the monarchy to swiftly crush once pulsing opposition protests, will not be extended further than June 1, two weeks ahead of the original deadline (al-Jazeera, May 8). The three-month state of emergency was declared on March 15, as pro-democracy protests developed into an anti-regime uprising and engulfed much of downtown Manama's financial district. A day prior to the emergency law's declaration, armored columns from Saudi Arabia poured into the tiny island nation via the 26 kilometer long King Fahd Causeway that connects Saudi Arabia's Eastern Province with the Bahrain archipelago (see Terrorism Monitor Brief, March 24). According to a statement from Bahrain's state news agency, Bahrain and Saudi Arabia "enjoy ideal relations," having stood together in solidarity when faced with "Iranian threats" (Bahrain News Agency, May 9). In a very unfortunate development for Bahrain's nascent pro-democracy movement, no sooner did the uprising devolve into violence than both Saudi Arabia and Iran turned the island into a sectarian propaganda proxy war. Neither side in the conflict has let up on the constant drumbeat of drama in a situation largely cast aside by both the global media and great powers. In an attempt to further agitate the situation, Iranian state television aired a documentary equating the Saudi intervention in Bahrain with the Israeli occupation of the Palestinian Territories, broadcasting footage of desecrated Shi'a mosques and hussainiyas (congregation halls for Shi'a rituals), as well as damaged Shi'a holy books (Press TV, May 9).

Bahrain's principal opposition party is al-Wefaq, which withdrew from parliament at the outset of the crisis to demonstrate its abhorrence at the crackdown (AFP, February 17). Al-Wefaq claimed in April that government forces had demolished no less than 30 Shi'a places of worship. Representatives of Bahrain's ruler, King Hamad bin Isa al-Khalifa, have issued thinly justified decrees that such "unlicensed" sites are being destroyed "regardless of any doctrine." Al-Wefaq released a statement refuting the regime's legal rationale: "Any attempt to showcase the measure as a legal action will neither be convincing nor objective" (AP, April 24). The bulldozing of Shi'a centers, some of them ancient, may be due to the growth of intolerant Wahhabi values in the Sunni-run security forces. These security forces have become stocked with recruits from Sunni communities in Pakistan and from poorer regions of the Sunni Arab world. Another possible driver in the attacks on Shi'a institutions may be an opportunistic attempt by descendants of Sunni settlers to erase the history of the island's indigenous Shi'a communities, which long pre-date the al-Khalifa dynasty established in 1783.

On the Ground

Jamestown paid a hurried visit to the besieged Persian Gulf kingdom in early April. During an attempt to visit the now notorious Pearl Roundabout, once the site of camping protesters in a pro-democracy uprising that began on February 14, Bah-raini National Guardsmen rushed over in an armored vehicle informing the author that the roundabout had been designated a closed area where photography was for-bidden. Not only was photography forbidden, but apparently simply looking at the heavily militarized zone with the naked eye was also unwelcome. Jamestown was instructed to leave the area shrouded in row upon row of concertina wire, entirely barricaded off from the rest of Manama's Central Business District. Forlorn South Asian migrant vendors milled about, unable to do any trade in fish or produce in the once bustling Central Market area after it became isolated from the other half of the city by Kevlar-clad troops.

Other areas of downtown Manama maintained the appearance of a war zone with tanks and armored personnel carriers careening around with abandon, driving over traffic medians and manning a plethora of intimidating checkpoints. Jamestown was told by a pair of bearded soldiers manning a checkpoint along King Faisal Corniche opposite Reef Island that walking in this zone was no longer permitted. These soldiers bore no national insignia on their fatigues, paid no attention to several Bangladeshi men casually bicycling by and attempted to detain this analyst for an unspecified vio-lation. A Sunni taxi driver who said he supported the regime described the Gulf Co-operation Council (GCC) intervention forces from Saudi Arabia and the United Arab Emirates as a "cocktail" in that they readily blended with Bahraini units so as to lessen the appearance of a foreign military occupation. A leaked U.S. Embassy cable from 2007 describes the Bahraini security forces as containing almost "no Shi'a," describing the use of Shi'a "community police" in Shi'a majority areas of the country.[1]

The author spoke with prominent dissident and Director of the Bahrain Center for Human Rights Nabeel Rajab about the festering crisis.[2] An outspoken critic of the al-Khalifa monarchy, Rajab viewed the announcement of the ending of the state of emergency two weeks ahead of schedule with a high degree of cynicism. He believed that the monarchy was essentially trying to save the economy from a total meltdown. The announcement, meant to forestall further capital flight from Bah-rain's once thriving financial services sector, was, in Rajab's view, principally driven by the need to preserve the prestigious annual Formula One Grand Prix auto race. While the 2011 race was cancelled before Saudi troops entered Bahrain, a decision on whether the 2012 race will still be held in that country is to be made on June 3, 12 days before the planned date to end the emergency (AFP, May 3).

Rajab described the Formula One issue as an important socio-economic indicator for the monarchy. A negative decision by the international sports body may further the continued outflow of foreign investment and Asian migrant workers on which the services sector is desperately dependent. The return of the Grand Prix may signify an economic lifeline. A denial by the sport body may be a walk to the gallows for Bahrain's endangered business sector as international confidence continues to ebb.

The Role of Iran

Nabeel Rajab scoffed at the constant talk of Iranian interference in Bahraini affairs. He spoke of a concerted effort by the Bahraini government to link the pro-democracy movement with Iran in any way possible. When asked about King Hamad's public talk of as yet unproven Iranian linkages to the crushed protest movement, Rajab asserted: "No Bahraini democrats see Iran as a system to emulate."

Rajab related recent appearances by both King Hamad and Crown Prince Salman bin Hamad bin Isa al-Khalifa—also the Deputy Supreme Commander of the 9000-strong Bahrain Defense Forces—in which they stated, respectively, that there was "no problem" with Iran and "no one [in Bahrain] has any relations with Iran." High-ranking Bahraini officials regularly make bellicose, though mostly unsubstantiated, accusations about their Iranian neighbors but do not seek to anger Tehran on a diplomatic level. Bahraini Foreign Minister Shaykh Khalid bin Ahmad al-Khalifa stated in a closed-door meeting of MPs that the Kingdom had no intention of severing ties with the Iranian state despite its "continuous interference" in Bahrain's internal dynamics (Gulf Daily News [Manama], May 10). Rajab sees the Bahraini government's contradictory stance toward Iranian President Mahmoud Ahmadinejad and Iran's Supreme Leader Ayatollah Ali Khamenei as evidence that Manama is in a bit of policy disarray: "The [Bahraini] opposition insists the uprising is an internal issue [unrelated to alleged Iranian agitation] . . . there are no formal political relations [with Iran]."

While the Bahraini government makes inconsistent declarations about its thoroughly rocky and complicated relations with the Islamic Republic, a formerly confidential quote appearing in a leaked embassy cable provides insight into the Iranian question vis-à-vis Bahrain. In a discussion with leading Sunni parliamentarian Ghanem al-Buanain during a 2007 visit to Bahrain by President Ahmadinejad, U.S. Ambassador Joseph Adam Ereli inquired as to why, when the regime regularly slams the Iranian president publicly, Crown Prince al-Khalifa still greets Ahmadinejad at the airport while King Hamad, in turn, sends him off. Al-Buanain replied: "Because we're Arabs. We don't like them [Iranians], but we need them."[3] It is interesting to note that, despite the official pleasantries bestowed on Ahmadinejad, he was whisked from the airport on the adjacent island of al-Muharraq, a Sunni stronghold, to al-Gudiabiya palace in central Manama, flanked by heavy security and with no way to personally interact with the country's Shi'a Arab populace, something Ahmadinejad would surely love to have done if provided the opportunity.

The Diversified Future of Bahraini Energy

For all of the bitter rhetoric between Bahrain and Iran since the February 14 uprising and the brutal, Saudi-backed crackdown, neither the al-Khalifa monarchy nor the Ahmadinejad government, both bound by pure economic realpolitik, wants to derail a protracted quid pro quo natural gas deal both sides have been constructing for years. Manama and Tehran have been in talks for several years about the expanded development of the South Pars gas field. South Pars is the world's largest natural gas field with a roughly 1/3–2/3 split between Iran and the State of Qatar, respectively (Mehr News Agency, June 15, 2010).[4] The potential of the massive deposits in South Pars could have massive mutual economic benefits for both parties if they can put their sectarian differences aside long enough to finalize an agreement.

To the dismay of American officials in the region, Ahmadinejad has been actively working to get Bahrain to invest heavily in South Pars in exchange for Iranian gas exports. Iran's then foreign minister, Manouchehr Mottaki, described the deal in a Bahraini pro-government daily: "According to agreements, Bahrain will invest in South Pars phases and Iran will take part in Bahrain's refining and petrochemical industries, and finally Iran's gas will be exported to Bahrain" (Gulf Daily News, June 30, 2010). Since an initial agreement was signed between the two Persian Gulf nations in 2008, intermittent ethno-religious tension

> *Bahrain is adept at maintaining a delicate balancing act between their larger neighbors, Saudi Arabia and Iran, as well as those further afield, including Britain, the United States, and now the Russian Federation.*

has been a persistent hindrance to a long-lasting, definitive agreement on South Pars. Bilateral energy sector ties are under severe pressure since the February 14 Shi'a-led uprising, but the process has not been derailed beyond repair. As recently as the fall of 2010, Iran's Oil Minister Masoud Mir Kazzemi met with Bahrain's Oil and Gas Affairs Minister Abdul Hussain bin Ali Mirza to discuss a deal on the export of Iranian gas to Bahrain. Iran's Deputy Oil Minister Javed Oji told Iran's semi-official news agency, "If [a South Pars deal is] finalized, a new natural gas pipeline will be built under the Persian Gulf waters; the pipeline is expected to transfer one billion cubic feet of Iran's gas to Bahrain" (Fars News Agency, September 5, 2010).

Bahrain's energy strategy does not simply rely on Iran. Bahrain has made it clear that not only is its domestic gas production in decline, but that it seeks to import gas on a global scale, thereby becoming a net gas exporter and greatly boosting the Kingdom's prosperity. Following months of turmoil, such a deal may be a means of reviving Bahrain's sagging economic outlook. Qatar, the world's largest producer of liquid natural gas, is considering a deal for Bahrain to install a floating re-gasification facility for LNG which would help Bahrain achieve its goal of becoming an energy exporter (Gulf Times [Doha], May 12). More interestingly, Manama's National Oil and Gas Authority signed a deal with Russian energy giant Gazprom to import natural gas to Bahrain coupled with a potential future pipeline deal or Russian-assisted deep exploration drilling (Arabian Business, October 28, 2010).

Conclusion

Relations between Bahrain and Iran have been historically tense since Bahrain's independence from the United Kingdom in 1971 was followed by Iran's Shah Mohammed Reza Pahlavi claim that Bahrain belonged to Iran. In post-1979 revolutionary Iran, Ayatollah Ruhollah Khomeini did little to ease Bahraini fears on Iranian claims of sovereignty over their country. Bahrain's sovereignty is currently ensured by the presence of the U.S Fifth Fleet / U.S. Naval Forces Central Command, which replaced an earlier British Royal Navy detachment in 1971. In another revealing U.S. diplomatic cable, an American official says that the al-Khalifas often tell their American partners that they are under constant threat of Iranian "subversion." The cable goes on to categorically state that the Bahraini claims of Iranian meddling have never been supported by any kind of evidence.[5] American officials based in Manama have never believed that the Shi'a opposition has had weapons supplied to them by Tehran nor do they believe they are involved in any kind of terrorism.

Bahrain is adept at maintaining a delicate balancing act between their larger neighbors, Saudi Arabia and Iran, as well as those further afield, including Britain, the United States, and now the Russian Federation. Caught up in labyrinthine web of regional ethno-religious demographics, layered with energy sector rivalries, King Hamad will continue to keep up this complex geo-political dance, playing the larger powers off one another while simultaneously trying to suppress his internal Shi'a opposition into submission, if only temporarily.

While Bahrain's rulers seek to portray a nation returning to a modicum of normalcy, the root causes of Shi'a unrest-turned-rage have yet to be genuinely addressed. Opposition members believe show trials are coming that will prosecute dozens of doctors and nurses, along with prominent jailed MPs like Matar Ibrahim Matar and Jawad Fairuz. As the regime prepares the legal cases against its enemies, Bahrain's stifled Arab Spring will likely be followed by a darker Arab Autumn.

Notes

1. To view the original cable, see: Shi'a Youth In Weekend Skirmishes with Security, Section 5(C), November 15, 2007, wikileaks.ch/cable/2007/11/07MANAMA1033.html.
2. Author's interview with Nabeel Rajab, May 10, 2011.
3. To view the original cable, see: Ahmedinejad Visit To Bahrain, Section 5(C), November 19, 2007, wikileaks.ch/cable/2007/11/07MANAMA1045.html.
4. The Qatari share of South Pars is called the North Dome gas-condensate field. The entire field totals 9,700 square kilometers in area and is estimated to contain approximately 51 trillion cubic meters of gas.
5. To view the original cable, see: Bahrain's Relations with Iran, Section 11(S), August 5, 2008, wikileaks.ch/cable/2008/08/08MANAMA528.html.

Bibliography

❖

The following books and articles provide additional information on this subject. Most of the noted articles are available on EBSCOhost databases.

Ajami, Fouad. "The Arab Spring at One: A Year of Living Dangerously." *Foreign Affairs*. Council on Foreign Relations, 24 Jan. 2012. Web. 10 Feb. 2012.

Anderson, Lisa. "Demystifying the Arab Spring." *Foreign Affairs* 90.3 (2011): 2–7. Print.

"The Assads: An Iron Fisted Dynasty." *Al Jazeera English*. Al Jazeera, 9 Dec. 2011. Web. 10 Feb. 2012.

Atzori, Erik. "Tunisia Leads the Way." *Middle East* Dec. 2011: 18–20. Print.

Bagnall, Janet. "Women's Gains in Arab Spring More Mirage than Miracle." *National Post*. National Post, 16 Dec. 2011. Web. 10 Feb. 2010.

Bröning, Michael. "The Sturdy House That Assad Built." *Foreign Affairs*. Council on Foreign Relations, 7 Mar. 2011. Web. 10 Feb. 2012.

Cassel, Matthew. "Bahraini Doctors Speak Out Against Torture." *Al Jazeera English*. Al Jazeera, 2 Dec. 2011. Web. 10 Feb. 2012.

Cropsey, Seth, and Arthur Milikh. "Democracy in Egypt: Applying the Tocqueville Standard." *World Affairs*. American Peace Society, May/June 2011. Web. 10 Feb. 2012.

Dickinson, Elizabeth. "Bahrain Commission Issues Brutal Critique of Arab Spring Crackdown." *Christian Science Monitor*. Christian Science Monitor, 23 Nov. 2011. Web. 10 Feb. 2012.

Dunn, Alexandra. "Unplugging a Nation: State Media Strategy During Egypt's January 25 Uprising." Fletcher Forum of World Affairs. *Fletcher Forum of World Affairs* 35:2 (2011): 15–24. Print.

Duri, Abd al-Aziz. *An Introduction to Arab Economic History*. (Arabic). Beirut: Dar al-Talia, 1969. Print.

Elgindy, Khaled. "Army May Be the Real Winner in Egypt." *CNN.com*. Cable News Network, 13 Dec. 2011. Web. 10 Feb. 2012.

Etzioni, Amitai. "Toward a Nonviolent, Pluralistic Middle East." *Middle East Quarterly* (Fall 2011): 27–38. Print.

Ismael, Tareq. *Middle East Politics Today: Government and Civil Society*. Gainesville: UP of Florida, 2001. Print.

Joffé, George. "The Arab Spring in North Africa: Origins and Prospects." *Journal of North African Studies* 16:4 (2011): 507+. Print.

Kamrava, Mehran. "The Arab Spring and the Saudi-Led Counterrevolution." *Orbis* 56:1 (2012): 96–104. Print.

Kaouther, Larbi. "Tunisians Mark Year After Ben Ali's Exit." *Yahoo!* AFP, 14 Jan. 2012. Web. 10 Feb. 2012.

Kenny, Charles. "Why Recessions Are Good for Freedom." *Foreign Policy* May/ June 2011: 31. Print.

Kinninmont, Jane. "Bread and Dignity." *World Today* 67.8/9 (2011): 31–33.

Kurkijan, Anousha. "Redrawing the Political Foundations." *World Today* 67.10 (2011): 11–14. Print.

Langendonck, Gert Van. "Libya Militias Taking Law into Own Hands." *Christian Science Monitor*. Christian Science Monitor, 4 Nov. 2011. Web. 10 Feb. 2012.

Malik, Adeel. "The Economics of the Arab Spring." *Al Jazeera English*. Al Jazeera, 13 Oct. 2011. Web. 10 Feb. 2012.

"No Bloom of Economic Freedom in Middle East/North Africa's Arab Spring." *Heritage Foundation*. Heritage Foundation, 12 Jan. 2012. Web. 10 Feb. 2012.

Rubin, Trudy. "Worldview: Economy Is Key to Egypt, Tunisia Democracy Quest." *Philly.com*. Philadelphia Media Network, 14 Apr. 2011. Web. 10 Feb. 2012.

Said Aly, Abdel Monem. "Egypt Will Never Be the Same Again." *BitterLemons International* 9.6 (2011). Web. 10 Feb. 2012.

Siddiqi, Moin. "After the Arab Spring: The Long, Hot Arab Summer?" *Middle East* Aug./Sept. 2011: 35–38. Print.

Spencer, Claire. "Moment in the Sun." *World Today* 61.2 (2011): 17–18. Print.

Springborg, Robert. "The Political Economy of the Arab Spring." *Mediterranean Politics* 16.3 (2011): 427–33. Print.

Talhami, Ghada Hashem. "A Nobel for Arab Women." *Progressive*. Progressive Magazine, 10 Oct. 2011. Web. 10 Feb. 2012.

———. "Syria: Islam, Nationalism and the Military." *Middle East Policy* 8.4 (2001): 110–27. Print.

Tarabay, Jamie. "Justice Denied." *National Journal* 27 Oct. 2011. Web. 10 Feb. 2012.

"Tunisia Constituent Body Holds First Session." *Al Jazeera English*. Al Jazeera, 22 Nov. 2011. Web. 10 Feb. 2012.

"Women and the Arab Awakening: Now Is The Time." *Economist*. Economist Newspaper, 15 Oct. 2011. Web. 10 Feb. 2012.

Wright, Robin. "The Arab Spring Is a Jobs Crisis." *Atlantic Monthly* 308.1 (July/Aug 2011): 58. Print.

Web Sites

❖

Council on Foreign Relations
http://www.cfr.org/region/middle-east/ri397

The Council on Foreign Relations is a nonpartisan membership organization that serves as an educational resource on world affairs. The organization is distinguished by its diverse membership, from journalists to government officials, and supports a variety of research, conference, and publishing initiatives relative to Middle East affairs.

Middle East Institute
http://www.mei.edu/

An independent, nonpartisan organization providing information and analysis on the Middle East. Promoting education on each country in the region, the organization sponsors presentations and classes conducted by leading scholars in the field.

United Nations Department of Political Affairs: Middle East and West Asia
http://www.un.org/wcm/content/site/undpa/main/activities_by_region/middle_east

The UN Department of Political Affairs monitors and evaluates political developments in the region with an aim to prevent and resolve violent conflicts. Web site provides information on peacemaking efforts, political analysis of US and regional relations, and efforts toward preventative diplomacy.

US Department of State: Bahrain
http://www.state.gov/p/nea/ci/ba/

US Department of State: Syria
http://www.state.gov/p/nea/ci/sy/

US Department of State: Egypt
http://www.state.gov/p/nea/ci/eg

US Department of State: Tunisia
http://www.state.gov/p/nea/ci/ts/

US Department of State: Libya
http://www.state.gov/p/nea/ci/ly/

US Department of State: Yemen
http://www.state.gov/p/nea/ci/ym/

The US Department of State provides background information, press releases, and updates on current diplomatic activities in other countries. In addition, the web site provides an archive of facts and records in the major areas of political affairs, business and economy, and social life.

Index

❖

Because of the variety of sources published in this volume and their different methods of romanizing or transliterating Arabic names, we have chosen what we feel to be the most common transliterations in the index below. Cross references are provided for those names commonly seen in several forms (e.g., Gaddafi and Qaddafi). For names beginning with an article such as al- or el-, see the specific Arabic name following the prefix (e.g., Bashar al-Assad will be indexed as Assad, Bashar al-).

About the Editor

❖

A Connecticut native, Paul McCaffrey was born in Danbury and raised in Brookfield. He graduated from the Millbrook School and Vassar College in Dutchess County, New York, and began his career with the H.W. Wilson Company in 2003 as a staff writer for *Current Biography*. He has worked on The Reference Shelf series since 2005, personally editing a number of titles, among them *The News and Its Future, Hispanic Americans, Global Climate Change,* and *The United States Election System*. As a freelance author, he has written several biographies for Chelsea House. He lives in Brooklyn, New York.